CW00656147

THE LOST TRIBES OF ISRAEL

By the same author

OPERATION MOSES
THE THIRTEENTH GATE
JOURNEY TO THE VANISHED CITY
THE ROAD TO REDEMPTION
THE JEWS OF PALESTINE
JUDAISING MOVEMENTS (With E. Trevisan-Semi)

The Lost Tribes of ISRAEL

THE HISTORY OF A MYTH

TUDOR PARFITT

Weidenfeld & Nicolson
LONDON

First published in Great Britain in 2002
by Weidenfeld & Nicolson

A CIP catalogue record for this book
is available from the British Library.

ISBN 0 297 81934 8

Typeset by Selwood Systems, Midsomer Norton

Printed and bound in Great Britain by
Butler & Tanner Ltd, Frome and London

Weidenfeld & Nicolson

The Orion Publishing Group Ltd
Orion House
5 Upper Saint Martin's Lane
London WC2H 9EA

For my father

CONTENTS

ACKNOWLEDGEMENTS

I am greatly indebted to a number of people and organisations: Dr Jack and Diane Zeller and Karen Primack in Washington D.C., Professor Norman Stillman of the University of Oklahoma, Professor Nathan Katz of the Florida International University, Professor Ivan Kalmar of the University of Toronto, Professor John Peel, Professor Andrew George, Ms Yulia Egorova and Dr Xun Zhou of SOAS, Dr Shalva Weil of the Hebrew University, Professor Emanuela Trevisan-Semi of the University of Venice, Dr Michel Gribinski, Professor Myer Samra, Mr Lionel Okun, Mr Neil Bradman, Rhian Luke, my agent Diana Finch and Richard Milner and Francine Brody at Weidenfeld and Nicolson, the Research Committee of SOAS and the British Academy. And mostly to Miss J and Sebastian for their forbearance.

TVP

Chapter One

THE LOST TRIBES OF ISRAEL

> These Tartars of cursed memory are the Ten Tribes who having forsaken the Mosaic Law, followed the golden calves, and whom Alexander the Great endeavoured to shut up in the rugged mountains of the Caspians with bitumen-covered rocks . . .
>
> Matthew Paris (*c.* 1200–59)

The quest for the Lost Tribes of Israel, like the quest for the Holy Grail, for Prester John or for the Ark of the Covenant, is one of the enduring motifs underlying Western views of the wider world. This book is both a history of that quest and a history of the myth it created. It is a history particularly of the way the myth has influenced the West and affected its perceptions of the outside world from the early mediaeval period to the present. We shall see that this myth is a vital feature of colonial discourse throughout the long period of European overseas empires, from the beginning of the fifteenth century, until the latter half of the twentieth.

How can I be sure that the Lost Tribes are indeed nothing but a myth? I am tempted to say, well I *am* sure and that's an end to it. But perhaps that will not quite do. The fact is that over the last two thousand years plenty of evidence of different sorts has been presented as proof of the continuing existence of the Lost Tribes. As far as I am concerned none of it is satisfactory as evidence. This is the standard view of scholars throughout the academic world.[1]

I am in a privileged position perhaps. For many years I have been involved with groups throughout the world who claim membership of the Lost Tribes, and I have written about some of them. I know too well how enticing their claims are and how easy it is to let drop one's scholarly guard. In 1984 I was researching a book on the Falashas of Ethiopia and witnessed them streaming over the border into Sudan at the height of the great famine, desperately wishing to get to Jerusalem – the precise location of which was quite unclear to them. I wanted to believe then, as they did, that they were a remnant of the ancient people of Israel struggling against all odds to rejoin their long-lost brethren.[2] When I subsequently wrote about the Lemba tribe and spent long months in their *kraals* in Zimbabwe and Vendaland in South Africa listening to their oral traditions, which connect them with ancient Israel, I *wanted* to believe them and had to make a great effort writing my book to be truly judicious with the evidence that came my way. And on other trips to Japan or Uganda or India or the United States, as I listened to pleas to be believed of earnest-faced men, I found myself yearning to do so. In other respects I am a normal, perhaps even somewhat cynical product of a certain type of British education. I am pretty careful about what I choose to believe and as I get older whom I choose to believe. But in the area of the mythology of the Lost Tribes I am still a potential sucker. As I wrote this book I became aware of the fact that I am not alone.

As will be shown, the myth of the Lost Tribes is one of the great universal myths. Its power to persuade is colossal. It has proved both potent and persistent and has allowed itself – volunteered itself – to be recruited to all sorts of causes, in every continent and just about every country. It has even been suggested that the Lost Tribes were involved in the destruction of Atlantis.[3]

What might the history of a myth involve? In this case it involves a certain historical background: we have to establish where the history of the Lost Tribes stopped and where the history of the myth of the Lost Tribes started. Subsequently our history will follow what happened to the myth throughout time and space, for it is a myth that has enjoyed travelling. And as it has travelled, like all good travellers, it has taken on the colouring of the places it has visited. As a myth it has a life of its own. With its appearance in different places and eras it acquired new significance and new trappings. The essentials of the myth were fairly constant but, as will be seen, it frequently spawned variants. It started life as a Jewish myth and was later taken up by Christianity. It is now a myth that is shared between these two faiths but it has importance for many others, including Islam. It has in addition played a seminal role in spawning completely new religions. It is a myth about ethnicity and also about religion. However the religious and ethnic elements are in constant flux. This is in part because in Judaism the term 'Jew' or 'Israelite' has always implied someone of the family of Israel, as well as someone who performs certain rituals. The confusion between these two definitions has haunted Judaism in the past and still does. The area of confusion has readily lent itself to association: confusion and ambiguity are velcro-strips to those seeking a new identity.[4]

The main vehicle for the initial spread of the myth of the Lost Tribes was the Bible, which launched a somewhat ambiguous tale upon the world. This biblical tale, with its haunting message of loss and redemption, became one of the key tools available to our European forebears in their courageous attempts to decipher a misty, unknown world beyond the horizon.

This is what we know of the *history* of the Lost Tribes. According to the biblical narrative there were twelve tribes of Israel. These were viewed as the descendants of the twelve sons of Jacob – Reuben, Simeon, Levi, Judah, Dan, Naphtali, Gad, Asher, Issachar, Zebulun, Benjamin and Joseph. The tribe of Levi was scattered among the other tribes, where its members served as a hereditary priesthood.[5] The remaining eleven tribes were restructured into twelve secular groups – the number twelve having sacred properties perhaps corresponding to the twelve months of the year. To achieve this the tribe of Joseph was divided into two tribes: Ephraim and Manasseh. The unity of the twelve tribes was short-lived: soon they were divided into two kingdoms, the northern kingdom, which consisted of ten of the tribes, and the southern kingdom, which included Judah, Simeon and most of Benjamin.

As a result of the invasion of the Assyrian kings, Tiglath-Pileser III (732 BC) and Sargon II (721 BC) the kingdom of Israel was brought down and the northern tribes were exiled in two stages chiefly to Assyria, Media and the lands neighbouring Aram-Naharaim. As the biblical account had it, 'In the ninth year of Hoshea, the king of Assyria took Samaria, and carried Israel away into Assyria, and placed them in Halah and Habor by the river of Gozan, and in the cities of the Medes ... So was Israel carried away out of their own land to Assyria unto this day' (II Kings 17:6, 23). Various hints in the Bible suggest that only a proportion of the Ten Tribes was indeed carried away and this is the view of most scholars today. Subsequently, a large proportion of the southern kingdom was exiled by Nebuchadnezzar to Babylon in 586 BC. In the case of the exile of the Ten Tribes an alien population – Cutha, Ava, Hamath and Sepharvaim – was settled on at least some of their lands and it is supposed that they were eventually absorbed by the Israelite population that had remained. The elements of the Ten Tribes exiled to Assyria may be presumed to have been absorbed into the Assyrian population, as had many others who fell prey to the Assyrian policy of forced assimilation and ethnic cleansing. There is some Assyriological evidence that individuals with Hebrew names were still to be found in Assyrian army units in the seventh century but there is no other clear evidence of the continued existence of the exiles.[6] To draw a sharp line between history and mythology is often complex and sometimes impossible, but in this case it would appear that this is the point at which the history of the Lost Tribes of Israel stops and the history of the myth of the Lost Tribes starts.[7] This is the moment the Ten Tribes disappeared from normal history and became an *imagined* community. After this Assyriological evidence even the most tenuous links between the Lost Tribes and factual history disappeared.

The fate of the ten tribes as an imagined mythical community started to assume great importance in the prophecies – for instance in Ezekiel 37:16 – where the final redemption of Israel was linked to the reunion of the Lost Tribes with the descendants of the southern kingdom. Similarly in Isaiah we read, 'And it shall come to pass in that day, that the Lord shall set his hand again the second time to recover the remnant of his people, which shall be left, from Assyria, and from Egypt, and from Pathros, and from Cush, and from Elam, and from Shinar, and from Hamath, and from the islands of the sea. And he shall set up an ensign for the nations, and shall assemble the outcasts of Israel, and gather together the dispersed of Judah from the four corners of the earth' (Isaiah 11:11–12). And Jeremiah cries out, 'O Lord, save thy people, the remnant of Israel. Behold, I will bring them from the north country and gather them from the coasts of the earth' (Jeremiah 31:7). The Apocrypha carried on the story of the Lost Tribes, revealing that subsequent to their deportation the tribes, 'formed this plan for themselves, that they would leave the multitude of the nations and go to a more distant region where mankind had never lived, that there at least they might keep their statutes which they had not kept in their own land. And they went in by the narrow passages of the Euphrates River. For at that time the Most High performed signs for them and stopped the channels of the river until they had passed over. Through that region there was a long way to go, a journey of a year and a half and that country is called Arzareth.[8] Then they dwelt there until the last times and now when they are about to come again the Most High will stop the channels of the river again so that they may be able to pass over' (II Esdras 13:41–7).

It is from these basic texts that the whole edifice of later Lost Tribes mythology was constructed. One of the features, which becomes axiomatic in the myth of the Lost Tribes, is their presence beyond a river that by the time of the historian Josephus (*c.* AD 37–100) was called the Sabbatical River and in later texts the Sambatyon, or some similar version of the name implying a relationship with the word 'Sabbath'. In each case this river observes the rules ordained for the Sabbath, which is to say that on the Sabbath it stops flowing.

In the passage in Esdras we can see that the Lost Tribes ensconced beyond the Sambatyon are now vigilantly keeping the law. No matter what sins they had committed in the past – sins that were responsible no doubt for their deportation – they were now living virtuous lives. Not only that but the river, which incarcerates and protects them and whose nature is much discussed in the later literature, also keeps the law because it too observes the Sabbath. Professor Giuseppe Veltri has suggested that as the keeping of the Sabbath was such a bone of contention between Jews and Romans (the Roman view was that the Jews were slothfully giving up one seventh of their life to total indolence), the legend of the Lost Tribes can be seen as, 'an attempt to explain Jewish law as a *lex naturalis* . . . a natural law to which natural phenomena are subject'.[9] In this imagined place, far away, beyond the unfordable torrent of the Sambatyon, a theoretical but perfect Judaism existed, which had nothing to fear from any competing religious system.

Certainty about the existence of the Lost Tribes passed effortlessly into the Christian canon. St Paul, for instance, referred to them, 'And now I stand and am judged for the hope of the promise made of God unto our fathers: Unto which promise our twelve tribes instantly serving God day and night, hope to come' (Acts 26:6–7), while St James addressed his Epistle, 'to the twelve tribes which are scattered abroad'. In a typically apocalyptic passage in Revelation we read, 'and there were sealed one hundred and forty-four thousand of all the tribes of the children of Israel. Of the tribe of Judah were sealed twelve thousand. Of the tribe of Reuben were sealed twelve thousand. Of the tribe of Gad were sealed twelve thousand,' and so on (Revelation 7:4 ff.). In general from this time on it is fair to say that Christians had two broad categories of Jews who played a hugely important role in the

Christian imagination. There were the actual Jews who lived, usually precariously, in European cities and who were by and large despised and hated, and there were the *imagined* Jews, of whom the Lost Tribes form a part and who usually provoked more admiration and interest. Christians had little interest in the history of actual Jews (indeed until the nineteenth century nor did the Jews themselves) but they had a great interest in imagined Jews, as one can see from the vast literature that was devoted to them over the ages. From the first Christian centuries the view is expressed that somewhere in the world there were warriors descended from the Lost Tribes who were biding their time but who would rally to Christ upon his return and help Him rout the forces of evil.[10]

The Jews were less obsessed by imagining Jews than were Christians. There was a somewhat fractured view of the Lost Tribes in Jewish circles. Josephus assured his readers that there were still, 'Ten Tribes beyond the Euphrates – where there are so many they cannot be counted.'[11] But his contemporary, the equally famous Rabbi Akiva (*c.* AD 40–135), who laid the foundations of what is called the Oral Law, which was later codified in the Mishnah, was of the opinion that the Ten Tribes had disappeared for good, 'just as the day goes and does not return so they too have gone and will never return', although his adversary Rabbi Eliezer opined, 'just as the day darkens and then becomes light again so the Ten Tribes – even as it went dark from them, so will it become light for them'. Jerome too, in the fifth century, is certain that the Lost Tribes still live under the yoke of the kings of the Persians, 'nor has their captivity ever been loosed'.

In the Talmud[12] one passage (Sanhedrin 110:b) says, 'the Ten Tribes have no portion in the world to come as the Lord rooted them out of their Land in anger and wrath and in great indignation . . .' The Sambatyon (here called the Sabbatyon) is mentioned only once in the Babylonian Talmud (Sanhedrin 65:b): Rabbi Akiva, possibly with tongue in cheek, replies to what he may have regarded as a somewhat daft legal question – how do you know that the Sabbath is actually the Sabbath? – that anyone who wanted to prove that the Sabbath was actually the Sabbath and that there had not been some awful error of calculation at some point in the past had only to go and observe the miraculous weekly arrest of the Sabbatyon. As the Sabbatyon's movements were clearly directed by some divine agency, it followed that they accurately reflected the divine calendar.

If, thus far, the imagined locus of the Lost Tribes is sketchily drawn, a passage in the Jerusalem Talmud put some long-enduring flesh on the bones of the myth. We hear that the Ten Tribes were carried away to three distinct places: to the other side of the Sambatyon River, to Daphne, and to a place where they were 'covered by the cloud which descended upon them', from where they will eventually be redeemed.[13] According to other versions, the tribes were supposed to have been covered not by a cloud but exiled 'inside the dark mountains', and this is the sense in the second-century Rabbinic historical work *Seder Olam* (Order of the World). These dark mountains were sometimes taken to represent Africa which, according to the Talmud, Alexander the Great had to traverse to get to Carthage.[14] A passage in the Midrash says, 'The Ten Tribes were carried to the Sambatyon but Judah and Benjamin are dispersed to all countries' (Bereshit Rabba 73:5). Another, in Pesiqta Rabbati, explains that when the Messiah comes the exiled Ten Tribes will be brought back along with those, 'who were swallowed in the earth. The latter he will bring by means of underground passages to a place under the Mount of Olives in Jerusalem. God will stand upon the mount and it will cleave open for the exiles and they will come out of it.'[15] This passage is somewhat obscure as there is no earlier reference to the Ten Tribes actually being swallowed up by the earth. Perhaps the sense is metaphorical and what is meant is that they had simply disappeared from view. The reference to underground passages reflects the Jewish tradition that Jews buried outside the land of Israel would be required to make their way by subterranean tunnels (during which they will endure *hibbut hakever* – the torments of the grave) to the Mount of Olives with the coming of the Messiah.[16]

Both the Talmud and the Midrash are concerned with the reasons that the Almighty might have had for banishing the Ten Tribes into outer darkness. The Talmud put it down to the evils of hard liquor, 'R. Helbo said: the wine of Perugita and the water of Diomsit cut off the Ten Tribes from Israel.' When a certain well-named sage, R. Elazar ben Arak, visited the Lost Tribes he joined them in their revels and as a consequence, not unnaturally, his erudition vanished overnight (Shabat 147:b). In the Midrash the Lost Tribes are accused of lewd behaviour of all sorts: debauchery, the worship of idols and adultery.

By and large the Talmud is muted on the subject of the Ten Tribes. The Talmud is interested in law rather than history so it is not surprising that there is not much discussion of events surrounding them but nonetheless the enduring reality of the tribes would have posed some tricky legal issues. If the tribes *had* been known to the sages of Babylon in the fifth and sixth centuries, their very existence would have given rise to endless discussions of their relationship with rabbinic Jews in matters of ritual purity, marriage and social relationships, among other things. Did they count as Jews for the purposes of marriage? Could one eat with them using their utensils? Drink wine with them? Take them as slaves? As there is no such discussion it is fairly clear that the rabbis had no direct or even indirect contact with, or knowledge of the Ten Tribes, and perhaps rather little interest in their whereabouts. Their interest in them, such as it was, was purely theoretical.

From time to time further information or misinformation about the Lost Tribes was added by reports of travellers or adventurers who had sighted them in one part of the world or another. One of the most famous and influential of these was the perplexing late-ninth-century Jew – Eldad ha-Dani – who is known to have visited Mesopotamia, Egypt, the Yemen and most famously the important community of Kairouan in present-day Tunisia. Here he made some extravagant claims: that he was a Hebrew-speaking member of the tribe of Dan, which he said was still flourishing in Havilah, in Cush (taken to be Ethiopia), along with Naphtali, Gad and Asher. The four tribes fought continuous wars against 'seven kingdoms with seven languages'. Eldad also spoke of certain of the tribes, Issachar, Zevulun and Reuben, who lived in the high mountains of Paran; Ephraim and one half of the tribe of Manasseh near Mecca; Simeon and the other half of the tribe of Manasseh in the 'land of the Babylonians'. In addition he gave information about the 'children of Moses' who were incarcerated beyond the River Sambatyon.[17] He said the four tribes on the far side of the Sambatyon could not speak to the tribes on the near side: the river was too wide and the noise it made too great. They communicated by carrier pigeon. Eldad paints a utopian picture of the life of the Lost Tribes. Children in that distant land never die in the lifetime of their parents. The Talmud there is written in the purest Hebrew. They are warlike, Spartan in their habits and wealthy. They are surrounded by the River Sambatyon, which is, 'full of sands and stones, but without water . . . this river of stones and sand rolls during the six working days and rests on the Sabbath day. As soon as the Sabbath begins, fire surrounds the river, and the flame remains until the next evening when the Sabbath ends.'[18]

What do we know of Eldad's origins? David Wasserstein has written: 'Speculation placed Eldad's origins in all the usual places just over the edge of the world which most people know about, and associated him with all those distant areas in which Jewish states with powerful rulers were said to exist.'[19] We do know that Eldad of the tribe of Dan was not, as claimed, a member of the tribe of Dan and we may be fairly sure that his name was not Eldad. If one takes the corpus of texts associated with him more or less at face value it may be possible to deduce, and a number of modern scholars have done so, that Eldad was a Jew from either the eastern Islamic world or perhaps from Ethiopia; he had a series of not entirely implausible adventures; he had been captured by cannibals but thanks to his slender frame was not consumed; he knew something about Jewish legal and literary materials; he arrived in Kairouan in about 883 and then perhaps continued on to Spain, at which point he disappeared from history.[20]

There are problems with this as Wasserstein shows: the material of *Sepher Eldad* is not homogeneous; the various claims that the source of Eldad's narrative and particularly the source of the Halakhah (Jewish law)[21] is to be found in some odd Jewish community or another – for instance the Falashas in Ethiopia, the Khazars, the north Yemenite community of Najran or even Somaliland – simply lack evidence to support them.[22] Some outstanding scholars in the twentieth century have seen in *Sepher Eldad* the first reference to the Falashas of Ethiopia but Steven Kaplan, the greatest contemporary authority on Falasha history, casts grave doubt on it.[23] Edward Ullendorff and Charles Beckingham have suggested that there may be an Arabic substratum to his Hebrew suggesting some sort of an Arabian origin and this has been echoed even more recently by Professor S. Morag.[24]

What we do know is that Eldad existed and made the claims outlined above. Clearly Eldad had to hail from somewhere and given that he comes to our notice in the North African desert, an Arabic-speaking background is by far the most likely. We also know that he has a great deal in common with a host of other characters who people the pages of this book, from David Reubeni to Sir John Mandeville, from

Antonio de Montezinos to Joseph Smith – the founder of the Church of Jesus Christ of Latter-Day Saints. His narrative was undoubtedly a work of the imagination and drew on what was known of the Lost Tribes in his day, on a certain knowledge of Jewish law and Jewish lore and a great deal more besides. What is the motivation for any troubador, storyteller or novelist? A modest gain? The pleasure of recounting a good tale? According to Heinrich Graetz Eldad was a Karaite and a 'proselytizer, a cunning man . . . who related wonderful adventures and made a great stir in his day . . . he belongs to a class of deceivers who have a pious end in view and who know how to profit by the credulity of the masses . . .'[25] This too was the view of Adolf Neubauer in 1889.[26] He may well have been a swindler and a fraud in some sense, as Wasserstein maintains, but the reasons for his fraudulence, as Graetz hints, may have been relatively benign. It could well be that his purpose, if he had a greater purpose (but storytellers often do not), was to 'raise the spirits of the Jews by giving them news of tribes of Israel who lived in freedom . . . the reports of the existence of such Jewish kingdoms undoubtedly encouraged and comforted Eldad's hearers by contradicting the Christian contention that Jewish independence had ceased after the destruction of the Second Temple.'[27] One might add that his message, if it was one, served a similar function in relation to Islam, and rather more immediately: somewhere in the hinterland of Muslim power there lurked a Jewish polity or polities that might threaten Muslim hegemony.

One way or another, Eldad's work was to have an enduring influence on the Jewish and European imagination. Until recently Eldad's story was regularly recited in Persian synagogues. According to some scholars Eldad's tale gave rise to the legend of Prester John (although there is always the possibility that while the Prester John letters are almost three centuries later than Eldad, some of the literary material associated with Eldad is much later than has been thought, so that it reflects the Prester John material, not the reverse).[28] Even if this is true, it does look as if elements of Eldad's fanciful tale may have been incorporated into the various versions, Latin, Hebrew and Provençal, of the Prester John letters. Eldad's Hebrew account, *Sepher Eldad*, was first printed in Mantua in 1480 and was to be translated into a number of languages including German, Latin and Arabic. It would influence the way the world was viewed – and particularly Africa – for centuries to come.

★

In 1160 Rabbi Benjamin ben Jonah of Tudela, perhaps the greatest of all the Jewish explorers, embarked on a remarkable thirteen-year journey that took him as far as the western reaches of the Chinese Empire. Returning via South Arabia, the Nile valley, Alexandria and Rome he brought back reports of long-lost Jewish communities in various places that are often difficult to identify. In Cush – thought here to indicate India or Ceylon – he discovered black Jews who were learned and observant. Elsewhere he reported that in Persia, coming from the mountainous areas beyond the River Gozan, 'in the hills of Nisbur there are four tribes of Israel – Zebulun, Dan, Asher and Naphtali – all descendants of the first exiles who were carried to this country by Shalmaneser, King of Assyria'. These Israelites were ruled by a Levite, possessed cities and castles, sowed and reaped, and waged war against Cush. According to Benjamin, the King of Persia had sent an expedition in search of the Lost Tribes and had managed to locate them and even to speak to emissaries from the tribes who were able to cross the Sambatyon.[29] It seems that the various traditions told by Benjamin about the tribe of Naphtali in the area of ancient Bactria is a confusion of the term Ephthalite – the Byzantine form of a group otherwise known as Evthalides, Elevthes, Talites, Hidalites, etc.[30] Benjamin also located some of the tribes – Reuben, Gad and half the tribe of Manasseh – in the Yemen.

A number of Jewish travellers or *shelihim* (emissaries) brought or sent back tales from the East in the following centuries, which corroborated and embroidered these accounts. The regularity and insistence of these reports about the Ten Tribes were frequently related to the general level of persecution of Jews, which in turn gave rise to Messianic hopes and expectations. These travellers who claimed to have found the tribes in a number of different places included Abraham ha-Levi in 1456 (Ethiopia),[31] Obadiah ben Abraham of Bertinoro in the fifteenth century (Ethiopia and Arabia), the sixteenth-century Kabbalist R. Abraham ben Eliezer ha-Levi (Ethiopia),[32] his contemporary Rabbi Moses Bassola of Ancona (Babylon and Ethiopia),[33] and the famous sixteenth-century character David Reubeni (Arabia and Ethiopia), who claimed that Israelite armies were patrolling on both sides of the Red Sea.[34] Obadiah ben Abraham wrote of hajj routes to Mecca, which were constantly under threat of attack by 'a tribe of formidable giants who spread terror in the land . . .'[35]

★

Reporting the latest news of the Ten Tribes was a joint Jewish-Christian enterprise. The Venetian traveller Marco Polo (1254–1324), for instance, spoke of Jewish kingdoms in the distant East: he claimed that in 'Georgiana' there was a king called David Melic, which, as he explained, 'signifies David King, who was subject to the Tartars'. Whereas in 'the great province of Abyssinia, which is in Middle India' he also found Jews with a mysterious mark on their cheeks.[36] Somewhat later a most telling reference to the Lost Tribes in the mediaeval world is to be found in the fabulous compilation supposedly by Sir John Mandeville, known as *Mandeville's Travels*.

Mandeville's Travels is some kind of a forgery, the reason for which is not clear, written by someone who was not Sir John Mandeville. In part because Mandeville was a figment of some unknown genius' literary imagination and the *Travels* a collection of lies, half-truths and borrowings from assorted sources, it may be viewed in some respects as a reflection of the imagined world of fourteenth-century Europe. In any event it became one of the most beloved literary works of the Middle Ages. There are many surviving manuscripts in German, Dutch, French, English, Latin, Old Irish, Danish, Czech, Spanish and Italian. Over three times as many manuscripts of the *Travels* exist as of Odoric or Marco Polo.[37] Insofar as it purports in many cases to be an eye-witness account, it has much in common with Eldad.

Mandeville's tolerance towards the unknown peoples of the East seems entirely remarkable for its time: but it should be remembered that there had already been a tendency to view the East in a benign way and sometimes as something akin to Paradise. The peoples of the East – at least some of them, and notably the distant Brahmins of the Indus area about whom something was known – were perceived as sort of honorary Christians.[38] Mandeville emanates a kindly benevolence towards many of the peoples he imagines into existence. His view of the Jews, however, was more typical of his age. His claim that a Jew had confessed to him that by means of a deadly poison from Borneo the Jews planned to murder all of Christendom was clearly part of a much wider discourse: accusations of well poisonings by Jews were widespread in the fourteenth century and particularly in 1348–9 at the time of the Black Death. As far as the Lost Tribes were concerned, Mandeville claimed they were to be found in mountain valleys in a distant land beyond Cathay: 'toward the high Ind and toward Bacharia'. It is here that:

> The Jews of ten lineages be enclosed, that men clepe Goth and Magoth and they may not go out on no side. There were enclosed twenty-two kings with their people, that dwelled between the mountains of Scythia. There King Alexander chased them between those mountains and there he thought for to enclose them through work of his men. But when he saw that he might not do it ... he prayed to God of nature that he would perform that that he had begun ... yet God of his grace closed the mountains together, so that they dwell there all fast locked and enclosed with high mountains all about, save only on one side, and on that side is the sea of Caspian ... And also ye shall understand that the Jews have no proper land of their own for to dwell in, in all the world, but only that land between the mountains. And yet they yield tribute for that land to the Queen of Amazonia ... And though it happen that some of them by fortune to go out, they can no manner of language but Hebrew, so they cannot speak with the people ... And yet nathles, men say they shall go out in the time of anti-Christ and that they shall make great slaughter of Christian men. And therefore all the Jews that dwell in all lands learn always to speak Hebrew, in hope, that when the other Jews shall go out, they may understand their speech, and to lead them into Christendom for to destroy the Christian people. For the Jews say that they know well by their prophecies ... and that the Christian men shall be under their subjection, as long as they have been in subjection of them.

The mouth of the valley system was guarded by the Queen of Amazonia and 'if it happen that any of them pass out, they can speak no language but Hebrew, ne they not speak with other men when they come among them'. These Jews, then, as we have seen, were also known as Gog and Magog and with the coming of the Antichrist could be expected to join forces with other Hebrew-speaking Jews in other parts of the world. They would then overcome the Christian nations of the world, turning them into vassal states.[39]

In Ezekiel 38 we are told that the Lord will bring Gog and Magog with his horsemen and horses out of the north along with Persia, Ethiopia and Libya. The prophecy is taken up in Revelation (2) where we learn that at the End of Days Satan will be released from his prison and will set out to deceive the nations and gather Gog and Magog to do battle against the saints. Many groups in the mediaeval period were identified with the hordes of Gog and Magog: the Goths, Tartars and

Scythians among others. But the identification of the Lost Tribes with the allies of Satan – Gog and Magog – was particularly popular. It is of striking interest that when Johannes Ruysch compiled his famous map of 1507 or 1508 he included the findings of John Cabot (*c.* 1450–98) who had discovered (or perhaps rediscovered) Newfoundland in 1496, thinking that it was part of the coast of China, and placed them either next to or actually in the realm of Gog and Magog.[40] The equation of the Lost Tribes with the elementally inimical forces of Gog and Magog and groups associated with them is significant: clearly the existence of a powerful and unfriendly Jewish state somewhere in the world was a justification for the anti-Semitism of the day (had one been needed) and provided a sound rationale for the massacres of the Jews, which had been such a feature of the previous centuries.

Mandeville's account is a promiscuous amalgam of Jewish and Christian myths and legends. However the common ground between Jewish and Christian legends and myths is best exemplified in the Prester John materials. In the twelfth century, Ethiopia, or part of it, was thought to be in the East, somewhere in the vicinity of the Caucasus. Gradually the idea took hold that a Christian kingdom existed, stretching from East Africa to the Indus and across Africa as far as the Atlantic Ocean, which was ruled over by the Priest King Prester John. In 1170 Pope Alexander III had referred to his 'beloved son John the illustrious and glorious king of India', and for centuries this figure of a saintly and almost supernatural Christian leader foreshadowing the returned Christ at the End of Days dominated the Western imagination. In the twelfth century a Latin version of a letter written to Manuel, ruler of the Romans, by Prester John started circulating in western Europe. According to this letter he ruled over the three Indies from the burial place of St Thomas in the south to the Tower of Babel in the desert of Babylon. Seventy-two kings were subject to him. Among his subjects lived the Ten Lost Tribes, the Amazons and the Pygmies, who were incarcerated behind the Sambatyon. Through his kingdom flowed one of the rivers of Paradise – carrying with it precious stones and gold – and the animals of the realm included elephants, camels, gryphons and the phoenix. His subjects were free of every vice, they refrained from adultery and theft, they would never lie, the animals did not harm human beings and no one was poor.[41]

The Hebrew version of the letter says that close to the land of Prester John is

> a high mountain called Olympus and underneath the mountain is a spring, more important than anywhere in the world, and it is said that it is near to Paradise, a distance of seven days, and in it there are many precious stones, close to Paradise and they are called diamonds ... and also in my country, at its edge, there is a great miracle, a sea of stones which makes waves as the ordinary seas do; and there is a big wind and it causes a great calamity; and no man is able to pass through this sea ... and you may know that from that sea of stones there issues a river which comes from Paradise and flows between us and between the great country of the great king Daniel, king of the Jews; and this river flows all the days of the week, but on the Sabbath it does not move from its place, until on the Sunday it returns to its strength. And when this river is full beyond its banks it carries very many precious stones and in this river there is no water ... and no one can cross it except on the Sabbath. But we are placing guards at the passages, for if the Jews were able to cross they would cause great damage in the whole world against Christians as well as Ishmaelites and against every nation and tongue under the heavens, for there is no nation or tongue which can stand up to them ... there are under the rule of King Daniel three hundred kings, all Jews, and all of them possess countries under the power of King Daniel. And also under his governance are three thousand dukes and counts and great men and we know that his country is unfathomable ... and furthermore I inform you that in his country they have many beautiful women and they are ardent by nature ...[42]

The Land of Prester John was also thought to be the land in which the Nile had its source – and the source of the Nile on the basis of a couple of verses in Genesis was equated in some way with Paradise. The general interest then in the various stories about Prester John was connected with the possibility of being able to locate the Garden of Eden. It seemed clear that the four rivers mentioned in Genesis were none other than the Nile, the Euphrates, the Indus and the Tigris. In his convincing way Mandeville modestly accepted that he had not personally visited Paradise but knew for a fact that it was to be found in the East.[43]

The sense that Paradise existed somewhere beyond the known

horizon was one shared by Christians and Jews. One of the things that might have appeared relevant to the early Spanish explorers of the Americas was the notion that an earthly Paradise was supposed by some to lie somewhere in the region of the western Atlantic – as suggested particularly by the eleventh-century work *Brendan's Voyage*, based rather loosely on the adventures of the Irish saint Brendan the Navigator (*c.* 484–577) who, with a group of monks, had sailed in a leather boat to 'the Land of Promise' somewhere in the Atlantic. This was perhaps not the most popular locus of Paradise: a more favoured one was somewhere in the Middle East. As we have seen, as late as the fifteenth century the Garden of Eden was being confused by Jews with Aden. A further factor that no doubt had some significance was the location of Mount Ararat – the landing place of the Ark: as humanity descended from the eight people who survived the Ark, where they landed had much to do with subsequent populations.[44]

One purely Christian myth that was important in terms of Europe's comprehension of the exterior world was that of the wise men. In his *Chronicon* Otto von Freising (1150) had made a connection between Prester John and Caspar, whom the later evangelists had identified as the King of India and one of the three Magi who journeyed to Bethlehem. Although there is only the vaguest mention of the Magi in Matthew, in the course of time their story was fleshed out: first their number, not mentioned in the New Testament, was fixed at three, and soon they were described as kings. In the sixth-century Armenian version they appear as King Melchior of Persia, King Caspar of Ethiopia-India and King Balthasar of Arabia. By the thirteenth century the image of the Magi had become symbolic of the three ages of man – thus of all humanity in all its stages – and at about the same time the Magi took on symbolic racial characteristics. It is usually in this guise that they appear in the countless artistic representations of the Renaissance, often with a youthful Caspar as an African, Balthasar as some sort of Oriental and the aged Melchior as a European. As late as the mid-nineteenth century a German explorer was invoking the myth of the three kings, along with myths of the Queen of Sheba and King Solomon, as a way of explaining some overgrown ruins in central Africa that for him were otherwise inexplicable.[45]

It has been suggested that the three kings were representative of the sons of Noah. In any event, Ham was associated with Africa, Japheth with Europe and Shem with the East. This threefold division of the world according to Rabanus Maurus in his famous tenth-century work *De Universo*, was no more than a reflection of the Holy Trinity.[46] So fixed was this notion for many centuries to come that a hundred years after Christopher Columbus (1451–1506) had discovered America, the world was still being described as having three parts (and the idea that vast tracts of the world were populated by Semitic peoples – descendants of Shem – is a discourse that as will be seen persists until today).

Rabanus Maurus had an over-arching numerical theory of the world: there were twelve winds, twelve regions of the Zodiac, twelve months, twelve hours of day and night, twelve patriarchs, twelve apostles and of course twelve tribes of Israel. Christ, the architect of this plan, as of the Holy City, was prefigured by the High Priest of the Temple who had twelve stones in his breastplate – representing the Twelve Tribes. This idea was taken up by other mediaeval writers, including the sixteenth-century French Christian Kabbalist Jean Thenaud, and echoes of these traditions are found throughout Lost Tribes discourse in areas as far removed as Japan, West Africa and South America.[47]

In the early Middle Ages Europe, then, had but the dimmest sense of what the outside world was all about. The world beyond was still replete with the wonder of the unknown. The basic text of Christian civilisation – the Bible – had nothing to say about Africa beyond the lower reaches of the Nile, nothing to say of the lands to the east of the Indus, nothing to say of the Pacific or the Americas. Some legends relating to Ethiopia had penetrated the West, but with respect to the rest of this vast unknown world barely a legend, barely a classical allusion had ever penetrated Europe. Maps, as Harvey has put it, 'were practically unknown in the Middle Ages . . . so far were people in the Middle Ages from our awareness of maps today that there was no word meaning map either in the languages of everyday use or in the Latin used by the Church and for learned writing.'[48] The sense then of what the denizens of this unknown world were about was inevitably an issue of the imagination. It was also an issue of theological controversy. There had always been a somewhat heretical suspicion that unknown lands lay in far reaches of the earth with a dubious population cut off from the rest of mankind. St Augustine had supposed that theoretically perhaps there were such egregious creatures, but doubted they were descended from Adam. But were there really inaccessible and unknown parts of the earth? How could the Gospel be preached 'in the four corners of the earth' if half of the world was cut off by, say, tropical fires, as Aristotle and indeed St Augustine had suggested? The Venerable Bede had staunchly resisted the idea that such a population could exist at all.

The period of the Crusades opened up some of the unknown parts of the world to a degree of Western scrutiny and in the wake of the Crusades a number of initiatives brought fresh information: the journey of Jean du Plan Carpini sent as an envoy to the Great Khan by Pope Innocent IV in 1245; Willem van Ruusbroec's journey on behalf of Louis IX of France in 1253 and so on.[49] But by and large the world beyond Europe and the inhabitants of that world remained for most people a dead letter. For such unknown populations throughout history and until our own day the myth of a quasi-universal Jewish presence – which explains everything – is used constantly. One aspect of this myth which was available to Europeans in their struggle to comprehend the strange peoples that resided beyond their gaze and beyond their ken was the device of the Lost Ten Tribes.

One of the earliest exploitations of the myth was with respect to the raiding hordes of Central Asia. When the Mongol invasion reached Germany in 1241 Matthew Paris (*c.* 1200–59), the Benedictine monk and abbey chronicler of St Albans, said of the barbaric, incomprehensible hordes that 'these Tartars of cursed memory are the Ten Tribes who having forsaken the Mosaic Law, followed the golden calves and whom Alexander the Great endeavoured to shut up in the rugged mountains of the Caspians with bitumen-covered rocks . . .'[50] And this was echoed by the Emperor Frederick II in a letter to Henry III of England: 'Tis said they are descended from the Ten Tribes who abandoned the Law of Moses.'[51] Moreover European Jews were accused of smuggling arms to their Mongol 'cousins' in wine barrels with the result that at a number of border posts Jewish merchants were killed on the spot. At the time Jews were hated in Europe as never before – the despised enemy within became the feared enemy without. The idea that the Tartars were descended from the Lost Tribes was frequently broached. The Dutch cartographer Abraham Ortelius (1527–98) in his map of Tartary in *Theatrum Orbis Terrarum* (Antwerp, 1573) includes the land of the *horda* of the Danites and a little further south the *horda* of the Naphtali. And an English traveller reported in 1611 that the Tartar 'until this day . . . retaine the neames of their tribes, the title of

Haebrewses, and circumcision. In al other rites they follow the fashions of the Tartarians.'

If the denizens of the unknown world were often imagined as Israelites, what of their language? In the Middle Ages Hebrew played a powerful imaginative role. In the first place it was widely considered as the first language of mankind. It was with the Hebrew words *vayhi or* (let there be light), after all, that God created the world. The Bible described the translucent language of Adam and followed its fall via the Tower of Babel into the convoluted languages of the myriad nations of the world. Hebrew was the original language: it was perfect and complete in every detail. It was spoken by God. In his *Comprehensive Grammar* (London, 1685) Jehudah Stennet noted that Hebrew was the 'Tongue of Adam' and thus the language in which everything was first named. It was the language with which God's finger engraved the law and was thus a 'tongue worthy to be wrote in Characters of Gold'.[52] Traces of Hebrew were discovered quite literally everywhere in the following centuries.

In early Christian times the three sons of Noah had been considered the founders of the three main groupings of humankind, along with their languages. Within a few centuries peoples such as the Scythians were also connected to the biblical genealogies of race and language. But by the time of the Renaissance historical etymology had started to play a role, as national pride began to assert that modern languages such as French[53] or Flemish could also be identified as the world's first language, or at any rate closely connected to it. In *De vulgari eloquentia* Dante mocked the remote hamlets wedded to the uplifting notion that their miserable dialect was the language of Adam and that they were privy to the secrets of the language of Paradise. But alongside these vainglorious claims on behalf of one's own language, nation and village there were still claims made on behalf of Hebrew. The idea that all languages ultimately derive from Hebrew is an ancient one, and it still has an altogether surprising number of adherents, as a few minutes on the internet will show. In earlier centuries one might mention Père Louis Thomassin's work of 1690: *La Méthode d'étudier et d'enseigner chrestiennement et utilement la Grammaire ou les Langues par rapport à l'Ecriture sainte en les reduisant toutes à l'Hébreu.*[54] This was followed by Daniel Defoe's *Essay upon Literature, or an Enquiry into the antiquity and original of letters proving that the two tables written by the finger of God in*

Mount Sinai was the first writing in the world and that all other alphabets derive from the Hebrew (London, 1726). Father Lafitau would have none of this: towards the end of his great work published in 1724 on the Iroquois Indians he observed tiredly that, 'We should wear ourselves out maintaining that the Hebrew language was the one spoken by men until the time of the Tower of Babel when it had the privilege of being kept alive in Heber's family and that it was transmitted by Abraham to the Jewish people who were his descendants. Those who, in this belief, try to trace back all the other languages to the Hebraic roots which they think they see in them put themselves to needless trouble for purely fictitious conjectures.'[55]

The motivating force behind the desire to show that Hebrew was the first language was simple enough. As the language of Adam (a popular image, particularly in the scientific domain, was that of Adam the philosopher in the Garden of Eden), Hebrew was a language of philosophy and clarity. As the language of the Kabbalah it was perceived throughout Europe as a key to arcane wisdom, to the wisdom of the East. If one could only recover the Hebrew of Adam in all its purity one could begin to understand the hidden secrets of the universe itself. As will be seen throughout this book the myriad peoples identified as Israelites were usually deemed to have some knowledge of Hebrew and the recovery of this language from among the Zulus, Maoris, Hottentots or Malagasy peoples became a hitherto unremarked aspect of the colonial enterprise: imperialism sought to bring back home anything of value – including the secrets of the universe.

The persistence of our myth of the Lost Tribes of Israel demands some explanation. It has persisted in part because it has become such a useful channel for understanding unknown peoples and races and a convenient means of labelling human entities. This myth has been used in the Western world as a device for understanding the 'other' – often the savage 'other' that is the imagined opposite of ourselves.

With the discovery of the American continent in 1492 and the rounding of the Cape of Good Hope a few years later, Europe was obliged to expand its sense of the other. Of course every society, including that of mediaeval Europe, consists of a myriad of 'others', some more familiar, some less. But the overriding 'other' against which the European stood pitted was essentially the 'other' of across the Mediterranean and this involved the Jew and the Moor. It was a European-Semite construction. Although this book is concerned mainly with the way in which the Jewish element of the Semitic world acted on the European imagination, the Arabs or Moors – as well as other ancient peoples – also played an important role. The way in which Muslims were used by Europeans as a metaphor for unknown people would be a study in itself. Throughout this book, however, it will be seen that there is a discernible linkage between Jews and Moors.

In mediaeval Europe 'Moorishness', like 'Jewishness', was the essence of 'otherness'. Hamlet's impassioned denunciation of his uncle reaches its peak with the term of abuse – Moor. During the reign of Henry VIII a 'Turk' was set on in the streets of London and the assailants charged, but the case was thrown out of court as Christians could not be prosecuted for an offence against infidels.[56] A contemporary-sounding seventeenth-century English immigration law taking 'Egyptian' as a description of 'Arab' or 'Moorish' stated, 'If any transport into England or Wales any lewd people calling themselves Egyptians, they forfeit £40.' The etymology of the word 'gypsy' (*gitane, gitano*) is derived from 'Egypt' – a reminder that even the 'other' within takes on the colouring of the Moor. (The linkage of Jews and Muslims in terms of 'otherness' is well illustrated by the fact that there is currently a discourse connecting Jews and Gypsies that claims the Gypsies too are descended from the Lost Tribes.)[57]

The Arabic language, like Hebrew, was the epitome of the unknown tongue (in France '*c'est de l'hébreu pour moi*' signifies an incomprehensible language). When Columbus arrived in the New World on his fourth voyage he observed that the people of the islands each had a different language and that they 'do not understand one another any more than we understand the Arabs.'[59] In the Veneto, which had a long history of symbiosis with Muslims, to this day *parlar turco* means to speak gobbledeygook and *cose turche* implies things that can scarcely be imagined.[59] Even those not convinced by the Israelite or Moorish origins of strange people still saw Jews and Moors as archetypal others: Amerigo Vespucci (1454–1512), at a loss to understand who the American Indians might be, noted, 'they cannot be called Moors nor Jews, but worse than gentiles ...'[60] In other words as Vespucci looked around for suitable 'others' to express the strangeness of the Indians, the most automatic first choice was a twinning of Jews and Moors. The Moors were the summation of intractability. Charles Lalemant in a letter of 28 February 1642 about the Iroquois, observed, 'as to coming to an agreement with them there is not the slightest possibility for he has been told not to expect this from them any more than if they were Arabs'.[61] The linkage of Jew, Moor and Heathen, already made in the *Book of Common Prayer* (1548) and the Collects for Good Friday was a frequent feature of later English writing. In Fielding's *History of Joseph Andrews* (1742) after an adventure in an alehouse one character complained that he had almost begun to suspect, 'that he was sojourning in a country inhabited by Jews and Turks'. There are no Jews or Turks in the novel so the term must represent an abstraction of foreignness. In *Tristram Shandy* Sterne noted in a couplet: 'A devil 'tis – and mischief such doth work / As never yet did Pagan, Jew or Turk.'

The creation of a European identity was to a substantial degree in opposition to these 'others'. Identity is as much a question of exclusion as inclusion and it was on the boundaries of these collectivities that a European sense of self was forged. The immediate boundary between European Christian and Jew or Moor was endlessly duplicated throughout the world as Europe confronted the hitherto unknown parts of the earth. What happened was that an essentially binary European-Mediterranean mould was obliged to incorporate a new and gradually revealed America, not to mention the other newly discovered lands in Africa and the Pacific that followed. Susanne Zantop has described how the relatively straightforward 'simple self–other, Occident–Orient dichotomies' were forced to absorb 'not just many others, but multiple, multivalent, constantly shifting "occidents". Anxieties about how to define the "other" in such new circumstances led to a new interest in questions of miscegenation, origins of people and comparative cultural phenomena.'[62]

Glimpses of strange and exotic peoples had been vouchsafed to mediaeval Europe before the great expansion that followed the age of exploration. Much of the interaction, with the Indian subcontinent and the Far East for example, slight though it was, came about as a result of the spice trade in its various forms. This interaction led to the exchange of desirable goods, strange and unlikely stories, artistic devices and motifs. Travellers' tales and travellers' books added to the store of knowledge and in due course themselves created a rich mulch in which Europeans' views of much of humanity were formed. However it was only with the establishment of physical (albeit fluctuating) frontier zones with these exotic societies, the frontier zones that were created typically at the beginning of the colonial era, that a real symbiosis started to occur. Symbiosis is perhaps not quite the *mot juste*: certainly in most cases eastern and African societies were much more influenced by the West than the West was by them: but nonetheless there was a flow both ways. Clearly in the sort of frontier situation typical of the colonial experience, a struggle for political as well as economic mastery is implicit, and part of this struggle is the not entirely innocent attempt to better understand the adversary. Both sides were compelled to engage in this difficult exercise of comprehension.[63]

The discovery of these new and, in some cases unsuspected lands can be seen as heralding European modernity. 'It literally opened up new horizons for Europeans: "virgin territories" were to be possessed and exploited; "different" realities were to be taken in, surveyed, and described; "strange" peoples were to be understood, integrated into existing categories, and subjected to European needs.'[64] The European attempt to articulate these new 'others' became a key part of colonial discourse. This may be defined as the sum of unspoken belief, stated ideology and assumptions that accompanied colonial societies in their colonising enterprise. This discourse can be reconstructed to some extent through an examination of a variety of texts: novels, political pamphlets, essays and colonial reports and indeed European oral traditions. All sorts of symbols and attitudes still enshrine many of these assumptions.

What concerns us particularly is the encounter between European and non-European which lies at the heart of the discourse. It is clear that its basis consists of comparisons between concepts of 'here' and 'there' and between the 'other' and the self. As may be imagined the discourse is affected by many things, including gender and sexuality, as has recently been shown by studies on British imperialism by Anne McClintock and Robert Young.[65] It is also heavily dependent on discussions of race: Homi Bhabha writes that the 'colonial stereotype', which he locates in 'racial difference', gives us access to 'the very heart of colonial fantasies'.[66]

A recent work by David Cannadine shows convincingly that the English class system too weighed upon and mitigated concepts of otherness. According to his analysis class was the key component before the Enlightenment and even when questions of race became more central in the nineteenth century, class issues were still critical.[67]

Until the eighteenth century it is clear that the majority of western peoples subscribed to a system of beliefs based essentially on the two Testaments. For mediaeval and even modern Europeans ancient Hebrew ethnology was the best documented 'primitive' way of life people knew about and it was natural to use this knowledge to explicate the new territories they discovered. First-fruit ceremonies, sacrifices to gods, lunar calendars, myths of floods and of Towers of Babel, purification rites and fasting and food taboos, endogamy, circumcision, pilgrimages and the veneration of objects recalling the Holy Ark all immediately evoked the religion of the Israelites and suggested the presence in unlikely places of the Lost Tribes of Israel or other Judaic peoples. The apogee of this kind of construction was from about 1880–1930, which coincides with the heyday of the British and French overseas empires. It also coincides with the unprecedented mass immigration into western Europe of Jews fleeing poverty, persecution and pogroms in the lands of the Russian Empire. It could be said that this process of creating Jews everywhere has something to do with the 'construction of affinities' – creating a ubiquitous mirror image of metropolitan society. As Cannadine has put it in the case of the British experience, 'Empire was about the familiar and domestic, as well as the different and the exotic: indeed it was in large part about the domestication of the exotic – the comprehending and the reordering of the foreign in parallel, analagous, resemblant terms.'[68]

Any history of the myth of the Lost Tribes of Israel is the history of an idea of the past that people have believed in and that has radically changed the way they view the world. From generation to generation and from place to place the *way* people believed the myth and precisely what it meant to them changed. In the colonial period the myth often seems like a kind of allegory on the relationship between the recording of the past and power. In contemporary society the myth is used, let us say in the African continent, for quite opposite ends by different groups: as a way of chastising an evil enemy; as a way of expressing features of a group's historical memory, which are otherwise inexpressible and which enhance the self-perception of the group. As Riccardo Orizio has put it in *Lost White Tribes*, 'all of us . . . belong to a lost tribe. We can all become minorities.' No doubt we can create minorities too, either in our own image or in opposition to it. The way we project ourselves on the world at large is the matter of this book: the way we create the flickering image of the 'other', which still haunts our imagination, endlessly throughout history and around the world.

Chapter Two

AS THE SAND OF THE SEA: ISRAELITES, THE SPANISH AND THE NEW WORLD

> They are all very like Jews in appearance and voice, for they have large noses and speak through the throat.
>
> Gomara's *Historia Generale de las Indias* (1553)

When Vasco da Gama (1469–1524) set off on his voyage of exploration he carried letters for the fabulous King Prester John and when Christopher Columbus set off on his great voyage he carried messages for the Great Khan, whom he expected to find on the other side of the Atlantic. Much of the motivation for such journeys of exploration was to make contact with places and peoples drawn from a common mythical memory. When Columbus arrived in the Americas in October 1492 he believed he had arrived at certain islands off the coast of the Chinese mainland, but in another sense he thought he had discovered a biblical land, or at least one that could be perceived as part of sacred history.[1] He remained convinced until the end of his life that he had discovered part of Asia in his four great voyages. As he left the Old World what did he expect to find?

No doubt he expected to find a remote part of the world he had left. That is to say he hoped to discover the outer reaches of the Old World and make contact with its peoples. Specifically he imagined he would encounter some of the nations that his contemporaries thought existed in the unknown parts of Asia. Among other things he supposed he might encounter some remnants of the Lost Ten Tribes, which were commonly believed to be in the land of the Tartars and Scythians – that is to say deep into Asia. He might have had some agenda of his own: there are some grounds for believing that Columbus' family may have been of Jewish origin. Certainly he took with him some former Jews: these included the ship's physician, the apothecary and most famously Luis de Torres (who, significantly, only converted to Catholicism a few days before the voyage) who had a knowledge of outlandish languages and was consequently taken along as the expedition's interpreter. Once they struck land his talents were called on.

On Friday, 2 November, as a reconnaissance party was about to be sent into the interior, Columbus, 'decided to send two men, Spaniards, one was called Rodrigo de Jerez,[2] who lived in Ayamonte, and the other was a certain Luis de Torres, who had lived with the *adelantado* of Murcia and who had been a Jew, and who, as he says, understood Hebrew and Chaldee and even some Arabic'. No doubt it was thought that de Torres' linguistic skills would be useful in the event the landing party encountered any Hebrew, Arabic or Aramaic speaking peoples.[3] Columbus believed that Española, the island he had discovered, was part of the Chinese mainland – Cathay – and he no doubt supposed that Hebrew might be an appropriate language for conversing with the Great Khan. Upon Columbus' departure de Torres was among those left behind on Española, where he was killed by the Indians.[4]

Divrei-ha-yamim lemalkhei Zarfat umalkhei beit Otman ha Togar, a work published in Hebrew in 1554 by Yosef ha-Cohen, the leader of the Jewish community of Genoa, still assumed that the first language of contact between the Spanish explorers and the Indians of the New World had been Arabic. Upon arrival on the shores of the Americas ha-Cohen observed, 'The men rejoiced much and rowed towards the dry land and went on shore. And they came into a small city, whose inhabitants were few and naked – yet they were not ashamed. And the Spaniards spake unto them, but they understood nothing except a little of the language of Ishmael.'[5]

According to Peter Martyr (Pedro Martir de Angleria), the fifteenth-century Italian historian, royal chronicler and author of *Décadas del Nuevo Mundo*, first published between 1511 and 1530, Columbus first identified Española as Ophir – 'the island from which King Solomon famously brought his gold'. The clear subtext to this was that if the island were indeed Ophir it followed that Solomon might have left behind soldiers – the ancestors of the Indians.[6]

The framework within which speculation about the Americas took place was essentially exegetical and deductive rather than empirical. There was an evident need for any discussion to be held within the framework of Christian belief and norms and for it to be based essentially on the text of the Bible and its commentaries. Thus the biblical chronology since the Creation had to be adhered to: as the time-span in question was thought to be only about four thousand years it was thought that the customs of people in all parts of the globe were likely to be fairly similar. So a morphological approach – comparing particular aspects of contemporary cultures with what was known of similar aspects of the cultures of the ancients – seemed a viable modus operandi.

Christopher Columbus' encounter with the Caribbean people known as the Tainos precipitated what S. M. Lyman calls, 'a crisis in biblically-based European cosmology'.[7] In addition to coming to terms with new and undreamed-of physical frontiers, Europe was obliged to critically expand its sense of the scale, extent and type of the world's human populations. More specifically, Europeans would have to incorporate into their world-view a new set of configurations concerned with the construct of what the 'other' might mean in these new circumstances. Of course every human society, including that of mediaeval Europe has almost infinite sets of 'others' – peasant, woman, gypsy, beggar, the degenerate inhabitants of the next village down the valley – all served as essential oppositions for some people. But the 'other' against which mediaeval Christian Europe defined itself in some important ways was the 'other' originally from across the Mediterranean: the Jew, the Moor. The Jews achieved this position largely as a result of theological factors and, of course, because they were the most obvious non-Christian minority throughout the lands of Christendom; the Moor largely because of the long centuries of conflict between the Muslim and Christian powers of the time. It is particularly worth remembering that Spain – the first of the great exploring nations – harboured a deep animosity against Moors *and* Jews, and that the expulsion of both from Spain in 1492 coincided with the discovery of the New World. The 'otherness' of these Semites could hardly have been more pronounced in the context of late fifteenth-century Spain. The linkage between the discovery of America and the expulsion of the Jews and Moors was frequently made by Columbus himself. At the beginning of his journal of his first voyage he wrote, 'Forasmuch as, in this present year of 1492, after that Your Highnesses have made an end of the war with the Moors who reigned in Europe . . . in this very month . . . Your Highnesses . . . determined to send me, Cristobal Colon, to the said regions of India . . . therefore, after having driven out all the Jews from your realms and lordships, in the same month of January, Your Highnesses commanded me, with a sufficient fleet, I should go to the said parts of India and for this accorded to me great awards . . .'[8]

It was frequently the case that Europeans' first encounters with the 'savage' led them to believe that they had no creed and no proper language. They were, in a sense, a void that had to be filled. Having seen that the Tainos did not know how to speak any of the languages with which his interpreters were familiar, and having assumed therefore that they did not know how to speak at all, Columbus observed in a letter to his Spanish monarchs Ferdinand and Isabella, 'Our Lord willing, at the time of my departure, I will bring six of them to Your Highnesses that they may learn to Talk.'[9]

The 'otherness' of Semitic languages was just as pronounced as the 'otherness' of the Jews and the Moors. The Arabic language was the epitome of the unknown tongue. By the time Columbus arrived in the New World on his fourth voyage he realised that the islanders did actually know how to speak – that in fact each island had its own language and their respective inhabitants did not, 'understand one another any more than we understand the Arabs'.[10] If Arabic was the antithesis of Spanish, so the religion of the Moors as well as that of the Jews was seen as the antithesis of Christianity: as late as 1730 Luis de Granada wrote, 'Those who hope for the temporal Messiah err no less than the Moors who hope for a sensual paradise. And for that reason we are obliged to snap our fingers at the Jews' Messiah and at the Moors' paradise, since each is as vile and base as the other.'[11]

With Columbus' momentous discovery this essentially binary European–Mediterranean configuration of oppositions was obliged to incorporate a new and gradually revealed western horizon, which kept retreating as the years went on, more exotic lands were encountered and as the complexity of the societies of these lands became dimly apparent. As we have seen, Susanne Zantop has suggested that the process of exploration 'expanded any simple self-other, Occident-Orient dichotomies, to include not just many others, but multiple, multivalent, constantly shifting "occidents". Anxieties about how to define the "other" in such new circumstances led to a new interest in questions of miscegenation, origins of people and comparative cultural phenomena.' In some ways this is true, yet the primitive architecture of identity remained much the same: European versus the rest. As Kirti Chaudhuri has shown this binary system of oppositions is still the case. He notes ironically, 'In the closing years of the twentieth century the "law of the excluded middle" combined with certain implicit and unspoken assumptions, underpins the division of the world into a "First" and a "Third World", a division in which the "Second World" was nowhere to be seen.'[12]

Chaudhuri has rightly remarked that in the wake of these discoveries a 'mental trauma' confronted the world: namely that with Ferdinand Magellan's circumnavigation of the globe in 1522 thinking people had little basis on which to contest what map-makers already knew by 1485: that the world was not in fact flat but was a sphere. 'Now the mathematical or the structural property possessed by a sphere or a circle is the fact that any point located within or on it cannot be identified absolutely in terms of its origin. There is neither a first nor a last point: that is, any extension of the point is topologically closed.'[13] In fact the world is not completely spherical and this fact contributes to the force of the poles, which as we know do permit us to define absolutely any point on the surface of the world. Chaudhuri's point may rather be taken metaphorically – what he was attempting to suggest is that following this grand but traumatic realisation of the shape of the world questions of origins were put on hold. The idea that everything radiated out from a fixed centre was no longer tenable. The new shape of the world – the new configurations – both demanded that a new social map, a new social architecture be invented. In the construction of this map it is indeed true that in the first few years the question of *origins* was not in fact the essential one.

How were Europeans to integrate the peoples who came under their sway into this new social map? For the first decades of Spanish rule the most essential question revolved around the respective rights and responsibilities of the Spanish and the conquered Indians. This was to culminate in the great debate between Bartolomé de las Casas (1474–1566) and Sepulveda in 1550. Initially the origin of the Indians was not at the forefront of the colonists' minds. There was still no conception of a *Mundus Novus* or New World: all that had been discovered as far as anyone was really aware was a new portion of the Old World. Believing until his death that he had merely discovered some islands off the coast of Cathay, Columbus clearly supposed the natives to be Asiatics of some description. As we have seen, the territories discovered had been placed firmly within the realm of European sacred history, with the suggestion that Española was the Ophir of the Bible. Even if it was not stated, there was already the lurking suspicion that the people inhabiting the islands might have something to do with the Israelites, via King Solomon's trading contacts with the illustrious gold lands.[14] Magellan's voyage might well have proved to thinking people that Jerusalem was not in fact at the centre of a flat world but that the sacred heart of Christendom still radiated significance throughout conquered and newly discovered territories. And as we know a ray has a starting point but is infinite.

In time, and particularly once it was understood that the Americas were a new and quite distinct continent, a veritable New World, questions as to the origins of its inhabitants multiplied. Who were these people? Were they descended from Adam and perhaps from Noah? How did their history fit in with biblical chronologies and what did the Bible have to say about them? And if they *had* made their way to the Americas in very remote times, before Noah, how come they had survived the Flood when no one else but Noah and his family had done so? This difficulty suggested strongly that they must be descendants of Noah. A number of theories were put forward connecting the Indians with the Phoenicians, with Arabia or perhaps, as we have seen, with the biblical Ophir. The point was that if the Indians were *not* connected with the biblical account and if the scriptures had *not* made allowances for them in some way, the Bible would appear to be incomplete. At the beginning of the sixteenth century Joseph de Acosta and Gregorio García insisted that the scriptures were not to be denied: it had to be accepted that the Indians were indeed descended from Adam and Eve.[15] Bartolomé de las Casas not only accepted that they were full descendants of Adam, but that they were the 'Elect' referred to by St Paul, who would be gathered up to join Jesus at the End of Days.

But from where had they travelled to America? Were they from China or Carthage or Atlantis or Canaan?[16] And what *was* America? Was it a *mundus alterius* – another quite distinct world where the laws of God did not apply – a world within a world? If America was part of the real world, it followed too that the Gospel must at some time have been preached there. Indeed supposed traces of Christianity in pre-Columbus America were found in Indian practices throughout the sixteenth century and would continue to be found for the next five hundred years. Such traces included the footprints and various other 'proofs' of the presence of St Thomas, representations of the Tower of Babel, several paintings and other representations of the cross and one picture 'emblematical of the five most precious wounds of the Redeemer'.[17] Within these discussions, notwithstanding that some people, including the Colombian historian Alonso de Zamora, Jerónimo de Mendieta and others, were pretty sceptical, the identification of the indigenous Americans as members of the Ten Lost Tribes played a significant part and was to remain part of a general discourse in North America until the time of Jefferson – and in more marginal groups until today.[18]

According to Juan de Torquemada it was las Casas, a contemporary of Columbus, and the so-called 'Apostle to the Indies', who first proposed that the native population was descended from the Lost Tribes. According to Lord Kingsborough,[19] 'the celebrated las Casas entertained no doubt that the continent of America had in early ages been colonized by the Jews; and he even goes so far as to say that the language of the Island of San Domingo was "corrupt Hebrew".'[20]

Torquemada himself was at a loss to explain the great temples and altars of New Spain:

> We do not read in Holy Scripture that any nation in the world has used temples and high altars of this kind built of masonry and elevated in the air, neither does profane history mention them: although Holy Scripture informs us in the Book of Joshua, that the two and a half tribes who did not cross the Jordan, but remained on the other side when the Children of Israel entered the Promised Land . . . erected an altar close to the said Jordan 'of infinite magnitude and height' . . . so that we are not informed nor do we know that a similar edifice has been constructed in the world in honour of the Devil, or so high an altar, except in the Kingdom of New Spain, where on the base of mason work of these high buildings, altars are placed and chapels built.

Elsewhere he explained that the altars and temples were indeed the work of the Devil who, envious of the sacrifices and sacred fires of the Temple in Jerusalem had commanded that 'not one but two altars' should be erected to him and that incense should be burned upon them, not only in the morning but during the whole day.[21]

The Indians, according to Torquemada, were literally of Israelite stock and had been persuaded by the Devil's wiles to worship him in something akin to their celebrated manner of worshipping God. One of the arguments adduced in favour of this proposition and quoted by Torquemada was that the population of the Americas was clearly the largest in the world. At the same time it was known from the Bible that no less an authority than the prophet Hosea had foretold, 'the number of the children of Israel shall be as the sand of the sea'. No doubt then this enormous American population was descended from the Israelites. Moreover, it was clearly understood that the local languages were no more than dialects of Hebrew and other Jewish languages. The fact that the name Cuba signifies 'helmet' in Hebrew was proof abundant that the earliest conqueror of the island must have been some Israelite chieftain noted for the magnificence of his headgear. Similarly Torquemada took the original name of Haiti – according to him Caitin-tateacuth – to be 'pure Hebrew'. The River Yuna was obviously named after the Prophet Jonah, the Yaqui after Jacob and the Haina was no more than *ayin* – the Hebrew word for fountain. These remarkable similarities, plus the parallels between a number of Jewish and Indian customs, were sufficient proof of the Indians' ancient pedigree.[22]

But not everyone was convinced of this. People had doubts as to the basic classification of the Indians. Were they actually human beings? This critical issue was resolved for some by the Papal Bull of 9 June 1537 in which the Pope declared them indeed to be human.[23] Amerigo Vespucci's first published letter (18 July 1500) described the Indians as naked, cannibals, brown and beardless and speaking various languages. Later, discussing the native populations of Brazil, he observed that they were ignorant of law, religion, rulers and the soul. Finally, at a loss to understand who the Indians were and casting around in the categories of classification available to him, he noted, 'they were neither Jews nor Muslims nor were they Christians. They were something worse.'[24]

Many of the early Spanish historians, however, took it as a matter of fact that the Indians in different parts of South America were, at the very least, strikingly similar to Jews. In the case of Peru, from the outset such similarities seemed evident to the Spanish. In Gómara's *Historia Generale de las Indias*, published in 1553, the author noted, 'They are all very like Jews in appearance and voice, for they have large noses and speak through the throat, the women cut off their hair and wear girdles, and they alone use rings. The men dress in short shirts, scarcely studying decency in their apparel, making themselves bald like monks, except that they shave off the hair from the front and the back of their heads and allow it to grow on the sides.'[25]

In around 1566 Diego de Landa of Yucatán, a Franciscan bishop largely responsible for the destruction of Mayan culture, having been recalled to Spain for exceeding his authority, wrote his *Relacion de las*

Cosas de Yucatán, where he noted, 'Some of the old people of Yucatán say that they have heard from their ancestors that this land was occupied by a race of people, who came from the East and whom God had delivered by opening twelve paths through the sea. If this were true, it necessarily follows that all the inhabitants of the Indies are descendants of the Jews: since having once passed the straits of Magellan, they must have extended over more than two thousand leagues of land which now Spain governs.'[26] He then formed the opinion that the Yucatán Indians were descended from the Lost Tribes and he feared that consequently they might well be harbouring crypto-Judaising tendencies.

At the beginning of the seventeenth century, in 1607, Gregorio García, the Spanish Dominican who became Grand Inquisitor, collected the many different theories about the likely forefathers of the Indians into a book, *Origen de los Indios del Nuevo Mundo* (Madrid, 1729). On balance, after comparing the claims of the Greeks, Scythians, Romans, Chinese, Egyptians, Africans, Phoenicians, French, Frisians and various others, he was perhaps inclined to give most weight to the claims of the Chinese and Scythians. But in fact he thought that a number of races had emigrated to southern America over many millennia, from the time of the Flood to more recently, and among these, in his view, were some Israelites. 'Many have supposed,' he wrote, 'and the Spanish generally who reside in the Indies believe, that the Indians proceed from the Ten Jewish Tribes who were lost in the captivity of Salmanazar, king of Assyria, of whom Rabbi Schimon Luzati ... says nothing is certain, nor is it known where they dwell. This opinion is grounded on the disposition, nature and customs of the Indians, which they have found to be very similar to those of the Hebrews: and although learned men condemn, and are uninclined to assent to such a belief, I nevertheless have bestowed great diligence upon the verification of this truth and I can affirm that I have laboured in this more than in any other part of my work: and from which I have found thereto relating, I shall lay such foundations for the edifice and structure of this opinion and hypothesis, as will be well able to sustain its weight.' And indeed García devoted the whole of the third book of his *Origen* to the similarities that he perceived between the laws, ceremonies, customs, sacrifices, history and idolatrous behaviour of the two peoples. His sixth chapter was devoted to a comparison between Mexican and Jewish morality and rituals, the seventh to a comparison of American languages and Hebrew (he pointed out that both the language of the

Peruvian Indians and Hebrew were guttural languages). Not all the points in common were flattering to the Jews. He observed, 'The Indians are cowardly, do not recognise Jesus Christ, and give no thanks for the good done to them.' Therefore, he concluded, they might well, in part, be Jews.[27]

Support for the presence of Hebraic rites was provided also by Father Joseph Gumilla. In *El Orinoco Illustrado* he affirmed, 'that the nations of Oronoco and its streams observed many Hebrew ceremonies in the time of their paganism which they followed rudely and blindly without knowing why or wherefore that had been transmitted by traditions handed down from father to son without their being able to assign any reason for the practice of them . . . from which customs and usages it is inferred that after America had been peopled by the descendants of Cham a certain number of Jews passed over likewise to that continent after the dispersion.'[28] Gumilla stressed similarities in circumcision practice of the Indians of Yucatán (both on the eighth day) and in the shared horror of pork, 'There is not that Jew in existence who holds the flesh of a sucking pig or of the domestic hog in such horror as the said gentiles.' Gumilla concluded one passage with the observation 'that if the spirit of covetousness and self-interest which is predominant in Judaism was lost it might be found entire and in full vigour amongst the nations of the Oronoco and its streams whose mode of addressing each other as regards the claim of kindred . . . is derived from the Jews.'[29]

A somewhat more sympathetic argument was advanced by the Dominican friar Diego Durán, who was born in Seville and died in Mexico in 1588. He soon began to be puzzled by what he saw as similarities between the ancient religion of the Israelites and the religion of the Aztecs in Mexico. After all, 'both Aztecs and Jews believed that in the beginning God created the heavens and the earth'. Similarly the Old World had its Tower of Babel and New Spain its great Pyramid of Cholula.[30] One day Father Diego heard that the Indians of Ocuituco had a precious and ancient document. Hoping that this might contain the answers he had been seeking he took himself to Ocuituco, only to find that they had burned it a dozen years before. As he put it, this might have been 'the Holy Gospel in Hebrew'. However the disappearance of the 'Hebrew' manuscript only spurred him on to greater efforts. On a further expedition he discovered a painting that appeared to him to be a depiction of St Thomas. He was convinced that at least at some time in the past someone had come to America and had preached the Bible. But the Old or the New Testament? For years he wavered between the possibility that Israelites or Hebrews had brought the Jewish religion there, or that Christian missionaries had introduced their faith. Or was there not a third option: that it had been the devil?[31] In his religious writing he also perceived striking similarities between Christianity and the religion of the Aztecs and even concluded at one point that Christianity must have been brought to Mexico by the ubiquitous St Thomas. However in his *History of the Indies of New Spain* he came down on the side of the Israelites and proclaimed that the Aztecs were in fact a Lost Tribe of Israel. As he put it, 'Because of their nature we could almost affirm that they are Jews and Hebrew people, and I believe that I would not be committing a great error if I were to state this fact, considering their way of life, their ceremonies, their rites and superstitions, their omens and false dealings, so related to and characteristic of the Jews.' The proof of their Israelite extraction he derived from the fact that both peoples had known earthquakes, both received divine manna, both knew about human sacrifice, both had made a long journey and both had multiplied greatly.[32] He argued that the Indians as descendants of the Israelites should be viewed in the same kindly light as the Hebrews of old.

The widespread sense that the local Indians were descendants of the lost tribes of Israel commended itself to the mainstream of Spanish colonists. The Indians were Jews who had no doubt been offered the chance of salvation, perhaps through the agency of St Thomas who, known to have reached India, might well have made his way to the Americas. The Indians were still Jewish-looking as far as the Spanish were concerned: they were dark and had large, aquiline noses. They also showed the same moral failings as the Jews: they were backsliders, idolators, they were mean and grasping, begrudging the Catholic priest his tiny stipend, allowing their aged and sick relatives to die of hunger. In addition their dress was Jewish and their meek manner was said to be due to the cowardly streak in the Jews that had been developed over the centuries during which they had laboured as slaves under the Pharoahs in Egyptian bondage. By the seventeenth century it is clear that a large number of Spanish settlers believed that the local people were of Israelite descent. The Israelites-in-America theory had struck root and would still be with us five hundred years later.

Chapter Three

THE INVISIBLE HEBREWS – A MYTH OF ALBION

> Jerusalem was, and is, the Emanation of the Giant Albion ... Your Ancestors derived their origin from Abraham, Heber, Shem, and Noah, who were Druids.
>
> William Blake

In 1290, after a period of horrific persecution, Edward I (1239–1307) had expelled the Jews from England and the edict of expulsion remained in force for almost four hundred years. From the time of the expulsion until the end of the seventeenth century there were officially no Jews in the British Isles. There was a small unofficial community of Spanish and Portuguese Jews who had ostensibly converted to Christianity – so-called Marranos – and perhaps a few others in the eastern part of London and elsewhere. But this went more or less unnoticed. Nonetheless, like a number of other countries throughout history without a Jewish community, Jewish issues loomed large and this was particularly so from the beginning of the seventeenth century. In the next chapter we shall examine the eschatological arguments that were important in the seventeenth-century debate over the readmission of the Jews to England and in the identification of a number of foreign populations as Lost Tribes of Israel. But within the British Isles there were other factors at play and as the discourses described in this book were largely, but not uniquely, generated in Great Britain and English-speaking countries, it is necessary to pay some attention to them.

The universal interest in origins, the quest to establish identity through one's ancestors, takes multiple forms – some of them innately bizarre. Societies throughout the world often construct a genealogically useful past in which unwanted narratives are dispensed with and others stressed, or even flaunted. In the European context attempts to establish group myths of origin frequently drew on Germanic models, while dynastic traditions drew on distinct and superior descents of all sorts. In England, as in other parts of Britain, however, there was a long-running discourse celebrating the notion that the English themselves were literally of Jewish extraction and that the ancestors of the English people were in fact Israelites. This view of the past chose to connect the mythical history of the English with the sacred history of the Chosen People. Perhaps this was a means of seeking legitimacy for a specifically English Protestant destiny that was viewed with such alarm by much of Catholic Europe; perhaps it was a way of fixing the chosenness of the English nation.

One of the first published expressions of an invented Israelite genealogy for the British was in *Rights of the Kingdom* (London, 1649) by John Sadler, one-time town clerk of London and MP for Cambridge, a student of Oriental literature and a friend of Oliver Cromwell. Sadler's book drew parallels between ancient English law and custom and those of the Israelites, and implied an Israelite descent both for the constitution of England and for the English people themselves. In 1650 Thomas Tany, a London silversmith, made the discovery that he was of the tribe of Reuben and announced that the temple would shortly be rebuilt in Jerusalem with him as High Priest.[1] In 1714 John Toland urged the bishops of the Anglican church to support naturalisation of the Jews on the grounds that they knew, 'how considerable a part of the *British* inhabitants are the undoubted ... offspring of the Jews ... and how many worthy Prelates of this same stock, not to speak of Lords or Commons, may at this time make an illustrious figure among us.' The year before an unknown poet addressed the British race with the words, 'Arise O Israel, know the Lord ... Happy *Israel* chosen tribe.' And in *Jubilate Agno* Christopher Smart (1722–71), a talented madman writing from a lunatic asylum observed that he was, 'the Lord's newswriter, the scribe evangelist' and noted that, 'the ENGLISH are the seed of Abraham and work up to him by Joab, David and Naphtali ... the WELCH are the children of Mephibosheth and Ziba with a mixture of David in the Jones's.' A perceptive contemporary critic observes that there is nothing 'idiosyncratic' about these observations – they were part of a general pattern of British identification with the Jews of old.[2]

Such notions went hand in hand with a deeply entrenched British philo-Semitism, which often led to the espousal of Jewish ideas.[3] For some individuals and groups Judaism, not simply as a construct of origin but as a religion, became an overwhelmingly attractive and seductive entity. One Judaising group was founded by John Traske, an

English minister who believed that the laws imposed upon the Jews in the book of Leviticus and elsewhere were binding on gentiles too. He attempted to live by Judaic precepts: he observed the Passover and the Sabbath and even had himself circumcised. Eventually he was convicted of offences against religion and was obliged to publicly recant. He subsequently became a Baptist.[4] One of his disciples was James Whitehall (b. 1587), a Master of Arts of Christ Church College, Oxford, who was given special leave to go on the ill-fated Orinoco expedition with Sir Walter Raleigh. On his return in 1618 he went back to Christ Church and to general consternation began to publicly preach Judaism. Before long he too was convicted and imprisoned. Escaping to Ireland he was for a while incarcerated in Dublin Castle, before being sent back to England in chains. Some of Traske's other disciples also escaped to Ireland. One of them, Christopher Sands, became a Jewish proselyte. The restoration of the Jews to the Holy Land similarly attracted a number of enthusiasts. One of them, an unbalanced Irishman called Grey, had such an acute desire to contribute to the restoration that he murdered his own child in order to plead the case of the Jews at his trial.[5]

In some sense the Jews of the time were perceived as honorary Britons and the national character of Jews and the English was taken to be somewhat similar. Dryden suggests in *Absalom and Achitopel* (1684) that a bloody-minded spirit of independence characterised Jew and Briton alike. Jews and British Protestants were perceived as being allies against the 'scarlet woman of Rome' and having a good deal in common besides. This putative alliance underlies the curious events surrounding the life of Lord George Gordon (1751–93) who sparked off the anti-Catholic Gordon Riots in June 1780. The mob that swept past the home of the Hebraising William Blake with its 'howlings and hissings, shrieks and groans and voices of despair'[6] provoked ten times more damage in London in one week than occurred in Paris throughout the whole period of the French Revolution. Gordon had been pro-Jewish for a period before his famous conversion to Judaism some time between 1786–7. In 1783 he had sent letters to the Jews of England, 'requesting those rulers to submit my best intended endeavours to the consideration of Judah and the tribes of Israel, whithersoever dispersed over the whole world'. He warned Jews that the 'tribes of Israel will soon be driven out of this pleasant land, like chaff before the wind, if they set themselves against God, and his People, to serve Idolators.

There is no time to be lost. The Protestants in Europe, as well as in America, will insist with vigour on your shewing yourselves on their side, against the Jesuits.'[7]

Christopher Hill has shown that the idea of a secret, occult wisdom runs through English thought and is often connected with a certain kind of religious and political radicalism.[8] By the 1780s there was a veritable explosion of anti-rationalism in Europe and perhaps particularly in London.[9] One expression of this was that with the arrival of the French Revolution speculation about the imminent End of Days increased. One notable eccentric who had a long-term influence on the diffusion of lost tribes ideology was Richard Brothers (1757–1824).[10] Brothers, who is tersely termed 'enthusiast' by the *Dictionary of National Biography* had a vision in which it was vouchsafed to him that he was none other than the Prince of the Hebrews, and as such the nephew of the Almighty. He fastened upon the glum prospect that he would in time be the ruler of the world. Brothers was born in Newfoundland, the son of a gunner, and eventually joined the British Navy where in 1783 he rose to the rank of lieutenant. On shore-leave he made the unsettling discovery that his wife had been living with another man whose offspring she had borne while Brothers was at sea. Cast down by this revelation he came to the conclusion that the military life was at odds with the teaching of Christ, retired from the Navy and in 1787 became a vegetarian and moved to London. In 1794 Brothers published a two-volume work that had a considerable success. *A Revealed Knowledge of the Prophecies and Times* predicted the date of the millennium and the role he was to play in it. Brothers worked out that he was in direct line of descent to King David via James, the brother of Jesus, and no doubt this distinguished lineage did much to bolster his appeal among his followers who were numerous and in some cases fairly influential. (One of his disciples was Nathaniel Brassey Halhet, MP for Lymington, an Oriental traveller recalled in Hansard as 'a memorable and melancholy instance of the eccentricity of the human mind', another, John Finlayson, a wealthy Scottish lawyer.) William Sharp, the engraver and friend of William Blake, was so convinced of Brothers' claims that he produced two plates of his portrait bearing the legend, 'Fully believing this to be the Man who God has appointed, I engrave his likeness.' Arrested for treasonable practices in 1795 (he had proclaimed that 'the Government of the Jewish Nation will, under the Lord God, be committed to me'[11]) Brothers was brought before the

Privy Council and in March of that year was condemned as a criminal lunatic and thrown into an asylum for the insane in which he was incarcerated for more than a decade. Brothers was convinced that the Second Coming would be on 19 November 1795. On this happy date he would be revealed Prince of the Hebrews and would lead the Jews back to Palestine along with the 'invisible Hebrews', the descendants of the Lost Tribes, some of whom were domiciled in England and other parts of Europe and some of whom were to be counted among his own disciples. His immediate influence waned somewhat after the failure of the world to come to an end at the expected time, but nonetheless he persevered and went on to write fifteen books. In *Correct Account of the Invasion of England by the Saxons, Showing the English Nation to be Descendants of the Lost Ten Tribes* (1822), as in most of the rest, he argued for the Israelite ancestry of the English.[12] One of the works Brothers composed after his release was *A Description of Jerusalem*. He was writing this at the same time as William Blake was writing his own more famous *Jerusalem*.[13] The two men in fact have a good deal in common. They were both Londoners, both of prophetic disposition, they were exactly the same age and shared some of their ideas. It is clear from the second book of Blake's *Jerusalem*, entitled 'To the Jews', that his views on the mythic ancestry of the British are almost identical to those of Brothers.

> Jerusalem, the Emanation of the Giant Albion! Can it be? Is it a truth that the learned have explored? Was Britain the primitive seat of the Patriarchal Religion? If it is true, my title page is also true, that Jerusalem was, and is, the Emanation of the Giant Albion. It is true, and cannot be controverted. Ye are united, O ye inhabitants of Earth, in One Religion – the Religion of Jesus, the most ancient, the Eternal and the Everlasting Gospel. The Wicked will turn it to Wickedness, the Righteous to Righteousness. Amen! Huzza! Selah!
>
> 'All things begin and end in Albion's ancient Druid rocky shore.'
>
> Your Ancestors derived their origin from Abraham, Heber, Shem, and Noah, who were Druids, as the Druid Temples (which are the patriarchal pillars and oak groves) over the whole Earth witness to this day.
>
> You have a tradition that Man anciently contain'd in his mighty limbs all things in Heaven and Earth: this you received from the Druids.
>
> 'But now the starry Heavens are fled from the mighty limbs of Albion.'
>
> Albion was the Parent of the Druids, and, in his Chaotic State of

Sleep, Satan and Adam and the whole World was created by the Elohim.

The fields from Islington to Marylbone,
To Primrose Hill and Saint John's Wood,
Were builded over with pillars of gold;
And there Jerusalem's pillars stood.
Her Little Ones ran on the fields,
The Lamb of God among them seen,
And fair Jerusalem, His Bride,
Among the little meadows green . . .

The direct propagation of Brothers' message was continued by his disciple Finlayson, who published a number of pamphlets and in 1849 a book, *The Last Trumpet and the Flying Angel*, where he set forth his belief that the Lost Tribes were to be found almost everywhere, 'So that nearly all the Germans, English, Lowlanders of Scotland, Easterlings of Ireland, are the descendants of the Hebrews. But two-thirds of France are also; as well as the Persians and those of the Barbary States – one half of the Russians, Poles, Swiss, Italians, Spaniards and Greeks are so, and they abound in the Turkish Empire and adjoining states, and even in China, Japan and Ethiopia – nearly all the North Americans are so.'[14] Brothers was followed by a number of other visionaries such as Joanna Southcott (1750–1814, just as tersely termed 'fanatic' by the *Dictionary of National Biography*) who in respect to Brothers' Messianic calling might be regarded his principal successor, although in fact she denounced some of his teaching. Southcott, the daughter of a small dairy farmer who worked as a shop assistant, believed she was the woman 'clothed with the sun' of the Book of Revelation (12:1) and that her destiny was to give birth, while a virgin, to the Messiah. Shortly before she died, to the excitement of her followers she showed some distinct symptoms of pregnancy confirmed by six of the nine medical practitioners who came to inspect her. A crib for the Messiah costing two hundred pounds was made to order by Seddons of Aldergate Street; one hundreds pounds was spent on 'pap spoons'. The London papers worked themselves into a fever of excitement over the case. Then she died. Crushed by her demise her followers believed she would imminently return, but to their alarm her anticipated resurrection failed to occur and she was buried in St John's Wood cemetery in London, near the final resting place of Brothers.[15] The Jewish aspect of Southcott's teaching was even more evident in the movements that sprung up among her followers following her death: one of her disciples, Mary 'Joanna' Boon, the wife of an illiterate cobbler, instructed her followers to observe the Jewish Sabbath as well as the law of Moses. Another was an unpleasant individual called John Wroe (1782–1863), the abused son of a farmer, worsted manufacturer and collier, who became the founder of the Christian Israelites.[16] Wroe, a beak-nosed hunchback who habitually wore a beard and a broad-brimmed beaver, was suspected of paedophilia, sent three innocent people to penal colonies, cheated his followers and delivered himself with some regularity of 'fatuous insipidities with a biblical twang'. He founded a movement in the Bradford area based on visions in which he was told by an angel to become a Jew and to convince Christians to observe the Jewish law. Wroe's angelic instructor bade him visit the Jews and with that end in mind he walked to Liverpool. Rejected by the Liverpool synagogues, he travelled throughout the Jewish communities of Europe announcing the need for gentiles to observe Jewish law. In April 1824 he was publicly circumcised in Ashton-under-Lyne where he lived until he was banished in 1831. His Israelite disciples also practised circumcision, wore long beards and maintained a Jewish dietary regime. His followers in Ashton included a number of respectable shopkeepers who wore broad-brimmed felt hats and closed their shops between 6 p.m. on Friday and 6 p.m. on Saturday. They were commonly known as 'Joannas', after Mary 'Joanna' Boon. In 1825 £9,500 was spent on a sanctuary for the movement in Ashton. Wroe divided his disciples into twelve tribes : his son Benjamin was to lead one of the tribes. He made a number of visits to Australia and the United States in both of which countries he had a considerable following. His Melbourne followers built him a splendid mansion near Wakefield – Melbourne House – which was inaugurated with due pomp in 1857 (it was purchased by the Christian Israelites in 1936 as their world headquarters). He wrote numerous books including *The Word of God* (Wakefield, 1834), *The Vision of an Angel* (Bradford, 1820) and *A Guide to the People Surnamed Israelites* (Gravesend, 1852),[17] and more recently he became the subject of a 1991 novel, *Mr Wroe's Virgins*, and a television film.

The Celts as a whole, and the Scots especially, were often associated in English thought, as well as their own, with the Jews. A widely held theory had it that the Celtic peoples were descended from Gomer, Noah's grandson, who was supposed to have sired the peoples of Asia

Minor and Europe. These Celts, it was thought, originally spoke Hebrew which eventually evolved into Celtic. The religious mores of the Celts were mediated by the Druids who had gained their insights and wisdom from Hebrew patriarchs. Another theory had it that the British nation was descended, at least in part, from the Hebrew-speaking Phoenicians who had come to trade for tin in Cornwall and who maintained colonies replete with their original culture in central and western Britain. The Celts were seen as being connected to the sacred history of the Jews and it was this that accounted for their special talents and for the peculiarly imaginative genius of their languages. Celts in the late eighteenth century are viewed in opposition to Germans on the one hand and to classical traditions on the other. The famous Ossian poems published by their clergyman author James Macpherson between 1760 and 1763 and presented as discovered fragments of a third century bard, a Scottish son of Finn (they were compared with the works of Homer at the time and influenced such diverse geniuses as Goethe, Napoleon and Blake) were in fact infused with a Hebraic spirit, 'Its Druid-Bard wisdom inculcated by Hebrew patriarchs is nobler than classical wisdom; its putative inspired, imaginative language stems from Hebrew and the God of the Hebrews who is Macpherson's God as well; its culture in part is the product of a people polished by commerce . . .'[18] The connection of Jews to the religion of the Druids was further explored by Godfrey Higgins (1772–1833) in *The Celtic Druids or, An Attempt to show that The Druids were the Priests of Oriental Colonies Who Emigrated from India; and were the Introducers of the First or Cadmean System of Letters, and the Builders of Stonehenge, of Carnac, and of Other Cyclopean Works, in Asia and Europe* (London, 1827) and since then by many more.[19]

Ireland already had a history of identification with Jews. In the *History of Ireland* Geoffrey Keating (*c.* 1570–1644) recounted how Milesius, the founder of the Irish race, son of Breogan, traced his descent through a genealogy that included twenty-two Celtic names and thirteen Hebrew ones going back to Japheth and Adam.[20] According to him the Irish were a tribe of Israel that had reached Scythia where their king, Fenius Farsaigh, had founded a great academy for the study of the languages of the world. From Scythia the tribe had crossed Europe into Spain and from there had gone on to Ireland. By the nineteenth century, with the development of British-Israel theory, Ireland came to have a significant role. According to some, the royal house of Ireland could be traced back to King David. One British-Israel writer opined, 'There is evidence that the tribe of Dan fled by the sea from their captors and colonised Ulster in Ireland, and Denmark . . .'

The theories connecting Gaelic with Hebrew, and the Celts with the Jews were parodied by James Joyce in *Ulysses*, 'The presence of guttural sounds, diacritic aspirations, epenthetic and servile letters in both languages: their antiquity, both having been taught on the plain of Shinar 242 years after the deluge in the seminary instituted by Fenius Farsaigh, descendant of Noah, progenitor of Israel, and ascendant of Hebrew and Heremon, progenitors of Ireland . . .'[21] Elsewhere in this discourse rebellious Ireland is seen as the offspring of Ephraim who rebelled against Moses. Even the Irish reputation for hard-drinking is connected with this distinguished lineage, 'Do you not see a fitness in this sad reminiscence of the old sin of Ephraim, when you remark that drunkenness is the besetting sin of our nation?'

In a more metaphorical sense, Ireland was often taken for Israel. The Irish saw themselves as the children of Israel enslaved by England's Egypt. In *Ulysses* this largely rhetorical device is mentioned frequently – Ireland as 'land of bondage', or Ireland's revolt against the English presented as the revolt of the young Moses against Pharaoh. As far as *Ulysses* is concerned, Joyce described it as 'an epic of two races (Israelite-Irish)', and called it elsewhere, 'the farced epistol to the hibruws'.[22]

A metaphorical identification with the Jews had been a key feature of the Puritan enterprise in England from the seventeenth century on. The more extreme English Puritans of that time believed they were God's chosen people, Old Testament Hebrews reincarnated, and appropriately chose biblical names for their children. In 1653, 'Praisegod Barebone' and other members of Cromwell's 'Little Parliament' replaced the English constitution with the Old Testament laws of Moses. Cromwell told his parliament that God's message to Israel in the sixty-eighth Psalm was addressed to them; they were chosen by God to preside over the establishment of His rule on earth.

In the British colonies in North America there had been a similar tendency from the very beginnings of Puritan settlement: as the Puritans made for the colonies they carried with them the notion which existed in Puritan circles in England well before the *Mayflower*, that they were the chosen people – the new Israel – and that North America was the new Zion. In 1629 on board the *Arabella*, the ship that brought the second group of Puritans to Massachusetts Bay, John Winthrop compared the vessel to Noah's Ark: the passengers would be the progenitors of a new race of people, while Europe would be destroyed for its manifold iniquities. A few years later a New England divine by the name of Samuel Wakeman preached a sermon, published in his book *Sound Repentance* (1685), in which he declared, 'Jerusalem was, New England is; they were, you are, God's own, God's covenant people; put but New England's name instead of Jerusalem.'[23] In about 1696 the famous Puritan clergyman Cotton Mather, acknowledged even by his enemies as the greatest scholar in North America, started calling himself 'rabbi' and took to wearing a Jewish skullcap. For Mather, as for other Puritans, the example of godly living was part of the process of redeeming the world, and their journey to the New World was the re-enactment of the wandering of the Israelites in the wilderness on the way to the Promised Land. In this scheme of things the Jews had a place: they had to be converted if the divine plan were to be realised.[24]

A key figure in the development of these ideas was Ezra Stiles (1727–95), a Puritan theologian and no mean Hebraist, who served as president of Yale College from 1778 to 1795. For Stiles, God's plans for the world were clear to see: it was the Americans who had created 'the City on the Hill', the working out of whose history was the realisation of sacred history. Stiles had a complex and somewhat ambiguous relationship with the Jews – with the old Israel. On the one hand he was sympathetic to their plight and had friendly relations with some individuals, but he did not believe that Jews could ever settle permanently in America unless they converted to Christianity. The Christian ethic, for Stiles, *was* America.[25] In the midst of the American Revolution Stiles transformed the Puritan idea of chosenness into a secular doctrine which argued that the creation of the new American republic was part of the divine plan for the world and would lead to the salvation of mankind. Anyone wishing to settle in this republic would automatically be covered by the glorious mantle of the chosen people. American Protestants were now the chosen people – any pretensions that any other group might harbour with respect to the status of chosenness were null and void.[26] The prevalence of this idea in the United States in the first half of the nineteenth century no doubt explains the visceral hatred many Americans had for the Mormons, who made similar claims for themselves. And it may very well be that the hatred of the Church of Jesus Christ of Latter-Day Saints fed into the development of the

British-Israelite movement, which essentially promoted the idea of the chosenness of Anglo-Saxon Protestants but, unlike the ideology of Stiles and others, did so in a woodenly non-metaphorical and literal way.

British Israelism is part of the wave of romantic nationalism that engulfed Europe in the nineteenth century. It may be seen as a somewhat feeble riposte to the Aryan theory, which posited an Indian origin for Germanic and other peoples and which held sway in much of Europe, commanding a good deal of respect throughout the nineteenth century (not least from Hegel). The Aryan myth in part sought to abandon an outdated biblical genealogy while the use of Indian fables, as the writings of Voltaire or Herder show, could be used to diminish the influence of biblical accounts. Leon Poliakov observed, 'among the ruins of the *ancien régime* Adam died as a universal ancestor', and he wrote tellingly of the 'lordly disdain with which Goethe attributed descent from Adam to the Jewish people alone.'[27] The Aryan myth was, in a sense, both anti-clerical and modernist, while the British Israelites were pro-clerical and deeply conservative. In the case of the British Israelites the nation's roots were found not in India, but in another distant place – the land of Israel – and also significantly in the various places where the Lost Tribes were supposed to have passed through after their dispersion, which is to say more or less everywhere. This was a handy stratagem for the creation of a tradition of origin for a master race which was identified with a world empire. Proofs were found for the theory in a wide variety of classical and other texts, and the wisdom of ancient Egypt – much in vogue since Napoleon's campaign of 1799 – was also pressed into service. The British Israelites were successors to a long line of Anglo-American-Celtic visionaries who had constructed for themselves an Israelite identity and history. At the same time, the movement grew in the second half of the nineteenth century from pretty marginal origins to an organisation that, by 1900, had some two million members. This was no doubt in opposition to different ideologies such as the Aryan theory, as well as similar ideologies notably among the Mormons in the United States and among the welter of miscellaneous groups in Africa, Asia and the Pacific who had been awarded Lost Tribe status throughout the Victorian age.[28]

The British-Israelite movement, which may be termed loosely an interdenominational Protestant fellowship, brought the Ten Tribes back into a properly Anglo-Saxon and orthodox Christian fold. The theory in essence posits that the Anglo-Saxons are the blood descendants of the Israelites and that Great Britain and its empire, along with her offspring – America – have inherited the covenant blessings given to Abraham.[29] The general notion of the Lost Tribes' descent for the Anglo-Saxons, unblessed with even a scintilla of evidence, found adherents in every corner of the globe – even, bizarrely, among the French, as may be seen from Roger Lambelin's *Le règne d'Israel chez les Anglo-Saxons* (Paris, 1921. It should be noted that Brothers' first important work was published in Paris in 1796 as *Prophéties de Jacques Brothers ou La Connaissance Révélée*).[30] In Europe the hostility shown by the British to Napoleon and to Russia was perceived, again bizarrely, as proof of their Israelite origin.[31] From the final decades of the nineteenth century until the present day thousands of books have been devoted to the British-Israelite idea, not one of which makes the slightest sense in purely historical terms.

The roots of the movement were no doubt nourished by the ministry of Brothers and by the work of the groups and individuals mentioned earlier in this chapter. However British Israelites usually dismiss the influence of Brothers, whom they regard 'as a person of weak intellect'.[32] Anton Darms in *Comprehensive Treatise* (New York, no date) instead argued that the movement could be traced back to a certain Dr Abadie of Amsterdam who is quoted as having opined in 1723, 'that unless the ten tribes have flown into the air or have been plunged into the centre of the earth, they must be sought for in the south and in the British Isles'. Elsewhere the Quakers of Skipton, who issued a treatise in 1660 maintaining that the English were descended from the Lost Tribes, were given the credit.[33] Others have offered the honour to Ralph Wedgewood whose book celebrating the defeat of Napoleon – *Book of Remembrance* (London, 1815) – attempted to demonstrate that the British Empire was 'the bow of Ephraim' and the 'peculiar possession of the Messiah'. Certain British-Israelite ideas were expressed by Godfrey Higgins (1772–1833) in *The Celtic Druids* already referred to, and in *Anacalypsis – An Attempt to Draw Aside the Veil of the Saitic Isis; or an Inquiry into the Origin of Languages, Nations and Religions* (London, 1833–6). However, British Israelites usually nominate as the true 'father of the rediscovery of Israel', the 'Christian phrenologist' 'Professor' John Wilson, the son of a Kilmarnock weaver. Wilson travelled throughout Ireland imparting the news (which can hardly have gone down well) that England was the lost Israel. He struck an immediate chord with his writing: in 1840 he published *Our Israelitish Origin*, which was the first coherent expression of Anglo-Israelism and went through five editions by 1876. In 1840 he also published *Lectures on Ancient Israel and the Origin of the Modern Nations of Europe*, which was to achieve a third edition by 1844. He adopted the idea that the European 'race', in particular the Anglo-Saxons, were descended from certain Scythian tribes, and these Scythian tribes (as many had previously stated from the Middle Ages on) were in turn descended from the ten Lost Tribes of Israel. Wilson's arguments were more or less refuted and the idea failed to gain anything like mass popular support, although he managed to maintain himself financially on the lecture circuit. Two periodic publications for which he was responsible, *The Time of the End and Prophetic Witness* (1844) and *The Watchman of Ephraim* (1866–8) were of short duration. Nonetheless his views did garner some followers, including C. Piazzi Smyth, the Astronomer Royal for Scotland, who believed that the Pyramids were expressions of divine Christian guidance containing within them spiritual and mathematical knowledge: indeed he argued that the passages within the Great Pyramid represented symbolically the progress of the whole of human civilisation.[34] Piazzi Smyth among other things deduced from the measurements of the Pyramids in Egypt that the English were descended from the Ten Tribes and went on to publish his theory in *Our Inheritance in the Great Pyramid* (London, 1864).

With the growth of British power in the world the idea that Europeans generally were descended from the Lost Tribes gradually gave way to the more useful notion of the British being owners of this proud pedigree. The first attempt to create an organisational base for 'Teutonist' ideas, which is to say that *all* the 'nordic' races were of Israelite stock, was at a meeting in 1871 chaired by Bishop Gobat who had been the Anglican bishop of Jerusalem since 1846.[35] An association was created, initially called the Anglo-Ephraim Association. To combat this the Anglo-Israel Association – peddling a specifically British version – was set up in 1874. Further unconnected associations, which also followed a more specifically British orientation, were set up in Bristol, Liverpool, Southampton and Dublin. Finally the Anglo-Ephraim Association was swallowed up by a new umbrella organisation for the British version – the Metropolitan Anglo-Israel Association – under the presidency of a former Indian civil servant, Edward Bird.

While these developments were taking place the interest of the general public was being aroused as never before by the publication of a book by Edward Hine, a poorly educated man who had taken up a career as public lecturer in the late 1860s, after the collapse of the Penny Bank in which he had been a deputy manager. Hine came to prominence with the publication of *Twenty-Seven Identifications of the British Nation with Lost Isael* (London, 1871) which sold a quarter of a million copies, and the appearance of a number of pamphlets including *Flashes of Light* and *Anglo-Saxon Riddles*. He also launched two British-Israelite magazines, *Leading the Nation to Glory* (later called *The Nation's Leader*) and *Life from the Dead*. Unfortunately for Hine he was related to an Oxford don – George Rawlinson – who attacked his work mercilessly: the attendant publicity was sufficient to launch a full scale controversy. Edward Hine toured England in the 1870s, spreading the good news and engaging in public debates – one carried on over a number of consecutive evenings in February 1879. In 1880 he published a riposte to Rawlinson and declared that the attacks on his theories had not dented his confidence, 'Not one objection has foothold as yet and I believe never can have. The identity of our Nation with Israel is purely God's work and no man has power to destroy it.'[36] Wilson, Hine and other Anglo-Israelites believed that as soon as their message had been accepted by the British people they would be joined by the tribes of Judah and Levi (the Jews) in the Holy Land.

In 1884 Hine set out for the United States to preach Anglo-Israelism. In New York Hines' *Israel with the Anglo-Celto-Saxons* was published and here he set out his mission, which was to include Americans in the British-Israelite dispensation. Specifically he suggested to them that they were descended from the tribe of Manasseh. A spate of publications followed in North America: these included a Toronto minister's sermons on the subject – William Poole's *Anglo-Israel or the Saxon Race*, which brought between the covers of a handsome volume speculation on the pyramids, the Druids and their connection to the Lost Tribes and the Saxon race – and a volume published in Philadelphia in 1892 by the Reverend Thomas Rolsing, which argued that the Jewish problem would only be resolved by the truth of British-Israelism.[37] As the theory developed into the twentieth century Great Britain continued to be viewed as Ephraim, and Manasseh as the United States. The general idea was that the Anglo-Saxon race would achieve permanent world supremacy. Hine gained a number of disciples, including

General Winfield Scott Hancock (1824–86), a brigadier-general on the Union side in the Civil War and a hero of Gettysburg. As the Democratic candidate for the US presidency in 1880 Winfield Scott Hancock was very narrowly defeated by James Garfield. Hine also attracted the support of Charles Latimer, the publisher of the *International Standard*, which campaigned fiercely against the metric system, on account of studies he too had conducted of the Pyramids. However Hine failed to marshal the financial support he needed and, deeply in debt, died a short while after his American mission.

In England, Hine by this time had lost ground to the more conventional Bird. Hine's claim to be 'Joseph, the shepherd of the state of Israel', his fierce espousal of Disraeli's imperialism and his vulgarity were rapidly putting him beyond the pale for middle-class audiences. Bird on the other hand had gone from strength to strength. He made Anglo-Israelism pay for itself and his publications established the essential views of the movement.

In 1928 Howard B. Rand (1889–1991), the manager of a construction company in Havervill, Massachusetts, who would become Anglo-Israelism's foremost crusader in the United States, accepted the post of National Commissioner of the Anglo-Saxon Federation of America. He put out an American Anglo-Israelite publication first called *The Bulletin*, then *The Message of the Covenant* and now entitled *Destiny*. Destiny Publishers, which he began in 1937, is still publishing books and pamphlets, as well as the newsletter *Special Alert*. One of the most important of the Anglo-Israelite churches is Bethel Temple in Spokane, Washington whose pastor publishes *Prophetic Herald News*. There are numerous other centres throughout the United States. A key figure in the movement is Herbert W. Armstrong and his World Wide Church of God, which has it headquarters in Pasadena, California. His message is propagated through his book *The United States and British Commonwealth in Prophecy* and a magazine – *Plain Truth*. He claims to have 125,000 co-workers. In an article in *Plain Truth* (February, 1973) Armstrong noted that his was 'a truly great worldwide operation serving 150 million people in all continents'.[38]

In England British Israelism became a sanctification and validation of the British Empire. 'We have many faults,' admitted one British Israelite in 1885, 'yet for all that it will be admitted that we are a great nation. What is the secret of Britain's greatness? If it is proved that the British are Israelites, the whole History of England will be understood with a right point of view; and that is, that God's dealing with her, being Israel, show forth that He is true, faithful, and "Covenant" keeping: this is the true secret of England's greatness.'[39] In *The Heritage of the Anglo-Saxon Race* (London, 1941) Gayer asked, 'What is British- or (Anglo-) Israel truth? Is it a new religion?' Gayer replied at once, 'Most emphatically not. British-Israel Truth is the Master-key with which all religions can unlock the problems of the Bible. With it the founding and purpose of the British Empire are demonstrated to be within the Eternal plans of God. The identity of the Anglo-Saxon race is historically established with the great Israel people of the Bible.' He asks again, 'Are the Anglo-Saxons then all "Jews"? No; the Anglo-Saxons are ISRAEL – not JUDAH. It is highly important to understand the difference in the Bible between Israel and Judah . . .'[40] (It should be noted that British Israelites have always been much drawn to the use of capitals for emphasis.) The rest of the book is a trawl through the Bible for support for this thesis.

The Anglo-Israelite argument has from the beginning been mainly based on a particular and very literal reading of the Bible or to a lesser extent the Book of Common Prayer, and as one wades, without any of the usual pleasure to be gained from wading, through this literature the quotations and arguments tend to repeat themselves endlessly. Israel was to change its name (Hosea 1:9), it would increase in size and dwell in islands (Isaiah 24:15), it would travel to the north (Jeremiah 3:12) and would ultimately become a great nation (Micah 5:8). It would spawn colonies (Isaiah 49:19). The American eagle is referred to in Ezekiel 17:3 and the British lion and the unicorn in Numbers 24:8–9. It should also be added that by and large the literature attacking British Israelism uses the same methodology and simply maintains that the British-Israelite reading of the Bible is fallacious. Anti-British-Israelite readings sometimes simply selected new victims for lost Israelite status: John Wilkinson's *The Ten Tribes: Where are They Not and Where are They?* – ostensibly a mild attack on the British Israelites – works up to the conclusion that the real lost tribes were the Nestorians of Kurdistan.[41] Wilkinson noted, 'About the year 1860 or '61 my morning daily paper announced the arrival in London of two representatives of this ancient people, and that they were located at the Home for Asiatics at Limehouse. My wife and I immediately went to see them. We saw them. I made myself understood through the Hebrew of which the Syriac is a cognate as well as the Chaldee . . . they told us there is no doubt of their Israelitish origin . . . anyone looking the elder one in the face would have no difficulty in perceiving at once the Jewish features.'[42]

In British-Israelite works there is often a hectoring tone, which combines dull stupidity with sanctimonious middle-class snobbishness: one example drawn from Captain B. de Weldon's *The Evolution of Israel: the Story of the English Race from 721 BC to the Present Day* (London, *c.* 1920) will perhaps give some idea of this.

> With the actual details of the journeyings of the people of Israel across Europe to the Land of Zion few of us, who were not students of this particular branch of history were probably acquainted. But there is no excuse for the Englishman who is ignorant of the fact that he is descended from Abraham and forms one of the children of Israel. He declares this to be the truth every time he attends morning or evening service in the Church of England . . . Nor does the preface to the authorised translation of the Bible permit a second sentence to pass without identifying England with Zion. After the dedication to King James it begins: 'Great and manifold were the blessings, most dread Sovereign which Almighty God the Father of all mercies, bestowed upon us the people of *England* when He first sent your Majesty's Royal Person to rule and reign over us. For whereas it was the expectation of many, who wished not well unto our Sion . . .' Now this version is published 'cum privilegio' by 'His Majesty's Express Command'. It is the only book in England of which the perpetual copyright is retained. Every edition is published with this preface; and with the words 'England' and 'Sion' in italics to show their importance. Are the statements in this preface to be considered of no value, are we to suppose them to be carelessly written? If so, we pay a very poor compliment to our King, our nation and our religion. The Church of England is the *Established* Church of the people of England; its Prayer Book is officially a schedule to an Act of Parliament. The views set forth in that prayer Book may not suit the taste of individuals or even of large sections of the community; this fact does not set aside the truth that by *law* this book expressed the religious opinion of the *nation* . . . But the most amazing fact is that the people is not the People of England but the People of *Israel.*

One can see Captain Weldon's finger wagging. Anglo-Israelite publications are also larded with frequent references to British and particularly royal history. An early variant on British Israelism expressed in *England, the Remnant of Judah* (London, 1861) maintained that the royal family of England was descended from the house of David. This took some ingenuity and absorbed a number of minds for considerable periods. In 1877 Stevens published a genealogical chart that explained the matter in great detail.[43] And this was followed by even more detailed schemes which included Scottish and Irish royal houses and finished up with Queen Victoria.[44] One of the favourite motifs of British Israelism is the British Coronation stone known as Jacob's Stone. According to British-Israelite history this stone was taken to Ireland by Jeremiah and his scribe Baruch where it was given the name 'Lia-Phail'. In *The United States and Britain in Prophecy* Herbert Armstrong tells the story of Jeremiah's journey to Ireland with a daughter of King Zedekiah of Judah:

> The real ancient history of Ireland is very extensive, though coloured with some legend. But with the facts of biblical history and prophecy in mind, one can easily sift out the legend from the true history in studying ancient Irish annals. Throwing out that which is obviously legendary, we glean from various histories of Ireland the following: Long prior to 700 BC a strong colony called 'Tuatha de Danaan' (tribe of Dan) arrived in ships, drove out other tribes, and settled there. Later, in the days of David, a colony of the line of Zarah arrived in Ireland from the Near East. Then, in 569 BC (date of Jeremiah's transplanting), an elderly, white-haired patriarch, sometimes referred to as a 'saint,' came to Ireland. With him was the princess daughter of an eastern king and a companion called 'Simon Brach,' spelled in different histories as Breck, Berech, Brach, or Berach. The princess had a Hebrew name Tephi – a pet name – her full name being TEA-TEPHI ... This royal party included the son of the king of Ireland who had been in Jerusalem at the time of the siege. There he had become acquainted with Tea-Tephi. He married her shortly after 585 – when the city fell. Their young son, now about 12 years of age, accompanied them to Ireland. Besides the royal family, Jeremiah brought with them some remarkable things, including a harp, AN ARK, and a wonderful STONE CALLED 'LIA-PHAIL,' or 'STONE OF DESTINY.'

According to British Israelites, 'the stone is kept because the kings and queens of Great Britain are the seed-royal to the House of David'. The throne of Britain is the continuation of David's lineage.[45] As one British-Israelite writer put it, 'When God appointed David's throne to reign over the house of David, he covenanted with King David that his throne would endure forever; as also his house and the kingdom of Israel, over which it was to rule. In other words, there is a house, and there is a people – these things which are to remain and we must find that throne, that people and that house. It is the throne of Westminster, it is the Commonwealth of British Nations.'[46]

The various proofs produced by the British Israelites were and are of a feeble composition even by the low standards of the genre. A feature of British-Israelite discourse is the importance granted to 'historical research'. Thus as a pamphlet of the Church of the Covenant in Pasadena has remarked, 'diligent research . . . in the records of heraldry, the findings of archaeology and in a study of ethnology and theology' support the British Israelite. One of the favourite tools of research is philology. The *Pall Mall Gazette* of 3 April 1894, for instance, announced, numbingly, that the proof the English were descended from the Lost Tribes was that 'Saxon' is clearly a corruption of 'Isaac's son'. It similarly follows that there must be traces of Hebrew in English and Celtic languages. In one of their publications it is announced, 'The declared opinion of eminent scholars is that the English language contains the roots of no less than eight hundred Hebrew words.' Some pairs of words purporting to indicate this are English sever – Hebrew *shaver*; hob – Hebrew *bab*; gum – Hebrew *gam*. Needless to say the Hebrew in most cases is non-existent in the sense implied, and in some cases in any sense at all, and it is difficult to know how anyone could have thought them similar or connected in any way. Nonetheless one British Israelite has noted, 'It is the sheer weight of evidence contained in all the ancient languages of the British Isles that is important and, combined with the incidence of significant place names, forms strong proof of our Shemite and Hebrew ancestry.' Some oft-repeated Hebraic proofs are that the Hebrew *brit* meaning covenant and *ish* meaning man are the base of the word British (men of the covenant); the word Britannia is derived from *brit* and *onia* meaning ship and thus Britannia means ships of the covenant (and of course Britannia rules the waves). Denmark is taken as the tribe of Dan and one can follow the process of Dan through Europe in the place names that to this day bear the tribal name: thus Mace*don*ia, Dar*dan*elles, *Dan*ube and *Dun*bar. Similarly there is supposed to be a connection between the *Khumri* of the Assyrians, the *Cimmerioi* of the Greeks, the *Cimbri* of the Romans and the *Cymri*. All these forms are said to be variations of the same name and traces of it are to be found in Crimea, Cumberland, Cambria and Gumbri (a Russian fortress on the banks of the Araxes, the place of the Israelite exile).[47] There is something touching about the ignorance that informs these views. No doubt the invocation of philology and other disciplines throughout British-Israelite discourse seems decisive to many of the poorly educated disciples of the movement who feel frustrated, as one of them put it to me tremulously, 'that a hundred and fifty years of relentless scholarship has failed to persuade the Establishment of Anglo-Israel truth'.

The deconstruction of British-Israelite ideology immediately suggests the striving of the ordinary man for a glorious, royal ancestry, replete with heraldic symbols which, in the normal course of things, he is denied. It also reveals the yearning of uneducated people for the trappings and vocabulary of scholarship. In the second half of the nineteenth century evangelical Christianity was still a fairly active wing of the Anglican Church. It dominated the Nonconformist churches and, as evangelicals clung tenaciously to a literal interpretation of the Bible, British Israelism could and did make some inroads. Moreover the second half of the century witnessed the rise of a newly literate class – the product of the educational reforms of 1870 and later – eager to acquire information about their heritage. British Israelism played well to both groups. The same period witnessed the apogee both of the British Empire and pride in its achievements and grandeur. British Israelism pandered to these tendencies too, insofar as it displayed an intense and intolerant chauvinism and racism which trumpeted the racial superiority of white Anglo-Saxon Protestants. Indeed the growth of British Israelism and more conventional racist ideologies in England, starting perhaps with the publications of Robert Knox's *The Races of Man: a Fragment* (London, 1850), occur more or less at the same time and no doubt draw on common sustenance. With the rise of social Darwinism biology became the science of reaction. As Hobsbawm puts it, 'Biology was essential to a theoretically egalitarian bourgeois ideology since it passed the blame for visible human inequalities from society to "nature".'[48] The rise in interest in eugenics, which at some level perceived the possibility of genetically creating a perfected race, is a backdrop to British-Israelite doctrines, which perceived in the British just such a perfected race derived – genetically – from the chosen people.

The ebb and flow of British-Israelite sentiment is to some extent a function of the political power of candidate nations at any given time. Thus as the United States developed into a world power towards the end of the nineteenth century it increasingly became viewed as Manasseh, co-equal with Britain's Ephraim. With the rapid rise in Japan's power the same thing happened: after the Anglo-Japanese alliance of 1905 a pamphlet appeared arguing that Japan, not America, was the true Manasseh, and this idea was to persist in British-Israelite literature for several decades to come.[49] As Wilson has noted, the remarkable success of the movement, given the excessive shakiness of its premise, may be attributed in part to the moment in history, 'for ... the age and the circumstances of Britain's economic, political and military position were peculiarly suitable and so, perhaps, were the attitudes and aspirations widely held among large sections of the population.'[50]

In a way, in the context of twentieth-century racial anti-Semitism, British Israelism can be seen as rather pro-Jewish insofar as British Israelites by and large were arguing that the British and Jews were racially not very different. A University of London scholar, Professor R. W. Chambers, objected to British-Israelite ideology precisely on these grounds that, 'the present-day Jew is typically different from the Englishman, Dutchman or German ... If he resembles them, it is generally because he is not of pure Jewish descent.'[51] But in another way it became anti-Semitic. Already in the 1870s there had been a split in the leadership of the movement between those who wished to make a priority of converting the Jews and those who wished to work with them. In time, many British Israelites considered the Jews rank impostors. This in turn led to the rabidly anti-Semitic rhetoric of the Christian Identity Movement whose arguments cast grave doubt on the Jewish connection with the land of Israel and who take upon themselves the mantle of Israel, literally as well as metaphorically. As Barkun puts it, 'the process of religious disenfranchisement in general, and the claim that at least some Jews have a distinct racial origin, was to contribute to Identity's most novel and sinister doctrine, the belief that Jews are the offspring of Satan.' In 1983 at Metaline Falls, Idaho an organisation usually referred to as the Order and known to its members as the Bruders Schweigen or Silent Brotherhood, was founded by Robert Mathews, a lapsed Mormon convert.[52] In its attempt to raise funds to wage the war against 'the Zionist Occupation Government' it robbed $3.8 million from a Brinks armoured car in Ukiah, California. In 1984 a Jewish talk-show host who was noted for attacking rightists on the air was murdered: the Silent Brotherhood had originally planned to murder Morris Deed, founder of the influential and quite splendid Southern Poverty Law Centre. Mathews was killed by the FBI in December 1984.[53]

The idea that the inhabitants of the British Isles or North America are descended from the Israelites is innately bizarre. Yet it is widespread and has had millions of adherents. Do we British have such a fractured sense of our own history? How can the force of the myth be explained? Perhaps the fact that so much of British history has been played out overseas is a factor. Sir John Seeley noted in 1883 in *The Expansion of England* that, 'the history of England is not in England but in America and Asia'. And more recently Salman Rushdie observed that the trouble with the English is that so much of their national history has 'happened overseas . . . that they don't know what it means'.[54] For some, no doubt, the historicity of the Israelite connection with its global implications – there were Lost Tribes everywhere – was an underpinning of empire. More than that, the process of absorbing this 'oriental' identity in itself contributed to the creation of a British identity. To be British, or European for that matter, 'involved more than the rejection of the Oriental, the rejection of the impossibility of being the other',[55] it implied too the absorption, internalisation and reproduction of non-European otherness and particularly that of the classical European others – the Jew and the Moor. The myth of the Lost Tribes was a critical element in this discourse. How the myth was used very largely by the British in their perceptions of the outside world will be the subject of the following chapters: a myth of Albion becomes a universal myth.

Chapter Four

THE PURITANS, AMERICAN INDIANS AND THE END OF DAYS

> The Cities of the Tribes shall be built againe, and inhabited by naturall Israelites, especially *Ierusalem*, which shall bee the most eminent city then in the world, or that ever was in the world.
>
> I. Archer, *The Personal Reigne of Christ* (London, 1642)

For several hundred years the idea, already explored by the Spanish, that the indigenous peoples of the Americas were Jews, or in part Jews, was a dominant discourse both in England and North America. As we have seen, there had been no Jews in England since the expulsion of 1290 but the position of the Jews in the imagination of the inhabitants of the British Isles had not been unduly affected by this, and myths and stories abounded about them in various parts of the world. The first English book to mention the Americas at all was published in Antwerp in about 1511, and in it already weird and wonderful tales of cannibalism and monsters are juxtaposed with a retelling of the Prester John stories and an account of 'the great kynge of Israhel'.[1] The fifteenth-century Italian historian and royal chronicler Peter Martyr's (Pedro Martir de Angleria) description of the New World, *Décadas del Nuevo Mundo,* first published between 1511 and 1530, which was translated into English by Richard Eden in 1555 as *The Decades of the Newe Worlde or West India,*[2] followed more or less in this direction. But in addition Peter Martyr was impressed by the heavenly qualities of the New World and by the Indians' nobility, beauty and innocence: for him they seemed to be a remnant of some lost golden age. In his report to Pope Leo X he observed that he supposed His Holiness would be pleased to know that the Indians of Yucatán had the sacrament of baptism.[3] He did not stress the Israelite-Indian theory particularly but he was struck that the language of the Indians showed such a remarkable similarity to Hebrew and that they, like the Jews, practised circumcision.[4] In addition he reported that Columbus had identified Española as Ophir. More explicit conclusions were drawn by the French cleric and cosmographer Gilbert

Genebrard's widely cited *Chronographia* (Paris, 1567), which overtly supported the Israelite-Indian theory, and Joannes Fredericus Lumnius' *De Extremo Dei Iudicio et Indorum Vocatione* (Antwerp, 1569) in which he followed the account in the apocryphal book of Esdras of the Ten Tribes' flight to Arzareth. (Lumnius identified Arzareth as India by which he apparently meant America, although he thought the two places were situated not far from one other.)[5] Another book published in England fed into the idea: William Bourne's *Booke Called a Treasure for Travellers* (London, 1578) argued that the Indians were descendants of Japheth, the youngest son of Noah. Japheth was blessed by his father for his delicacy in averting his gaze while he lay in a drunken stupor in his tent. The blessing 'may God enlarge Japheth and let him dwell in the tents of Shem' was sometimes taken to mean that the descendants of Japheth – variously taken in earlier times to be Greeks or Anatolians – would participate in the religion of Israel. However Bourne understood the term, one may be sure that his intention was to place the Indians within the realm of Christian sacred history. If the Indians were not Israelites they were something along those lines. With these and other hints the Indian-Israelite theory entered English consciousness, but it was not for another seventy years that the motif of the Lost Tribes, on American soil, became a predominant issue in England.

The first English work to deal at length with the issue of the Lost Tribes was Giles Fletcher's *The Tartars or, Ten Tribes*, which was written between 1609–11. Fletcher's view, following numerous earlier writers, was that the Ten Tribes were to be found among the Tartars. This he proved through the similarity of a number of Tartar and Hebrew names and certain customs, including circumcision. An anonymous English traveller to the Orient in 1611 offered a cautious addendum to this: he noted that in fact the Tartars consisted of more than one ethnic group. The Jews were just one element among them – those 'Tartars who are far situated from the residue, and inhabit that remote Scithian promontory . . .' He reported that these Tartars, 'until this day . . . retaine the neames of their tribes, the title of Haebrewses, and circumcision. In al other rites they follow the fashions of the Tartarians.'[6] In 1614 Edward Brerewood (who taught astronomy at Gresham College but who was interested in the analysis of languages) published his seminal work *Enquiries Touching the Diversity of Languages and Religions through the Chief Parts of the World*, which was followed by new editions in 1622, 1635 and 1674. It dealt at length with the origin of the Tartars who, as he explained, were frequently identified with the Lost Tribes because of their customs – even their name, it was said, was derived from a Hebrew word *totari* meaning remnant. Brerewood did not accept the identification of Israelites and Tartars however: he thought the Indians were descended from Tartars: they clearly had not come from Europe, 'for they have no rellish nor resemblance at all, of the Arts, or learning, or civilitie of Europe', nor were they from Africa, 'their colour testifieth they are not of the African progeny'.[7]

The hypothesis of the Tartars and the Lost Tribes had been espoused in 1575 by the famous French historian, Guillaume Postel in his *Des Histoires Orientales*. But in addition Postel thought that many of the peoples of central Asia, despite appearances, were in fact descended from the Lost Tribes. In the same year as Postel's book appeared André Thevet (1504–92), royal cosmographer of France during the second half of the sixteenth century, wrote of the discovery of a Hebrew inscription in America from which he concluded that the ancient Israelites had not only settled Palestine and moved to Asia but were to be found throughout the world.[8] A few years later another theory was advanced. The French Calvinist explorer, Jean de Léry (*c.* 1534–*c.* 1613) who had travelled in Brazil in 1556–8 and written *L'histoire d'un voyage fait en la Terre du Brésil* (1578), felt sure that the American Indians, or at least the local people he had encountered – the Tupinambas – were most likely to be the descendants of the Canaanites who had been expelled from Palestine at the time of Joshua. This was taken up by another Frenchman, Marc Lescarbot, in *Histoire de la Nouvelle France*, first published in 1609. He based his argument in part on the fact that both Canaanites and Indians were cannibals (he thought it likely that Noah had built a second ark to take people to North America), and by William Strachey in his *History of Travell into Virginia Britania*, written in 1612 but unpublished until 1849.[9]

Reports on and interest in the Lost Tribes waxed in the first half of the seventeenth century. This was in part due to difficulties in the Jewish world. In Jerusalem in 1625–6 the Jews were harassed by a particularly rapacious pasha, which meant that they had to send far more emissaries than usual to raise sorely needed funds from Jewish communities in Europe. The emissaries carried hopeful tidings of imminent redemption in which the Lost Tribes would play a decisive role and these tidings reached the wider community. Similarly the massacres in the Ukraine of 1648–9 triggered by the Cossack rising against Polish landowners, Catholic clergy and the Jews, led by Bogdan Chmielnicki (1593–1657), played a very significant role. According to a contemporary account, 744 Jewish communities were wiped out in the Chmielnicki massacres and hundreds of thousands of Jews were killed. One result of this was that the communities affected by the massacres could no longer send funds to Palestine to support Jewish communities there, and many other Jewish communities in Turkey, Italy and Germany felt obliged to help their brethren in the Ukraine rather than the Jews of the Holy Cities. Consequently emissaries from the Holy Land made more fund-raising visits abroad and returned with increasingly imaginative tales. One Rabbi Barukh Gad, recently back from a mission to Persia, recounted how on his travels he had encountered a member of the Lost Tribes called Malkiel who had given him a letter from the sons of Moses which was addressed to the tribes of Judah and Benjamin who inhabited Jerusalem. This forgery, presumably perpetrated by Barukh himself, was based to a significant degree on the *Book of Eldad*, but also had material calculated to elevate the importance of Jerusalem and its community of pious Jews in the eyes of other Jews of the world. The epistle became well known throughout Europe and the Jewish communities of North Africa and the Middle East, and was used by many emissaries at the time and for the next two hundred and fifty years.[10]

In the 1650s detailed reports started arriving in Europe of the discovery of remnants of the Lost Ten Tribes in South America. In England and Holland these rumours soon took on a particular and long-lasting importance. At the time Jews had no right of abode on English soil. There may have been some who stayed on covertly and there are scattered references to Jews in sixteenth- and seventeenth-century English literature: from a passage in *Every Woman in her Humor* (1609), for instance, we may assume that Jews frequently worked as old-clothes dealers in the larger cities. From *Wandering Jews telling Fortunes to Englishmen* (1640) we hear that 'Jewes we have in England; a few in court, many in the citty, more in the countrey.'[11] Whereas in the immediate aftermath of the 1290 expulsion it may be supposed that few Jews dreamed of returning to a country that had treated them so harshly, once the large Jewish population had been expelled from Spain in 1492 there were those who thought England might provide the shelter they needed. Some Spanish Jews had chosen to remain in Spain and accept conversion: some of these forced converts, known as *conversos* or Marranos, successfully sought refuge in western Europe, including England. But nonetheless the ban on Jews officially persisted.

The growth of the Puritan movement in the Church of England, with its emphasis on the importance of the study of the Old Testament and of the Hebrew language, meant that increasingly proposals were heard both from Puritan and *conversos* circles advocating the official right of asylum for Jews being persecuted in Europe. This was not entirely altruistic. Since the days of Queen Elizabeth many Puritan theologians had stressed their conviction that in time the entire Jewish people would be converted to Christianity and that this event would form a key element in the lead up to the End of Days. This belief was largely based on a reading of Romans 11:25 ff where Paul speaks of some kind of mass conversion of Israel just before the Second Coming of Christ. This reading of Romans was followed by the influential Geneva Bible whose 1557 and 1560 editions explained that Israel here signified the nation of the Jews, while the 1599 edition stated categorically that the Old Testament prophesied the future conversion of the Jews to Christianity. Works by the rabbinic scholar Hugh Broughton (d. 1612) also stressed this view. The majority of Puritans believed that there would be a restoration of the Jews to the Promised Land following their conversion to Christianity. Some held that the conversion of the Jews would bring manifold blessings upon the Church, others further believed that following their conversion and restoration an era of untold glory would ensue and the kingdoms of the world would be blessed by the rule of mercy and righteousness. During this period, as one English millenarian put it, 'the Cities of the Tribes shall be built againe, and inhabited by naturall Israelites, especially *Ierusalem*, which shall bee the most eminent city then in the world, or that ever was in the world.'[12]

These convictions had become an essential, even dominant, element in Puritan discourse by the middle of the seventeenth century. According to Hugo Grotius (1583–1645), the great Dutch scholar and founder of international law, some eighty books expounding the nature of the End of Days were published in England in the first four decades of the seventeenth century.[13] Another aspect of this discourse was the question of the Jews themselves. It is clear, as one scholar has put it, that, 'all the Messianic speculation of the day was related in an essential way to Israel'.[14] But how did the real-life Jews of the day fit into a Christian scheme of things? Earlier in the century Grotius himself had been asked to try and define the legal and social status of the burgeoning Jewish community in Amsterdam, the so-called Jerusalem of the North. In European thought, millenarians and Messianists like Isaac la Peyrère and Peter Serarius tended generally to the view that the social situation of the Jews in their own time was a purely temporary one and therefore of little importance: after all they would be recalled to the Holy Land at any moment. There was, it is true, some argument as to whether they would return as Jews or as converts to Christianity. Menasseh ben Israel, whom we shall meet later in this chapter, thought they would return as Jews, la Peyrère as Jewish Christians.[15] This discourse was largely Christian, but there was a good deal of exchange and common ground between Christians and Jews. Amsterdam had been obliged to absorb thousands of Jewish refugees from eastern Europe, South America and elsewhere: these refugees included some former Marranos who attended the synagogue but who were also connected with Christian congregations.[16]

With the execution of Charles I in 1649 and the establishment of the republican government of England known as the Commonwealth, the question of the Jews had already taken on a fresh significance. During the period of the Commonwealth the question as to whether the Jews should be formally readmitted into England remained a critical matter of government and public interest. It created in its wake a wider and wilder discourse in which the Jews were both lionised and vilified: it was rumoured for instance that the Jews would pay handsomely for the right of return, that they thought Cromwell barely 'a man of flesh and blood' but some 'divine composition issued from on high'. According to some, Cromwell was in fact a Jew – a delegation of Jews from Asia and Prague was reported to have gone to Huntingdon to establish from the parish registers if he were indeed of Jewish descent and perhaps of the Davidic line. Indeed a pamphlet was said to have been published entitled *Cromwell, Lion of the Tribe of Judah*.[17]

This rumour-mongering had some impact. However for most sober Englishmen the main issue remained that the Jews were supposed to play a central role in the events leading to the End of Days. For many the Second Coming was not a distant event. It has been shown that some seventy per cent of churchmen who left published work were actively concerned with doing all in their power to facilitate the return of Christ and believed it to be imminent.[18] For these millenarians there was, therefore, everything to be gained from allowing the Jews to settle in England: there they would see with their own eyes the peculiar piety and godliness of the English nation (as opposed to the corrupt ways of the Catholic Church with which they would have been only too familiar in Europe). Once the Jews were restored to their ancient land and converted to the religion of Christ, other non-believers would follow. The Anti-christ pope would be destroyed and a new religious world order would descend. It was thought likely, as J. J.'s *The Resurrection of Dead Bones* (London, 1655) makes clear, that the role of the Church of England in bringing all this about by proffering a palatable and inspiring version of Christianity to the Jews and others would be significant. In any event the return could not take place until such time as there were Jews in every land on earth, including England. In Howard Weinbrot's neat formulation, 'Since their expulsion from England ... they were effectively barred from their ultimate home in Jerusalem by being barred from their temporary home in London.'[19]

Quite apart from eschatological considerations, a number of Englishmen had been arguing for the readmission of the Jews on grounds at least partly of religious tolerance. Thus in 1614 in a tract entitled *Religious Peace or a Plea for Liberty of Conscience* the Baptist, Leonard Busher, argued that the Jews should be readmitted in part so that they could engage in free discussions with Christians. In *A Word to the Army and Two Words to the Kingdom* (1644) the independent preacher Hugh Peter suggested that readmission should be granted on grounds of freedom of conscience. The following year in *Objections answered by way of dialogue, wherein is proved . . . that no man ought to be persecuted for his religion* another Baptist, John Murton, proclaimed that there should, henceforth, be no further persecution of Jews. Dissenters who were keen to be tolerated themselves may have had their own self-serving agenda. But even outside Dissenter circles there were those who argued that the original expulsion of the Jews from England had been wrong and that the present ills besetting the country were divine punishment on the nation that had so ill-treated God's people.

The seemingly rather advanced spirit of tolerance shown in Puritan tracts and sermons was not restricted to purely ecclesiastical circles. In 1648 at Whitehall, the Council of Mechanics passed a resolution demanding universal toleration for all religions, 'not excepting Turkes, nor Papists, nor Jews', and on Christmas day of that year the policy was given the endorsement of the Roundhead Council of War. It narrowly missed being included in the constitutional document known as the

Agreement of the People, which was then under discussion. Nonetheless the pressure for much broader toleration continued and in January 1649 the Council of State received a plea from Ebenezer and Joanna Cartwright, two English Baptists living in Amsterdam, petitioning the new government to permit the Jews to enter England to trade, as they were allowed to do in the Netherlands. The Council promised to deal with the matter as soon as the trial of King Charles I was over. Charles was executed shortly afterwards. Even as this matter was being discussed a further polemical tract was with the printers. *Apology for the Honourable Nation of the Jews* by Edward Nicholas, which achieved a very wide circulation, claimed that the most heinous crime of the English nation had been to banish the chosen people of God. There was the risk, he argued, that by keeping out the Jews England would lose 'God's favour and protection'. Rather, he argued, the English should, 'for the glory of God, the comfort of those afflicted people, the love of my own sweet native country of England . . . show ourselves compassionate and helpers of the afflicted Jews.'[20]

A further factor, which no doubt played an important role in creating an atmosphere in which Jews were well viewed as well as creating an interest in the Jewish people, was the great interest in Hebrew in seventeenth-century England.[21] Certainly there were often connections, not always acknowledged, between Christian Hebraists and Jews and it could be that this led in some sense and in some cases to better relations. However the revolution in interest in Hebrew was Europe-wide and indeed some of the major work had been by European pioneers such as Johannes Reuchlin (1455–1522), the grand uncle of Melanchthon, Pico della Mirandola (1463–94), Jean Thenaud (d. 1542) and others. Yet it is difficult to see anything even remotely paralleling the English interest in Jews, which the historian David Katz rightly describes as 'unique'. It must also be remembered that a prime motive for the European revival of interest in Hebrew studies was polemical: for Protestants it was yet another weapon in the fight against Papists; for the Papists a weapon against Protestants; and for both, at least theoretically, a weapon against Judaism.

One of the great enthusiasts for the readmission of the Jews to England was the Scottish ecumenical churchman John Dury – a 'hereditary rebel' who had been educated at the Walloon Seminary in Leiden.[22] Dury, a member of the Society of Divines, was convinced that the Lost Tribes of Israel would reappear just before the millennium which he believed would occur in 1655. Before the millennium, Jews would have to be sought and found in every corner of the globe. It was for this reason that Dury had been so excited by the work of German mystic millenarians such as Abraham von Frankenberg[23] and later by the reports of New England missionaries, particularly John Eliot, of their work among the Indians. And it was with this in mind that Dury 'practically started the first agitation' in favour of admitting the Jews to England (although he was later to turn against the project).[24]

As part of this project he entered into a correspondence with Menasseh ben Israel of Amsterdam (1604–57).[25] Menasseh, the great champion of the readmission of the Jews to England, was a remarkable man by any standards. The man Lord Middlesex called 'my dear brother the Hebrew philosopher', was a scholar (he knew eight languages) and kabbalist, probable teacher of Spinoza and a prolific correspondent with friends and contacts throughout Europe (including Rembrandt, who supplied engravings for some of his work). He was among other things a theologian, business man, historian, activist and printer. He was visited by princes and the greatest scholars of the age. Dury's contact with Menasseh was the Honourable Robert Boyle (1621–91), Dury's uncle by marriage. Boyle, one of the greatest natural philosophers of the age, as well as an accomplished student of Hebrew, rabbinics and other oriental matters, was an old friend and correspondent of Menasseh.[26] Dury had read the manuscript of a tract entitled *Jewes in America or Probabilities that the Americans are of that Race* (1650) by Thomas Thorowgood – a Norfolk preacher who had prepared this text on behalf of the New England missionary society. The society was active in trying to convert the Indians but suspected they might be Jews and realised they had better be prepared for an arduous task. Thorowgood's tract argued that the native population of North America were descendants of the Ten Lost Tribes. In it he referred to what was generally known or suspected at the time. He mentioned a letter he had received from the radical New England Puritan Roger Williams ten years before, which had pointed to the 'biblical' Indian custom of separating off menstruating women in a little wigwam. He described the Indian belief in a god who made heaven and earth, listed dozens of parallels between Jewish and Indian rituals and customs, and included a long list of biblical and post-biblical Jewish legends that were known to the Indians. In addition he noted the similarities between Indian languages and Hebrew: Hebrew words were to be found in the daily speech of the Indians: had not explorers often enough observed that the Indians were fond of saying 'Hallelujah'?

One of Thorowgood's correspondents was quoted with approval. He had observed that the Indians:

> 1. Themselves constantly affirme that their Ancestors came from the south-west, and thither they all goe dying.
> 2. They constantly and strictly separate their women in a little wigwam by themselves in their feminine season.
> 3. And beside their God Kuttand to the Southwest, they hold that Nanwitnawit (a God over head) made the Heavens and the Earth, and some taste of affinity with the Hebrew I have found.

Dury was clearly fascinated by this work (he later went on to write a long introduction to the book where he included among other things, a report of an emissary from the Ten Tribes who had recently appeared in Palestine). The findings of Thorowgood were subsequently incorporated into tracts that described the missionary work among the New England Indians. In one of these, *The glorious progress of the Gospel amongst the Indians in New England* (1649), Dury wrote an appendix on the Ten Lost Tribes. In another, *The light appearing more and more, towards the perfect day* (1651), the author advanced the theory (perhaps taken from the writings of the rabbinical scholar Hugh Broughton) that the American Indians were descendants of Eber, the son of Shem, who had migrated eastward and found their way overland to North America. He cited in addition a Captain Cromwell who had found circumcised Indians in America, which to him too suggested Jewish antecedents. Dury himself had also heard rumours from a Jewish jeweller in The Hague that elements of the Lost Tribes had been found somewhere to the east of the Holy Land – perhaps in Persia or Afghanistan.

But suddenly there were rumours of a specific sighting of a lost tribe in the Americas. Dury wrote to Menasseh and asked for further information about a story apparently brought back from South America by a new Christian of Jewish descent called Antonio de Montezinos, which seemed to corroborate rather wonderfully the information he already had. On 27 November 1649 Dury received an account of Montezinos' story which had been confided to Menasseh under oath on 19 September 1644. Menasseh assured him that Montezinos 'sware in my presence yt all he declared was trueth'. This information was published as an appendix to *The Jewes in America* (1650). Dury went on to envisage the Lost Tribes, including both Caraites and Red Indians, marching on Jerusalem at the End of Days.[27]

Montezinos' story fell on fertile ground at a very particular time in history. There was an acute sense of Messianic expectation among Christians, especially Protestants, during the first half of the seventeenth century. These stirrings had been stimulated by the appearance of the great comets in 1618, 1648 and 1652; by devastating epidemics, especially in the United Provinces; by the mass slaughter and loss of life of the Thirty Years War; by the Civil War in England, which overturned the monarchy and the natural order of things; and by the execution of King Charles I in 1649. For Jews the massacres in the Ukraine in 1648–9 allied with the persecution of the Marranos in Spain and Portugal had a similar effect. But all of a sudden there were new signs and portents. For Dutch Protestants the 1648 Treaty of Westphalia which marked an end to the Thirty Years War (in which between a third and a half of the population of the Holy Roman Empire perished) and which confirmed Dutch independence from Catholic Spain (thought by some to be the Antichrist) seemed very specifically to suggest the dawning of a new age. It was in 1650 that Rembrandt painted his *Vision of Daniel* based on a biblical passage with powerful Messianic associations for Jews as well as Christians. For Jews like Menasseh, who had been brought up in an atmosphere of persecution and torture, the new life of freedom in Amsterdam must in itself have suggested Messianic days.[28]

It is nonetheless difficult to accept that Menasseh believed Montezinos' tale at first. Given the stupendous nature of his revelation, for Jews as for Christians, why did it take him five years to make the matter public? It may be that as Menasseh slowly digested the news, he perceived a way of using the story as part of a wider campaign to get the English government to readmit the Jews into their territory. Menasseh, while cautious and circumspect, was a cunning man and not the innocent he has been taken for by some historians.[29] But it could also be that he really came to believe the tale. It was long ago suggested that it was the news of the burning to death of the Dutch Marrano Isaac de Castro-Tartas in Lisbon by the Inquisition in 1647 that provided the emotional backdrop to the evolution of Menasseh's views on the subject. These views would eventually be incorporated into a famous book where the terrible persecutions of the Jewish people were set against the hope of redemption to come.[30] It would certainly be wrong to ignore the background of Menasseh. His early years were marred by the Inquisition, his father was tortured and his eyes were constantly fixed on the persecution of his people in Spain and Portugal. As far as he was concerned the 'fourth beast' referred to in the book of Daniel was none other than the Inquisition. The background was indeed one of 'death, torture and *auto-da-fé*'.[31]

Menasseh, who in England as well as Europe was considered 'the principal exponent of Jewish science',[32] had canvassed support for his démarche in favour of the readmission amongst European Jews. In a sense he was speaking for Jewry. In his negotiations with the English, Menasseh expressed the view that the first inhabitants of the Americas had been Jews who had fled from China, and specifically from Kaifeng, in fear of being overrun by Tartar forces and had settled in the Americas – crossing either by way of a land-bridge or by boat across the 'Streight of Anian'. The Tartars who crossed after them were the ancestors of some of the Indians, the Jews ancestors of others. These Jews still considered themselves as Jewish. As Michael Pollack shows, Menasseh's argument was based on, 'three separate and seemingly unrelated sources: a verse from the book of Isaiah, Matteo Ricci's discovery of an old Jewish community in the heart of China and Antonio Montezinos' reported encounter with members of the Lost Tribes in the wilds of South America.' Isaiah (49:12) imagines the return of the dispersed of Israel in these terms, 'Behold, these shall come from far and lo, these from the north and from the west; and these from the land of Sinim.' Menasseh explains Sinim as China following Ptolemy. This was proof that there were Jews in China at the time of Isaiah. Matteo Ricci's discovery in 1605 of the previously unknown Jewish community in Kaifeng corroborated what the Bible had already foretold and the revelations of Montezinos provided yet further testimony.[33]

As we know from Inquisitorial records, Antonio Montezinos had been born in Villaflor, Portugal and was descended from Jews who converted in 1497. He set off for the Americas where he lived until 1644. According to research carried out by a collateral relation of Antonio, Elisabeth Levi de Montezinos, her ancestor was incarcerated in the secret prisons of the Holy Office in Cartagena, Colombia between September 1639 and February 1641.[34] Montezinos arrived in Amsterdam on 19 September 1644. He announced that in the Cordilleras (the Andes) in New Granada he had made contact with Jews who practised certain Jewish rituals, recited the elemental Jewish prayer, the *Shema Yisrael* (Deuteronomy 6:4–9), and were members of the lost tribe of Reuben. Initially Menasseh showed little interest. It has been suggested that this was because the story had little or no resonance in terms of Jewish tradition and because it seemed to confirm other similar tales thought to be of Jesuit origin. However after the beheading of King Charles, Menasseh came to see that the story was a splendid proof of the divinely ordained nature of the dispersion of God's people. He perceived, or pretended to perceive, that this dispersion had to occur in its fullness before the restoration of the Jews to the land of Israel could take place. But essentially it served his great purpose: to bring about the return of the Jews to the British Isles. There were Jews in South America (and apparently in North America as well) but there were no Jews in England. As the mediaeval Hebrew name for England could be rendered as 'the ends of the earth' – perhaps an attempt to convey 'Angleterre' – it seemed to be the case that once England was settled the dispersion of the Jews would be complete.

Menasseh set to work on a book that was to be the first serious attempt to harness to Jewish secular interests the theory of Israelites in America. The first edition was in Spanish – *Miqweh Israel. Esto es Esperança de Israel.* In 1650 there followed a Latin edition published in Amsterdam – *Miqweh Israel. Hoc est Spes Israelis* – complete with a dedication to the English Parliament. Then two further editions in English appeared in 1650 and 1651, translated by Moses Wall, the millenarian friend of John Milton. The first English edition of *The Hope of Israel*, as the frontispiece explains, set out to show, 'the place wherein the Ten Tribes at this present are, provd partly by the strange relation of one Antony Montezinus, a Jew, of what befell him as he travelled over the mountains Cordillaere with divers other particulars about the restauration of the Jewes.' The book then begins with 'the relation of Antony Montezinus' concerning his encounters with Jews in the Andes. The rest of the book is divided into forty-one sections, which deal with the general dispersion of the Twelve Tribes and various expert views as to their present location. In the second English edition the translator added 'some discourses' under his own name entitled 'Considerations upon the point of the Conversion of the Jews', which set out Wall's view that it was incumbent upon English people to engage forthwith in the great matter of the conversion of the Jewish people. Wall, like Dury, believed that this event would happen soon and that the seventh trumpet referred to in the book of Revelation would blow in 1655, ushering in the millennium. Then angels would gather together the Twelve Tribes of Israel from the distant corners of the earth and lead them back to the Promised Land.

Montezinos' account differs from many of the analogous ones over the centuries in that he was not merely offering an opinion about the origin of the South American Indians or presenting an explanation of their manners and customs. Instead he was presenting an account of events that he solemnly swore had taken place, which he was widely known to have solemnly sworn, and which proved that some American Indians were Jews.

Montezinos' account has a number of features in common with earlier stories. But his tale is extremely specific. He explained that he had set out on an arduous journey from Honda to Cartagena accompanied by a number of fellow travellers, including an Indian called Francisco who was addressed by everyone as *cazicus*, which we learn is the Indian term for chief. Trapped by a mountain storm the group lost its baggage but were urged by Francisco not to despair because times were set to improve: the 'hidden people' would soon swoop down on the Spanish and take revenge for all the persecution the Indians were suffering at their hands. Imprisoned by the Inquisition upon arrival in Cartagena, Antonio decided that when released he would try to find out more about the intriguing 'hidden people' mentioned by Francisco. In time he was freed, and successfully tracked down Francisco. Impulsively he asked the Indian to go on a journey with him. Off they set, and once out of town Montezinos vouchsafed that in fact he was a Jew of the tribe of Levi. Hearing this Francisco agreed to take him to the 'hidden people'. However he laid down a number of conditions: that Francisco be considered the leader of the expedition; that they only travel by foot; that they eat nothing but parched maize; and that in retelling the story afterwards Montezinos omit nothing, not the slightest detail, of what happened. In due course they arrived at a river and a woman and three men crossed over in a boat, greeted Francisco and recited the *Shema Yisrael*. The men are described in some detail: they are of dark complexion but are pleasing to look at, they have fine ornaments on their wrists and ankles and wear a linen headdress. They explained to Montezinos that their ancestors were, 'Abraham, Isaac, Jacob and Israel, and they signified these four by the three fingers lifted up; then they joined Reuben, adding another finger to the former three.' They then observed that, 'Joseph dwells in the midst of the sea, they making a sign by two fingers put together, and then parted them', adding that they would shortly, 'go forth to see, and to tread under foot; at which word they winked and stamped their feet. "One day we shall all of us talk together, they saying 'ba, ba, ba'; and we shall come forth as issuing out of our mother the earth." '

After more of this Montezinos managed to get further information from Francisco. According to him the Jews had defeated the local Indians in battle so comprehensively that the entire local Indian population had been wiped out, save for the old men and women. The local chiefs had been told that they could only approach the Jews five at a time and no chief younger than three hundred moons would be admitted into the Jews' secret lore. In addition these secrets were not to be repeated unless all five *cazici* were present, and even then only in secret meetings out in the desert. The chiefs were only allowed to visit the Jews every seventy months except for very special occasions, and during the lifetime of Francisco these occasions had consisted solely of three momentous events: the coming of the Spanish, the sighting of ships in the South Sea and finally the coming of Montezinos himself. Anyone who attempted to make contact with the Jews at any other time would be killed. The Indians believed that in time the Jews would deliver them from the Spanish and that at the End of Days these people would rule the world. As the Indians are said to have put it, 'these sonnes of Israel shall goe out of their habitations, and shall become Lords of all the earth as it was theirs before, if you will be happy, joyne yourselves to them.'[35]

Fragments of this somewhat fantastic account had done the rounds in England in tracts and pamphlets, particularly among members of the clergy. But the appearance of *The Hope of Israel* in its English translation had an even greater impact. Menasseh appears to have believed the basic story. However he was careful to distance himself from the theory that posited an Israelite origin for *all* the American Indians. He stressed that the descendants of the Lost Tribes living in the Americas, the first settlers of the continent, had nothing to do with the Indians who had arrived later 'by that strait which is between India and the kingdom of Anian'. He pointed out that there had indeed been previous sightings of the Lost Tribes in the Americas, 'white and bearded men were found who had never commerce with the Spaniards; and whom you cannot affirm to be any other than Israelites, because also as they could never be overcome so shall they never be fully known.' He mentioned the history of Pedro Simon, which told of the discovery of a warlike people somewhere in Venezuela. As Menasseh says, 'It is probable that they are Israelites.' He wrote too of the discoveries of a Dutch mariner who at 'seven degrees towards the north between Marañon and the great Para' met 'white men, and bearded, well bred, well clothed and abounding in gold and silver . . . some of us guessing them to be Israelites had proposed to send him again to enquire more fully. But he died suddenly last year . . .' He also referred to other groupings of the Lost Tribes in the world: in China, and Tartary, stories about the Horda of Naphtali,[36] according to him, 'relics of the Jews of the tribe of Naphtali', and the accounts of Eldad and David Reubeni.

It was against this background that in 1650 an English delegation was sent to Holland to negotiate a trade agreement. The delegation spent time with the important Jewish community of the city and the question of the readmission of the Jews was broached. Menasseh ben Israel wrote to the Council of State in September 1651, but it was not until November 1652 that he was issued with travel papers to enable him to enter England. The first Anglo-Dutch War (1652–4) then broke out and prevented him from travelling. Nonetheless the issue was brought up in the English Parliament in 1653. With the conclusion of the war in 1654 three English admirals drew up a petition to admit Jews into England.[37]

In the same year Menasseh's son arrived in England and reported back to his father that he had been awarded a doctorate at Oxford University. Although this was false (the certificate was forged) Menasseh was well pleased and in September 1655 he arrived himself. Shortly before leaving Amsterdam Menasseh met an emissary from Jerusalem called Rabbi Nathan Shapiro who had brought with him a copy of the epistle from the sons of Moses, a covering letter from the Jerusalem community recounting the tale told by Rabbi Baṛukh Gad and some details about the epistle, 'from our brethren the sons of Moses who live beyond the Sambatyon'.[38]

Along with his retinue of three rabbis Menasseh was lodged in some style on the Strand as the guest of Cromwell, the Lord Protector. On the last day of October he formally petitioned Cromwell for the readmission of the Jews to England, which met with vocal opposition on all sides. With little support Cromwell, who as we have seen was suspected by some of being a Jew himself, was forced to call a conference to debate the matter. Economic arguments claiming that the Jews would have a positive impact on trade were not at the forefront of the debate. Indeed an economic argument was usually advanced as a reason for not allowing the Jews entry.[39] At the Whitehall Conference, which was called in December 1655, Menasseh stressed the potential usefulness of the Jews to England, while the English merchants and City men argued that the Jews would inevitably be in contact with their co-religionists in Holland and by these means wealth would be transferred to the Dutch – England's deadly rival.

The Whitehall Conference played into the hands of the opponents of the scheme. There was too much opposition for formal readmission to be carried, despite Cromwell's efforts.[40] A cleverly presented booklet by the outstanding pamphleteer William Prynne called *A Short Demurrer* raked up mostly forgotten memories of the Blood Libels surrounding William of Norwich in 1144 and Little St Hugh of Lincoln in 1255, and recalled the anti-Jewish decrees of the thirteenth century. Foreign Jews were rumoured by some to have bought the most precious books from the Bodleian and Cambridge University libraries. Others said the Jews were all set to buy the famous Oxford library in its entirety and others yet that the Jews planned to transform St Paul's Cathedral into a great synagogue.[41]

Despite the enthusiasm on the part of the majority of the theologians who attended the conference, or who otherwise made their views known, that the Jews should be admitted, England would not, as Menasseh had hoped, become an immediate refuge for persecuted Jews in Europe. But it was acknowledged that there was in fact no law in force to impede Jewish immigration, and tacitly it was decided that henceforth Jews would be permitted quietly to trade and to settle in England in small numbers joining the Marranos and few Jews already there.[42]

At the time that Menasseh's theory was being given such prominence and having such striking effects, other explanations of the remarkable state of the world were being advanced. Arise Evans, author of *Lights for the Jews or the means to convert them in answer to a book of theirs called the Hope of Israel* (London, 1656), argued that Menasseh had got it all wrong and that in fact King Charles was the long-awaited Messiah (John Milton thought he was the Antichrist).[43] Henry Jesse in Holland published *On the Speedy Glory of Judah and Israel* in Dutch, which looked forward to an imminent millennium. The Christian Bohemian alchemist and mystic Paul Felgenhauer wrote *Good News of the Messiah for Israel – that the Redemption of Israel from all its Sufferings, its Freedom from Captivity and the Glorious Advent of the Messiah is Nigh for the Comfort of Israel.*

Similarly quite different theories on the American Indians were being concocted. One or two of the more discerning participants in this debate were pretty sceptical about Menasseh's theories. As we have seen, there had already been considerable controversy on the subject of the origin of the Indians. Quite apart from the work of the Spanish historians there had been the fierce debate in the 1640s between the intellectual heavyweight Hugo Grotius, mentioned above, and Johannes de Laet, a historian and director of the Dutch West India Company, which gave no support to the Israelite theory. Grotius thought that Indians north of the isthmus of Panama were originally Norwegians, those of Yucatán, Ethiopian Christians and those more 'refined minds' in Peru undoubtedly descendants from the Chinese. He dismissed the Lost Tribes theories on the grounds that Esdras was 'full of vain dreams'. De Laet's view was that the Indians were of Tartar or Scythian stock. Grotius took de Laet's criticisms rather poorly and reviled him in a very personal way, while de Laet nobly refused to be provoked. In any event the dispute became well known and a number of contemporary thinkers were drawn into it.[44] So the idea that peoples other than the Israelites had been involved in Indian origins was widespread. Sir Edward Spenser and Thomas Fuller expressed their doubts about Israelite origins in a scathing tract, *An epistle to the learned Menasseh ben Israel, in answer to his, dedicated to Parliament* (1650). The authors demolished the theory in a sardonic, teasing way:

> Some conceive the modern Americans of the Jewish race, collecting the same from resemblance in rites, community of customs, conformity of clothes, fragments of letters, foot-steps of knowledge, ruins of language (though by casual coincidence some straggling words of the Athenians may meet in the mouth of the veriest barbarians) . . . and lately a Jewish Rabbi of Amsterdam tells us that beyond the Corillera hills and river Maragnon, a fair people are found with long beards, and rich in clothes, living by themselves, different in religion from the rest of the Indians, whom he will have to be the Ten Tribes there remaining in a body together. His arguments so prevail on some, formerly contrarily minded, as to turn the tide of

> their judgement to concur with his, with others they make it dead water, not to oppose his opinion, whilst a third sort listen to his relation, as only privileged from confutation by the remoteness thereof. For mine own part, I behold his report as the twilight, but whether it will prove the morning twilight, which will improve itself into full light, or that of the evening, darkening into silence and utter obscurity, time will discover. When the eleven tribes (so virtually may I term them) brought news that one lost tribe (Joseph) was found, Jacob's heart fainted, for he believed them not (Genesis 45:26), till afterwards he was convinced on clearer evidence. How much more then may I be permitted to suspend my judgement, when one man brings tidings of ten lost tribes, all found in an instant, until farther proof be made thereof?

The attacks on Menasseh continued. In 1652 Sir Hamon l'Estrange published *Americans no Jewes, or Improbabilities that the Americans are of that Race*. His view was that the Americas would have been populated from the first but that, like everywhere else, the population had been wiped out during the Flood. Subsequently he wrote, 'What hinders to believers but that Shem and his children who were true believers and children of God and lived quietly and peaceable ... and kept their Hebrew language, and were not engaged in the action of the Babel Tower and suffered no interruption by that confusion but travelled to the East multiplicated and grew very numerous. And as the progeny of Japheth or Ham approached nearer towards them so they removed still more East, and soon after planted and peopled the nearest, and more parts of America, and so verified that in Genesis 9:19 the Three Sons of Noah over spread all the Earth.' However L'Estrange concluded that the parallels drawn between the Jews and the Indians were lacking in substance and that many of the supposedly common practices were common to mankind. In addition there were many things the Indians did that the Jews patently did not: no Jew for instance would eat unclean meat, whereas the Indians would eat anything; no Jew would marry a whore but all Indian women were whores.

Thorowgood replied with a second edition of his book with a foreword by the missionary and so-called 'apostle to the Indians' John Eliot (1604–90): this edition was entitled *Jews in America or Probabilities that Those Indians are Judaical, made more probable by Some Additions on the Further Conjectures* (London, 1660). John Eliot's foreword was clear and carried some weight, since he was a translator of the Bible into an

Indian language – the first Bible printed in North America – and he knew the Indians intimately. 'I conceive that the first planters of America to be not only of Shem, but Hebrewes of Eber' and 'therefore we may not only with faith but also with demonstrations say that … these naked Americans are Hebrewes, in respect of those that planted first these parts of the world.'[45]

Whichever position they took, by the 1660s the theories about the Lost Tribes had a power and a fascination for most people that could hardly be denied. Growing interest on the part of Christians in the fate of the Lost Tribes was further stimulated by the remarkable career of Shabbetai Zvi (1626–76), the false Messiah from Smyrna, which reached its apogee in 1665. Some Christians as well as Jews accepted that Shabbetai was indeed the Messiah, and believed Nathan of Gaza's prophecy would indeed come to pass, that Shabbetai would shortly enter Jerusalem riding on a lion with a seven-headed serpent as bridle. In addition, the end of the world was widely predicted to be 1666 and this brought in its wake all sorts of wild speculations.[46] It is entirely possible that the rise in the incidence of sightings of the Lost Tribes at this time was linked with the Messianic fervour inspired by Shabbetai, and in the widespread expectation that the end of the world was at hand.[47]

David Katz has suggested that by the end of the seventeenth century the identification of the Indians with the Ten Tribes was totally discredited.[48] Certainly by this time in addition to the attacks on the theory listed above,[49] a number of scathing rhymes and ditties had attacked Israelite theories. A New England preacher by the name of Nicholas Noyes tartly observed that the Indians were, 'Conjectur'd once to be of Israel's Seed, But no Record appear'd to prove the Deed,' while William Penn's publicity man Richard Frame observed in a humorous poem written in 1692 about the Indians, 'Some men did think they were the Scattered Jews / But yet I cannot well believe such News.'[50]

But despite this the outcome was hardly 'sterile', as Katz would have it.[51] In the British colonies in America the idea had already found very fertile ground. Hertzberg has concluded that in America the Israelite theory was abandoned as soon as the Puritans 'became better acquainted with the Indians'.[52] In fact, as missionaries to the Indians in Massachusetts became more familiar with their manners, they found all sorts of features of their languages that seemed reminiscent of Hebrew, and various practices and customs that seemed to be Judaic. Daniel Gookin, who was appointed captain of the military company in Cambridge, Massachusetts in 1644 and subsequently was made superintendent of Indians in Massachusetts in 1656 and 1661, wrote *Historical Collections of the Indians of New England* in 1674.[53] He starts his book off with a chapter on the origins of the Indians where he observes that 'there is nothing of certainty to be concluded'. He was convinced however that all Indians throughout the Americas were descended from the same people. After all, the Indians on this vast continent looked much alike, 'not unlike the Moors in Africa'. As he pointed out, there were a number of theories about their origins concerning the Indians of new England and elsewhere. Among other contenders he discussed the Tartars or Scythians, 'that live in the north-east parts of Asia which some good geographers conceive is nearly joined unto the north-west parts of America ... a third conjecture of the original of these Indians, is, that some of the tawny Moors of Africa, inhabiting upon the sea coasts ... have put off to sea and been transported over in such small vessels as those times afforded.' A principal conjecture (though by no means everyone supported it) was, 'that this people are of the race of the Ten Tribes of Israel ... but this opinion, that these people are of the race of the Israelites, doth not greatly obtain. But surely it is not impossible and perhaps not so improbable, as many learned men think.'[54]

English colonists such as the Quaker William Penn (1644–1718), who obtained a grant of land in 1681, found all manner of signs of Judaism among the Indians in Pennsylvania: after his first few months among the Red Indians he observed that there were so many Jews around it was like being in a Jewish quarter in London. He noted of the Indians:

> Their eye is little and black not unlike a straight-looked Jew ... their language is lofty, yet narrow; but like the Hebrew in signification; like short-hand in writing, one word serveth in the place of three ... For their origin I am ready to believe them of the Jewish race; I mean of the stock of the ten tribes, and that for the following reasons; first they were to go to a 'land not planted or known' which, to be sure, Asia and Africa were, if not Europe; and He that intended that extraordinary judgement upon them, might make the passage not uneasy to them, as it is not impossible in itself, from the Easternmost

> parts of Asia, to the Westernmost of America. In the next place, I find them of like countenance, and their children of so lively a resemblance, that a man would think himself in Duke's Place or Bury Street in London, where he seeth them. But this is not all; they agree in rites, they reckon by moons; they offer their first fruits; they have a kind of Feast of Tabernacles; they are said to lay their altar upon twelve stones; their mourning a year, customs of women, with many things that do not now occur . . .[55]

Let us return briefly to the man who was responsible for so much of all this – Antonio de Montezinos. His account, as we have seen, was more than speculation – it was narrated as fact. He swore that while he was in the Cordilleras in New Granada he had made contact with Jews who practised certain Jewish rituals, recited the *Shema Yisrael* and were members of the Lost Tribe of Reuben. He also swore on his death bed in Brazil in 1647 or 1648 that his story was true. Was Montezinos making it up? Did he hope to enrich himself in some way? Was it a hugely successful hoax? It is very difficult to see what motive he might have had for a hoax. He had had a difficult life. He had been persecuted, probably tortured. The story he told was unlikely to win him friends in the Holy Office of the Inquisition. We know that he made no attempt at all to raise financial capital from his account while he was in Amsterdam: he received no alms from the Jewish 'nation' of Amsterdam in 1644 and 1645 and refused even offers of hospitality.[56] Was he simply enjoying the telling of a good tale and the fame or notoriety that went with it? But nor does this seem likely: according to Elisabeth Levi de Montezinos her ancestor turned down an offer to go to England to tell his story because he wanted to keep the location of the tribe of Reuben secret.

Edward P. Samiljan has written a short privately printed pamphlet, *In search of conversos in Ecuador*, which describes some days he spent there in July 1997 looking for 'lost' communities of Spanish Jews forced to convert to Christianity. He found some interesting things, including a group of dwarfs in Loja, a small town in the Cordilleras not far from the Peruvian frontier, whose form of dwarfism, says Samiljan, appears to be shared uniquely by some Sephardi Jews in Tel Aviv. Is there any connection between the dwarfs, other possible ex-*conversos* groups in Ecuador and the people discovered by Montezinos? It does seem not unlikely that what Montezinos came across was indeed a group of *conversos* who had settled in as remote a place as possible, intermarried with Indians, and put themselves beyond the reach of the Holy Inquisition. By the time Montezinos came upon them they had only a garbled version of their past: they may have left Spain almost one hundred and fifty years before – plenty of time to forget some things while remembering others, and eventually disappear. Whatever the basis for his story, the spark ignited by Montezinos inflamed hearts and minds in the seventeenth century and was destined to carry on doing so for the next three hundred years.

Chapter Five

A STAR IN THE WEST: ISRAELITES AND THE AMERICAS

> I came across the Mohican tribes near New York and asked them, 'Whose descendants are you?' They replied, 'We are of Israel.'
>
> Joseph Wolff 1845

The question of the origin of the Indians of the Americas was not dead. Indeed in different ways their origins and anthropology became central to a variety of important debates. A number of missionaries, for instance, were to hold on to the idea of the Indians as representatives of a lost and ideal world. The most important of these was Father Joseph François Lafitau, a Jesuit from Bordeaux, who spent the years 1712 to 1717 as a missionary among the Iroquois Indians on the south shore of the St Lawrence opposite Montreal. Lafitau was not content merely to describe the habits of the people among whom he lived: he had a greater project – the construction of a science of culture achieved through the comparison of the manners of savages with those of the people of antiquity. During his time with the Iroquois Lafitau became famous throughout Europe because of his discovery in Quebec of ginseng, a herb that had been in use among the Iroquois Indians and was in great demand in China. Indeed the Indians' use of the herb was one of the features that led him to connect their customs with those of Asiatic peoples.

Lafitau's great work, *Moeurs des sauvages amériquains comparés aux moeurs des premiers temps*, was published in 1724. His central idea, which was rather fashionable at the time, was that primitive cultures of his day could illuminate the cultures of ancient societies, and vice versa. In terms of the origins of the Indians his view was that at least some of their population, and particularly the Huron and Iroquois Indians, were descended from the barbarous people who once inhabited Greece. His view of native Americans, which was essentially respectful, would lead into the ideas of the Noble Savage later in the century and contribute to the discussion about the nature of primitive man which evolved during his lifetime. Lafitau was only too well aware of the various theories on the origins of the American Indians. He referred to the great debate between Hugo Grotius and Johannes de Laet almost a century before, but was unwilling to be drawn too deeply into it. While allowing that there were some difficulties in explaining away apparent vestiges of Judaic culture in America, he himself was not in favour of this explanation. 'In respect to the Jews,' he wrote, 'many people have persuaded themselves that the Ten Tribes of Israel carried into captivity in Medea by the Assyrian kings . . . had made a route for themselves to go into the New World. [This theory] is founded . . . on many traits of resemblance found between the legal observances and other civil customs of the Jews and the practices of the Americans. I myself have seen many missionaries on whom this had made an impression and who came near believing that all the Americans in general originated from the Hebrew people.' Lafitau thought this was an untenable view – or almost – he seems to catch himself in mid-phrase, 'at least I believe that no substantial enough proof of it can be brought'. In general, he concludes the Jews of old had various practices that were common to all Jews and gentiles alike: as he puts it, 'no conclusion can be drawn from these general practices'.[1] Moreover in his view there was no trace of Hebrew in Indian languages, 'It is very certain that the American languages have no analogy with it, neither with those related to it.'[2]

Throughout the eighteenth century there was further discussion in England and elsewhere on the theological implications of the Lost Ten Tribes. Joseph Eyre published a work on prophecy in 1771 in which he made the point that the 'great happiness' mentioned in the Old Testament referred not to the Church but rather, 'to the conversion and restoration of the literal Israel, the Jews and Ten Tribes, in the latter times, and to that reign of Christ when the Church shall be triumphant.'[3] It is against this backdrop that the Indian-Israelite theory continued to be played out. As we have seen, in America the numerous similarities had impressed both simple folk and some weighty thinkers. Many of the supposed similarities were seen as culturally advanced. Purification rituals among women reminiscent of Israelite practice, for instance, were particularly approved of – they were seen to be 'civilised'. On the other hand there were aspects of Indian practice that were not. The Anglican bishop and philosopher George Berkeley (1685–1753) started off in favour of the Israelite theory and became obsessed with a plan to set up a college in the Bermudas to promote 'the propagation of the Gospel among the American savages' on account of their Israelite origins. He sailed for America with his newly married wife in 1728 with this end in mind. It was not until he came across a bunch of drunk Indians in Newport, Rhode Island that his views changed.[4]

Another enthusiast of the theory was Charles Beatty, who was appointed by the synod of New York and Philadelphia to visit the 'frontier inhabitants' and Indians to see what could be done with respect to bringing them the Gospel. He set off on 12 August 1766. All sorts of strange theories about the Indians abounded in these frontier zones: it is interesting to observe how Beatty's account picks up a number of earlier ones, including a Welsh-origin theory: one version of this theory by a David Powell, published with approval by Richard Hakluyt, had it that Prince Madoc (*c.* 1170) had fled Wales and settled with his followers in America.[5] On his journey, then, Beatty came across a certain Levi Hicks who as a boy had been taken captive by Indians and raised among them. Hicks told him of an Indian tribe, 'on the West side of the Mississippi River, who talked Welch'. Another former captive of the Indians called Sutton, whom Beatty met on his way, made a similar claim, 'He said he saw a book among them which he supposed was a Welch bible.' Sutton told Beatty the story of a Welsh-speaking clergyman who was captured and sentenced to death by some Indians. But just in time the Indians realised that they all spoke the same language. They showed the clergyman their book – a bible – which was in Welsh and which he was able to read to them: in this way he was saved. But Sutton had more than one mythic tradition to call on. 'Sutton farther told us that among the Delaware tribe of Indians he observed their women to follow exactly the custom of the Jewish women in keeping separate from the rest seven days, at certain times, as prescribed in the Mosaic law.' In an appendix to his book *Journal of a Two Months Tour* (London, 1768) Beatty explained how he himself had found traces of Israelites among the Delaware Indians, 'I had taken pains,' he wrote, 'to search into the usages and customs of the Indians in order to see what ground there was for supposing them to be part of the Ten Tribes: and I must own, to my no small surprise that a number of their customs appear so much to resemble those of the Jews that it is a great question with me whether we can expect to find among the Ten Tribes (wherever they are) at this day, all things considered, more of the footsteps of their ancestors than among the different Indians tribes.' He cited the separation of women during menstruation, 'conduct ... perfectly agreeable to the Law of Moses', feasts of first fruits, a feast that resembled the Passover, chants that resembled 'hallelujah'. He observed that a hundred of them were a match for one thousand British troops 'in the wilderness', 'and were not the Jews of old remarkable for their courage, and high sense of liberty? And was it not customary, in the days of Saul and David to bring home testimonies of the number they had slain in battle, not very different from the scalps of the Indians.' In addition the Indians had, it was claimed, once owned a book. 'So long as they kept it and acted according to it, their God was kind to them and they prospered: but that the white people at length bought it off the Indians whereby they learned a great many things and prospered while the Indians on the other hand began to decline ... In these and other particulars I believe you will observe, with me, a strong resemblance between the ancient Jews and Indians ...'[6]

With the rise of scientific anthropology in the eighteenth century the question of Indian origins took on a new significance. One of the tasks of this new discipline was to try and explain the different varieties of the human race while staying within the framework established by the Bible. Georges-Louis Buffon (1707–88), the French naturalist whose work foreshadowed the theory of evolution, and the Swedish botanist Carolus Linnaeus (1707–78), who is considered the father of modern taxonomic botany, believed it was possible to divide humankind into four or five species. They and others considered the apparent shortcomings of the Indian and black races open to remedy – through changes in education, diet and so on – and viewed them as descendants of Adam and Eve and therefore part of the biblical framework. Others argued that different branches of mankind had come into being at different times and different places: David Hume (1711–76) supported a theory of polygenesis that established the innate and irremediable inferiority of the black races; his cousin Lord Kames supported the theory that some human groups including the American Indians, were created after Adam and Eve and therefore had no part in the world of the Bible. Bernard Romans' *Natural History of East and West Florida* (New York, 1775) provided a detailed dismantlement of the Jewish-

Indian theory in the context of the Indians of Florida, suggesting rather the alternative of divine multiple creations.

But the Israelite theory refused to die. In 1775 James Adair, an English aristocrat who had traded with Cherokees, Catwawbas and Chikkasah in the southern colonies for forty years and had observed them closely, wrote his *History of the American Indians particularly those Nations adjoining to the Mississippi, East and West Florida, Georgia, South and North Carolina and Virginia*, in which he attempted to prove in the greatest possible detail that they were 'lineally descended from the Israelites'. He advanced twenty-three arguments in favour of this proposition. His first argument concerned the similarity between the tribal system of the Indians and the Israelites, including the insignia of sub-tribes, clan loyalty and so on. His second argument concerned the Indian name of God which he rendered as 'Yo-he-wah', resembling the Hebrew divine name YHWH, written in European languages as Jehovah. Other arguments included similarities of language, belief, their system of counting and even parallels in ornamental styles. Adair's work was even more fantastic than most of his predecessors: as one critic put it, 'He tormented every custom and usage into a like one of the Jews and almost every word in their language became a Hebrew one of the same meaning.'[7] In 1799 Charles Crawford noted that even if there had been 'visionary elements' in Adair's works, his book could clearly be shown 'to prove the descent of the Indians from the Jews'. Adair had come up with many exact parallels according to Crawford, but he would have proved his point to the satisfaction of the greatest sceptic in the continent if he had been able to establish just two points, 'the separation of their women at a certain time by the Indians, and their dance in which they sing Hallelujah Yo-he-wah. We know the former custom to prevail universally, and the latter frequently among the Indians particularized by Mr Adair. Must not the first custom have sprung from a higher source than the indelicate mind of a savage? And could they have found Hebrew words in the desart?' No doubt the Indians were different from the Jews in some respects but these differences could be accounted for. They did not circumcise, for instance, but this could be explained, 'from the loss of their sharp knives as they passed through the desart'.

Adair's book was written in part because he believed that Florida should be wrested from Catholic Spain: as the Florida Indians were descendants of the Israelites it hardly seemed decent to leave them at the mercy of anti-Jewish Catholics. Subsequently the book was to provide an ideological justification for the American Revolution, in that it seemed to associate the Americas in the most intimate way with the working out of God's plan for the world.

A few years later Charles Crawford, mentioned above, wrote *An Essay on the Propagation of the Gospel* (Philadelphia, 1799). Crawford took it for granted that the Indians were descended from the Jews. 'There is,' he wrote, 'a strong argument in favour of the Indians being converted to Christianity, their being descended from the Jews . . . the aborigines of America were probably the descendants of Noah, that is, America was first peopled by the sons of Noah, before the division of the globe. The sons of Noah are said to have wandered over the earth . . . Afterwards, it is probable that America was further peopled by the ten tribes, who were taken captive by Shalmaneser, King of Assyria.'[8] Crawford, too, was convinced that America's role was to be instrumental in converting the Lost Tribes and thus to bring about the End of Days. In a later expanded edition of his work he was to take heart from the fact that a rabbi who had converted to Christianity had settled in Philadelphia with the Indians of the Lost Tribes and planned to lead them to Jerusalem. After a while, however, the erstwhile rabbi, 'proved to be an impostor and is now in an elevated station in the Church of Rome'.[9] In this edition Crawford brought some startling new evidence, 'I think that scalping may have been practised by the Jews, from an expression in the 68th Psalm: "God shall wound the head of his enemies, and the hairy scalp of such an one as goeth on still in his trespasses." ' In addition he advanced a new and not uncompelling argument: he insisted that the 'whole people of America' should treat the Indians 'with as much lenity and forbearance as possible'. The reason for this was that 'all the descendants of the House of Israel among which are many Indians will be restored to the land of their forefathers. The time is not far distant when this restoration will be effected. Many of the Indian will then voluntarily relinquish their lands to the white people.'[10] What was the point of fighting this redoubtable people when the exercise of patience might achieve the same goal?

What was true of the United States was also true of the northern reaches of Canada. Samuel Hearne, in *A Journey from Prince of Wales's Fort in Hudson's Bay to the Northern Ocean* (London, 1795), claimed that the Indians in the Hudson Bay area had a dance during which they sang out 'Hee-hee, hoe-hoe', and had a number of practices that seemed biblical: after killing a band of Eskimoes all those involved were prohibited from 'cooking any kind of victuals, either for themselves or others'.[11] Similarly, on the west coast of Canada such theories were commonplace. The imprint of Jewish influence on the customs of the coast Indians was seen by many: the theories had it either that the Lost Tribes made their way to the area or that Jewish war vessels involved in 'Kublai Khan's thirteenth-century expedition against Japan' were blown off-course and finally landed in the Queen Charlotte Islands or the Nass River. Alternatively it was suggested that Jewish traders from China might have crossed the Pacific. A recent historian of the Jews of British Columbia has observed that indeed there are a number of features of coast Indian societies, 'suggestive of Hebraic ceremonies such as: purification rites, fasting from sunset to sunset, measurements of time and seasons, and customs enforced upon female adolescents. The ceremonial dress of the Medicine Man or Chief is reminiscent of that of the biblical Jewish priest: mitred headdress, breastplate and wearing of fringes. Father Jean Marie le Jeune, Catholic missionary to the Indians and expert linguist, reported that he had discovered Hebrew words in every native dialect west of the Canadian Rockies.'[12]

As we have seen, traces of Hebrew were found everywhere. A work by Jonathan Edwards (1745–1801), the pastor of a New Haven church and a member of the Connecticut Society of Arts and Sciences, *Observations on the Language of the Muhhekanneew Indians* (New Haven, 1788), demonstrated 'some instances of analogy' between the Muhhekaneew language and Hebrew. Edwards' work was referred to subsequently in an article in *The American Museum or Universal Magazine* of 1791 edited by the political economist Mathew Carey (1760–1839), who observed that it was, 'no small proof of their Jewish descent that the Mohegan language so nearly coincides with the Hebrew in the pronouns and persons, the prefixes and suffixes, in which it differs from all the ancient and modern languages in Europe'.[13]

The apparent similarities between Hebrew and Indian languages also caught the imagination of Elias Boudinot (1740–1821), one of the leaders of the American Revolution (he was head of the revolutionary state at the end of the war) and the founder of the American Bible Society. Boudinot was undoubtedly one of the most important Americans to take up the Indian-Jewish theory. Fired with enthusiasm he sent out a friend with some knowledge of Hebrew to investigate the language of a Cherokee tribe that had had no contact with Europeans.

The friend spoke to them in Hebrew and was convinced by their answers that they were Jews. Boudinot went on to write *A Star in the West or a Humble attempt to discover the long Lost Tribes of Israel preparatory to their return to their beloved city, Jerusalem* (New Jersey, 1816). In his book he made a number of grammatical comparisons between Hebrew and the various Indian languages: among other things he noted that Hebrew shared with native American languages the absence of pronouns. Similarly he found a number of words in Indian languages that were derived from Hebrew: the word for heaven in Charibbee – *chemim* – was similar to the Hebrew *shemim* (I am using Boudinot's inaccurate form of the Hebrew), while the word for man – *ish* – was identical to the Hebrew. In Creeks, *halleluwah* was clearly similar to the Hebrew *hallelujah* and *abba*, the Creeks for father, was identical to *abba* in Hebrew. In most cases, however, the supposed Hebrew equivalent does not in fact exist: thus *na* is not Hebrew for now; *guir* is not Hebrew for assembly; *li hene* (*liani* in Charibbee) is not Hebrew for his wife, and so on. However if Boudinot got the whole thing hopelessly wrong he was disarming about it. He finished this section with an apologia, 'As the writer of this does not understand either the Hebrew nor Indian languages, so as to be a judge of their true idioms or spelling he would not carry his comparisons of one language with the other too far.'[14]

This book was marked by a spirit of compassion and tolerance remarkable in any age (Boudinot had adopted and converted a Cherokee youth who went on to have a controversial career). He stressed the persecution of the Jews in Europe, as well as their shoddy treatment in America, and asks forgiveness. Similarly he described the nobility, courage and morality of the native Americans. He was convinced that the Indians would have an important part to play in the End of Days and that this conclusion to human history was not far off (he thought that Napoleon was the Antichrist). With the coming of the Messiah the Indians could be expected to return to Zion. Moreover, Boudinot noted, 'Who knows but God has raised up these United States in these latter days for the very purpose of accomplishing his will in bringing his beloved people to their own land.'[15]

It was inevitable that this entire crucial issue would sooner or later be taken up at the highest level of state. Thomas Jefferson (1743–1826), the third president of the United States, served as vice-president under John Adams, the second president. He asked Adams what he thought of the Indian hypothesis. They were both trained as lawyers and they went to the most available text – that of Adair. Both men concluded that Adair's evidence was slim. It seemed to them that the Indians were ordinary people descended from the progenitors of the human race like everyone else. There was no reason to suppose, therefore, that they would soon be trooping off to Jerusalem. It has been shown that Jefferson's decision to buy two million square kilometres of land from France in Louisiana (the Louisiana Purchase 1803) was at least in part because he wanted to find space to settle the Indians in US territory: it implied that the United States as a rational, secular state would endeavour to redeem its own people, if necessary, quite out of the context of divine history.[16]

Notwithstanding what Jefferson thought, some American scientists were still not convinced that the Indians formed a normal part of humankind. American ethnographers led by Samuel Morton examined cranium size among Indians and Negroes. Morton came to the conclusion that both peoples formed separate races, which had separate origins from the rest of mankind. They had nothing to do with the Bible; they were clearly inferior to Caucasians or Asiatics and therefore could hardly be expected to play a special role in human destiny. Indeed, it justified enslaving them as an inferior species. As Popkin puts it, 'The application of ethnology to the Indians justified taking away their lands, driving them westward, and decimating them.'[17] Morton's methodology involved filling the cranium with pepper seeds and then weighing them. According to Stephen Jay Gould the evidence in any case was slanted to fit the thesis that Negroes and Indians were racially inferior.[18]

The nineteenth century saw a spate of new publications in support of the thesis on the Israelites in America: E. Howitt's *Selection from Letters* (New York, 1820); the Vermont pastor Ethan Smith's *View of the Hebrews or the Tribes of Israel* (Vermont, 1823); Israel Worsley's *A View of the American Indians: their General Character, Customs, Language, Public Festivals, Religious Rites and Traditions Shewing them to be the Descendants of the Ten Tribes of Israel* (Plymouth, 1828); Joshua Priest's *American Antiquities* (New York, 1834); J. Finlay's *On Jews and Wyandottes* (New York, 1840) and G. Catlin's *Letters and Notes on the Manners, Customs and Conditions of the North American Indians* (London, 1841). However the most lavish production of the century was Lord Kingsborough's splendidly produced and illustrated nine-volume work *Antiquities of Mexico* (1829–31), which argued that the codices of the

Aztecs showed similarities to Hebrew lore and that the Indians, certainly those of Central America, were Jewish.

Edward King, Viscount Kingsborough (1795–1837)[19] was the first-born heir to a noble Irish family. His interest in the subject of the lost tribes was first fired in the Bodleian Library at Oxford where he came across some Mexican codices. After coming down from Oxford he was elected MP for County Cork in 1818 and again in 1820, but resigned his seat in favour of his brother in 1826. This appears to have been partly because of a disillusionment in politics in general and partly because of his new passion. For the next twenty-odd years he attempted to prove his thesis. From his father he had inherited substantial debts: ignoring these he continued with his life's work, lavishing care and money on the project. He imagined his book to be in essence the new sacred scriptures for the Americas – it followed that it had to be produced in as splendid a way as possible. Four copies were printed on vellum with hand-coloured plates; one of these was presented to the Bodleian library, another to the British Museum. But the ordinary copies of the book were pretty lavish too. In all they cost £32,000 to produce. Financial ruin resulted. Kingsborough was flung into debtors' prison three times (for debts of £508 10s 6d, £26 4s 11d, and £118 17s 7d). His third stint was in the sheriff's prison, Dublin where he died of typhus fever, unmarried, at the age of forty-two. This last time he was gaoled on account of a debt of his father's for which he was guarantor.[20]

Kingsborough's book contains beautifully drawn facsimiles of Mexican hieroglyphs and incorporates documents from royal and other private libraries: its full title is *Antiquities of Mexico comprising facsimiles of ancient Mexican paintings and hieroglyphics preserved in the Royal Libraries of Paris, Berlin and Dresden; in the Imperial Library of Vienna; in the Vatican Library; in the Borgia Library at Rome; in the Library of the Institute at Bologna and in the Bodleian Library at Oxford.* Kingsborough's own views are expressed in the notes that start in the sixth volume. His methodology is essentially morphological: that is, he finds connections between Mexican and ancient Jewish practice, which are taken to prove that the Jews settled in Mexico in remote times.

The first topic to engage his interest is the similarity in terms of sacrifice. As he notes, 'In nothing did the Mexicans more resemble the Jews than in the multitude of their sacrifices ... It is probable that the Jews, immediately on their arrival in the New World revived the sacrifices which the old law ordained as a perpetual memorial of their flight from Egypt and committed to paintings the principal events recorded by Moses to have preceded and followed that flight.' But truth to tell he found parallels everywhere: to phenomena found in the Bible and rabbinic literature from the dress of the native Peruvians – which he thought was similar to that of the Israelites of old – to the breastplate of the Mexican priests, which was identical in his view to the breastplate of the Jewish High Priest described in the twenty-eighth chapter of Exodus. Kingsborough summarised his views and revealed some of the motives that underlay them in a telling passage in the sixth volume, 'The Jews had in very early ages colonized America, established an empire in that continent of more than a thousand years' duration, revived their old law in its full vigour, and, to show their hatred and contempt for Christianity, introduced into their religious rites and ceremonies many observances calculated to turn into ridicule its most sacred rites and mysteries and thereby as they imagined practically to demonstrate that they could not be sacred which could with such impunity be profaned.'[21] Unlike the Puritan writers of the seventeenth century there was no philo-Semitism in Kingsborough's work: the worst interpretation is put on the mores of Mexican Jews – the project to discredit Christianity.

Lord Kingsborough's extraordinary work was published at a time when such theories were being diligently pursued – at about the same time as Joseph Smith's translation of the Book of Mormon (1830) and Godfrey Higgins' *Anacalypsis – an Attempt to Draw Aside the Veil of the Saitic Isis; or an Inquiry into the Origin of Languages, Nations and Religions* (London, 1833–6). Given the *Zeitgeist*, Kingsborough soon acquired a substantial following: one enthusiast, Barbara Simon, author of *The Ten Tribes of Israel Historically Identified with the Aborigenes of the Western Hemisphere* (London, 1836), noted that the importance of the work could hardly be overestimated. It was no less than, 'an illustration and confirmation of Scripture testimony, in disclosing the Hebrew origin, history, experience, and genius of that grand division of the Hebrew nation, which, although cut off for a series of ages from their own, and the nations of the earth, have nevertheless occupied a prominent place in the prophetic pages'.[22] Mrs Simon was followed by many, many more, including a Frenchman, Brasseur de Bourbourg, the author of *Histoire des Nations Civilisées et de l'Amérique Centrale durant les Siècles antérieurs à Christophe Colomb* (Paris, 1857), who defended Kingsborough passionately.

One of the best known of the supporters of the Indian theory of this period was the Jewish-American diplomat, publisher and author Mordecai Manuel Noah (1785–1851). Born in Philadelphia, then the capital of the United States, he was perhaps the leading American Jew of his generation. He had a varied career. At the age of twenty-eight he was appointed US consul to Tunis and subsequently became Sheriff of New York County, Grand Sachem of Tammany Hall, publisher of several newspapers, surveyor of the Port of New York, playwright and associate judge of the New York court of sessions. He came up with an ambitious plan to create 'Ararat – a City of Refuge for the Jews' on Grand Island in the Niagara River. Noah imagined that poor Jews from North Africa and eastern Europe would flock to this refuge where they would be joined by Karaites and the Jewish American Indians. This city was to be a temporary staging post for the scattered Jews and Ten Lost Tribes before their final return to the land of Israel. Noah's ideas were no doubt mediated by developing European perspectives on Jews. It has been suggested that Masonic lodges may be responsible to some extent for the development of the image of the 'noble Jew', and this construct is found in colonial Lost Tribe discourse at the time. A connection between such conceptions of native 'nobility' and the Masons may be illustrated in the grand ceremony organised by Noah. As the first step in his ambitious plan to create a state for the Jews in America, on 11 September 1825 he led a magnificent procession of uniformed militia, Masons in their Masonic regalia and the Lost Tribes in the form of American Indians with feathered headdresses, including a certain Chief Red Jacket. However the Jews he planned for never materialised and the plan came to nothing.[23]

A year before Noah's death a work was published in Philadelphia which gave tremendous support to the idea that the Lost Tribes were still to be found somewhere in the world. Joseph Schwartz's *A Descriptive Geography and Brief Historical Sketch of Palestine* (Philadelphia, 1850)[24] included a chapter devoted to the efforts that had been made by Jews in Palestine to find the Lost Tribes. As we see elsewhere these efforts seemed to have been fairly fruitful: definite sightings had been made and a letter from the Lost Tribes had actually turned up in Jerusalem. This and other sightings throughout the world reinforced the Israelite-American theory. If there were Lost Tribes in the Arabian desert or in Ethiopia, why not in America? Another Jewish book translated into English may also have had some impact. J. J. Benjamin II's *Eight Years in Asia and Africa from 1846 to 1855* was in great part a quest for the Lost Tribes, which he had no difficulty pinning down in a number of countries. He implicitly accepts many of the American-Israelite theories by saying that the 'islands of the west' were none other than the West Indies.[25] Further encouragement came with the discovery of a number of artefacts in America which purported to prove that Jews had once inhabited the continent. In *Natural and Aboriginal History of Tennessee* (1823) Justice John Haywood reported the discovery of Roman coins from the second century AD in Tennessee. Hubert Howe Bancroft gave detailed descriptions of Hebrew relics in the western parts of the United States. Earlier there were discoveries of a Hebrew inscription in New Milford, phylacteries in an Indian burial mound in Pittsfield, Massachusetts and a Hebrew tomb in Ohio. In *Publications of the Ohio Archeological and Historical Society* for 1904[26] R. E. Chambers referred to the Hebrew writing on the Newark holy stones in Ohio and, taking the same line on the subject that had been taken by Josiah Priest in *American Antiquities* (New York, 1798), affirmed the builders of the neighbouring mound to have been the Lost Ten Tribes. He also referred to the Black Hand Rock, above Licking River. According to him the hand, 'pointed to the mound that contained the last rabbi who ministered at the altar ... the hand on the rock pointing to the place of his burial'.[27] Similarly a purported Phoenecian inscription was found in Brazil (conclusively shown to be a forgery).[28] In 1932, 1952 and 1967 Hebrew coins were supposedly found in Louisville, Clay City and Hopkinsville, Kentucky. Frauds have been frequent and include the Newark holy stones, the Grave Creek tablet, the Pemberton axe, the stone from the Grand Traverse Bay and many others. The best known of these pieces of 'evidence' for the Israelite theory was the excavation carried out by the Washington-based Smithsonian Institute in 1894 where an inscription – the so-called Bat Creek stone – was unearthed at a burial site, which at first was taken to be a Cherokee inscription of no great antiquity. It has been suggested that this was a forgery made by a field assistant for the Smithsonian – a certain John Emmert – an alcoholic who was afraid of losing his job and wanted to secure his future with one great 'find'.[29] However in about 1969 Cyrus Gordon, a well-known and distinguished biblical scholar, identified it as a Hebrew inscription from about AD 100, of the Hebrew letters LYHWD – 'for Judah'. Gordon, who thus far has received no scholarly support for his identification, concluded that the burial site had been created by Jews who had fled Palestine at the time of one of the rebellions against Rome. However he also concluded that in his view some segments of the Ten Lost Tribes probably did migrate to the shores of America, although for the moment there is regrettably no hard evidence to hand.[30]

Theories that traces of Hebrew are to be found in South America are still advanced: in 1977 Father Miguel Santamaria, a member of the Colombian Society of Aboriginal Linguistics, argued in *Escritura Aborigen de Colombia* that there are eighty-three ancient Hebrew rock inscriptions in Colombia.

As Popkin shows, by the end of the nineteenth century mainstream opinion had turned its back on the Jewish Indian theory. Increasingly Indians were perceived as being perhaps of Mongolian origin. In any event they were seen as a primitive group – the most disadvantaged in the United States. Why try to connect this band of miserable, drunk outcasts to the sacred history of the Jews, which was also the sacred history of Western civilisation? As one historian said contemptuously of the Jewish-Indian theory in 1872, 'This truly monkish theory ... lunatic fancy, is possible only to men of a certain class, which in our time does not multiply.'[31] Connecting the Lost Tribes to the Anglo-Saxon master race was perhaps a different thing. It might still be possible to perceive something of 'a providential people' in the British Israelites – who, after all, could doubt the technical abilities of Victorian Britain? – but the Jewish-Indian theory, at least for the intellectual elites, was a dead letter. It was, as Popkin puts it, a 'bad joke' or 'an intellectual pariah'.[32]

However, as far as many people in the United States were concerned, the idea was live and well and particularly in religious, sectarian circles. In the first half of the nineteenth century, both in England and the United States, there was renewed and intense speculation about the Ten Tribes, which was one aspect of the religious revivals of the period known as the 'Second Great Awakening'. One of the most important of these new religious expressions was Mormonism and with its inception the theory of the Ten Tribes entered a fresh phase replete with new texts and mythologies.

The Church of Jesus Christ of Latter-Day Saints is a religious movement that derived from Joseph Smith (1805–44) and *The Book of Mormon*. In 1820 Smith, of Methodist farming stock, was surrounded by a brilliant light and confronted by God the Father and the Saviour who told him that the teaching of all Christian churches was false. Two years later, with some divine assistance, Smith discovered the location of certain gold tablets on which were written the words of God. At about this time, according to Smith's detractors, he came across a manuscript compiled by a Presbyterian preacher called Solomon Spaulding, who had written an imaginary account of the early inhabitants of the American continent called *Manuscript Found*. According to these sources a former Baptist minister, Sidney Rigdon, compiled *The Book of Mormon* from this text and with the help of Smith, 'perpetrated one of the greatest religious hoaxes of the century.'[33] Comparison of *Manuscript Found* with *The Book of Mormon* reveals little in common however. It is much more likely that the source of Smith's idea was one of the countless enthusiasts for the theory about Israelites in America mentioned in this chapter. On 24 April 1887 a somewhat convincing link was made in *The Cleveland Plain Dealer* between Spaulding and Ethan Smith (1762–1849), the noted New England congregational minister and author of *View of the Hebrews* (1823). It was a staunch defence of the theory on Israelites in America. The *Plain Dealer* quoted Ethan's grandson, who maintained that his grandfather had written another book that he had never published. As the paper noted:

> Taking as its foundation the migration of the lost tribes of Israel to the western continent, it [the book] described the hegira from Palestine, the establishment of the Jews in what is now Central America and Mexico, the founding of a great empire and its gradual decline and fall. It told of magnificent cities inhabited by an enlightened and Christian people. The author claimed for them a civilization equal to that of Egypt or Jerusalem. Hundreds of years passed and the history of the eastern Jews was repeated on the western continent. Quarrels between the various tribes sprang up, bloody wars were waged and the process of disintegration began. Gradually the people were scattered, their cities destroyed and all semblance to a nation was lost. Thousands perished by pestilence and the sword and the remnants of a once mighty nation relapsed into a state of barbarism. Their descendants, Dr Smith claimed, were Indians of North America, and the Aztecs of Mexico. This is almost exactly similar to the story told in *The Book of Mormon*.

Both Spaulding and Ethan Smith studied at Dartmouth College and according to Ethan's grandson were friends. In any event in 1830 Joseph Smith published a translation of his tablets which disappeared in mysterious circumstances. These describe the Lost Tribes of Israel, the Jaredites and the Lamanites, who came to America. The Jaredites soon disappeared from view and the Lamanites turned against the Nephites. It was Mormon who wrote the tablets and Moroni who buried them near Palmyra, New York, in AD 438.

The Mormon version of Israelite history based on *The Book of Mormon* is a 'distinctively American revelation'.[34] It shows that America was settled by Jaredites after the period of the Tower of Babel. The Jaredites first travelled to the Valley of Nimrod (Ether 2:1), dwelt in tents in Moriancumer near 'the great sea' for four years (Ether 2:13), were instructed by God to build barges (Ether 2:16–17), to gather together flocks and herds and to embark on the said barges (Ether 6:4). This they did and after 344 days at sea arrived in the promised land – America (Ether 6:11–12). They became exceedingly rich (Ether 6:28), divided into two kingdoms (Ether 7:20) and were destroyed in the final wars. However an Israelite called Lehi and his followers came to America from Jerusalem in about 600 BC. God had told them, 'Ye shall prosper and shall be led to a land of promise; yea, even a land which I have prepared for you' (1 Nephi 2:20). His followers split into two groups: the Nephites and the Lamanites. The Nephites built the great pre-Columbian cities of Central America and the Andes but died out in the third century AD. Specifically the Nephites engaged in periodic slaughter of other tribes or were slaughtered by them (Helaman 11:13), grew exceedingly rich (Helaman 6:9), transgressed, backslid and were destroyed. But the last twenty-four (Mormon 6:7–15) were hunted down and destroyed in their turn (Mormon 8:2). The Nephites perished in a great final battle near the hill of Cumorah in New York State where the sacred tablets were buried, and then removed in 1827 by Joseph Smith. The Lamanites had a similar history: they fought the Nephites (Jacob 1:13–14), slaughtered (Alma 56:12), became exceedingly rich (Helaman 6:9), prevailed over the Nephites (Mormon 6:7–15) and rejected the teaching of Christ (Ether 4:3). The Lamanites did not die out and indeed may still be seen in a 'degenerate condition' in the native Indians of the American continent. Mormon beliefs also extend into the Pacific. In about 55 BC some Israelites left the western coast of America and, according to one Mormon source, went on to populate New Zealand, Samoa, Tahiti, Tonga and other Pacific islands.

Indeed in 1843 Mormon missionaries were sent to labour among the Polynesians in the belief that they were of 'Israelitish origin and descendants of the people of whom *The Book of Mormon* is a history'.[35] The Latter-Day Saints apostle, Orson Pratt, in 1875 reflected an early Jewish tradition when he suggested that the location of the Lost Tribes might be under the surface of the earth.[36]

Mormons claim that material has been discovered to support their holy texts which shows that Israelites went to America rather than Babylon at the time of the destruction of the First Temple; that Jesus preached to them in America and that these, the Latter-Day Saints, would form the vanguard of the millennium. Features of the Mexican Maya culture are taken by Mormons to resemble the Christianity that once flourished in the continent, particularly the similarities between the Mayan god Quetzalcoatl and Christ (Quetzalcoatl has elsewhere been identified with a range of other notables including St Thomas, Atlas, Osiris, Dionysus, Bacchus, Poseidon and Hotu Matua – the culture hero of Easter Island in the Pacific). Mormons find parallels between *The Book of Mormon* and the *Annals of Ixtlilxochitl*, which had been written in the sixteenth century by a Mexican Indian, Fernando de Alva Ixtlilxochitl, grandson of the last native king of Tezcuco. Various other proofs are adduced in favour of Mormon belief: for instance that the stylised tree of the well-known sculpture in the so-called Temple of the Cross in Palenque, Mexico, was actually a depiction of the Christian cross and as such proof that Christianity had come to America before Columbus. Many other pieces of 'evidence' were collected in Thomas Stuart Ferguson's exhaustive and exhausting study, *One Fold and One Shepherd*, first published in Salt Lake City in 1958. This argues that the American Indians are descended from Mesopotamian Jaredites who landed on the Gulf coast of eastern Mexico in the third millennium BC and from two groups of Israelites descended from Joseph, who crossed the Atlantic in the sixth century. In one section he lists 298 'elements of culture' that central America and the ancient Near East had in common, from A – adobe huts to Z – signs of the zodiac.[37] In recent times one well-known non-Mormon scholar, Cyrus Gordon, has supported these views. He has written about a Mayan monument 'with Jewish connections'. 'It is,' as he puts it, 'the "Phylactery Stele" from Tepatlaxco, Veracruz, now on permanent display in the National Anthropological Museum in Mexico City. Specialists in Mayan art date it between AD 100 and 300. The wrapping of the thong (securing the phylactery) seven times around the forearm, followed by winding it around the hand and fingers, is perpetuated by observant orthodox Jews to this day.'[38]

The Mormons insist that the followers of their leader, Joseph Smith, will be joined in due course by remnants of the Lost Tribes, who for the time being remain hidden somewhere in the Arctic. The *Doctrine and Covenants* (110:11) describes a vision manifested to Smith in the temple at Kirtland, Ohio in 1836 in which, 'Moses appeared before us and committed unto us the keys of the gathering of Israel from the four parts of the earth, and the leading of the Ten Tribes from the land of the north.' And similarly in a revelation given through Smith at Hiram, Ohio on 3 November 1831, 'And they who are in the north countries shall come into remembrance before the Lord; and their prophets shall hear His voice, and shall no longer stay themselves ...' *Doctrine and Covenants* (133:26). One of the Articles of Faith of the Mormon church is belief, 'in the literal gathering of Israel and in the restoration of the Ten Tribes', and another is, 'that Zion (the New Jerusalem) will be built upon the American continent'.

Mormonism was widely detested by non-Mormons on the American continent from the outset. The concentration of power in the hands of the founder of the movement in Nauvoo (which had grown from a village of religious refugees and new converts to the point where it almost rivalled Chicago as the largest city in Illinois) was understandable: Smith was mayor, commander of the Nauvoo Legion state militia, justice of the peace, and university chancellor. It may have caused resentment that he ran for the office of the president of the United States in 1844. In addition there was general dislike of Mormon doctrines and suspicion about the mysterious origins of the new scriptures, as well as a distaste for polygamy, which had been introduced in 1843 after Smith received a revelation permitting 'plural marriage'. In the wider community Smith's message never earned him much more than a generous measure of ridicule. Perhaps the greatest crime of the Mormons was that they had effectively hijacked Christian and Jewish sacred history and had taken upon themselves, very substantially at any rate, the mantle of Israel – to the point that the varying degrees of the Mormon priesthood carry the names of Aaron, the founder of the Jewish order of priests, and Melchizedek, the King of Salem who blessed Abraham 'in the name of God the Most High'. The Zion of the earliest American settlers, the 'City upon a Hill', was threatened by the American Zion of the Mormons. The violent death of Smith at the hands of a mob at the age of thirty-eight on 27 June 1844, is symbolic of the general hatred and disdain for the sect and dramatically concluded the founding period of the Church of Jesus Christ of Latter-Day Saints.[39]

The Mormons have contributed greatly to keeping Lost Tribes ideology alive and well into the twentieth and twenty-first centuries. The American Zion that has been created in Utah commands the allegiance of over ten million Americans and millions more elsewhere in the world. Partly thanks to the Mormons 'Lost Tribes in America' ideology has more adherents in the United States than elsewhere in the world and more than at any time in history.

In the current context this remarkable myth has entered the political, religious and cultural arena of the United States in a number of unexpected ways. The amusing scene in Mel Brooks' 1974 film *Blazing Saddles*, where a band of Indians led by a Redskin chief (played by Brooks himself) speak Yiddish to each other and comment on a wagonload of African Americans as *schwarzers* – an American-Jewish designation of black people – brings this myth into the visual world of modernity. As Lester Friedman has observed, 'It seems comically appropriate that the West's most conspicuous outsider, the Indian, should speak in the tongue of history's traditional outsider, the Jew.'[40]

A number of Afro-American groups in the United States have also come under the spell of the Lost Tribes. No doubt the chief mechanism for their enchantment was the Bible, to which they had been introduced on the slave farms of the south. Among the clamour of other claimants for a Lost Tribe pedigree in the United States there were few whites who bothered to advance Afro-Americans as descendants of the Israelites. This did not matter, for they were to do it for themselves. The Church of God and Saints of Christ was founded in 1896 by W. S. Crowdy on the claim that the Ten Lost Tribes were the ancestors of black people. The rival Commandment Keepers defined the black peoples as the tribe of Judah, but claimed that the Lost Tribes were in fact the white race. A separate discourse, which had established a Jewish origin for so many of the inhabitants of the African continent, certainly had an impact upon the Afro-Americans of the United States. In the 1920s the rabbi of the black Jews of Harlem declared that, 'the African-Hebrew Heritage belonged to blacks alone and included Falashas, the Queen of Sheba and tribes of West Africa.'[41] In other words the real

Jews were Africans and only Africans – the white Jews were fakes.[42] The discourse connecting black American 'Jewish' groups with West African 'Judaism' was bolstered by a parallel discourse suggesting that the origins of American black Judaism were to be found in Ethiopia. As Emanuela Trevisan-Semi has shown, many Afro-Americans gradually came to create an identity in opposition to, and in imitation of, the American-Jewish community and to this end adopted an imagined Ethiopian and Falasha identity. According to one black American leader, the death of King Solomon forced two of the Twelve Tribes to migrate to East Africa: the other ten were conquered by the Philistines and scattered throughout the world. The black Jews were the direct descendants of Jacob, while the white Jews were descended from the red-haired Esau.[43]

One recent book, *The African Origins of Modern Judaism*, has argued that Abraham and all the people he converted went to Ethiopia where they became known as Falasha.[44] Trevisan-Semi writes tellingly of American black Judaism's 'interest in the possibility of sharing a myth that spoke of royal descent, lions of Judah and Abyssinian princes', as a strategem for transcending the bitter memories of slavery and creating a noble history that could compare favourably with that of white Americans.[45] In this they had much in common with other groups, notably the British Israelites.[46] Once the actual existence of the Falasha community of Ethiopia became known in the United States, it seemed to settle once and for all and in a suitably scientific fashion the question of the legitimacy of Afro-Americans' Israelite origins.[47] Today there are hundreds of thousands of black Israelites in the United States with links to other black Jewish organisations and movements elsewhere in the world. Some of these have a sympathetic relationship with white Jews, others do not. The Yahwists, a black Israelite community based mainly in Florida and led by Yahweh ben Yahweh, currently serving an eighteen-year prison sentence for assault, firebombing and fourteen murders, are violently opposed to whites, whom they regard as 'white devils'.

The chief agents for the dissemination of theories about the Lost Tribes throughout the world, both among colonists and native peoples, were Christian missionaries of one sort or another. This was as true of the United States as elsewhere. Within this discourse both Christians and Jewish converts to Christianity were active. In the 1780s a Jewish convert to Christianity came to Philadelphia to preach the Gospel: he said that, 'many of the Indians in America were the descendants of the Ten Tribes. He said his design was to go and live among them to learn their language, that he might teach the Gospel and proceed with them in person to Jerusalem; to obtain which he supposed an expedition would soon be entered upon . . . he died a natural death, it is supposed, some little time after being among the Indians.'[48] In 1848 Joseph Schwartz, a Jew from Jerusalem, visited Philadelphia on a fund-raising trip on behalf of his community in Jerusalem to get his book on Palestine translated and published.[49] No doubt his presence did much to further speculation about the Lost Tribes, at least among the Jewish community.[50] Ten years before, Joseph Wolff, another Jewish convert to Christianity and no stranger to the discourse surrounding the Lost Tribes of Israel, went to Philadelphia, Washington and Baltimore where he, too, preached the Gospel. He remarked that the idea that American Indians were of the Lost Tribes had 'lately been so much mooted', although he was somewhat sceptical. His scepticism is in itself pretty revealing: he had had little trouble finding Lost Tribes just about everywhere else. He went on to write, 'Worthy people in America desired me to travel about with them in order that I might convince the Indians of their extraction from the Jews.' Eventually he was fortunate enough to encounter some Indians who believed in the theory, 'I came across the Mohican tribes near New York and asked them, "Whose descendants are you?" They replied, "We are of Israel." I asked, "Who told you so?" and expected to learn much ancient tradition. To my great surprise they said, "Mr and Mrs Simons of Scotland." '[51]

In the West the ideology of Lost Tribes found fertile soil, which will no doubt keep generating new expressions of Israelite identity in the service of new needs and anxieties. It could serve Jewish nationalists, American patriots, Indian supporters or detractors, white supremacists and black supremacists, crooks, dreamers and countless others of less determinate callings. But as we shall see equally fertile ground was to open up in the East.

Chapter Six

FROM THE CHI'ANG TO THE KAREN: ISRAEL IN THE EAST

> Despised, persecuted, broken, here are the residue of a race who have never bowed the knee to Baal, or forsaken the faith of their fathers.
>
> The Reverend Thomas Torrance, 1923

Since early mediaeval times it was assumed that the Lost Tribes would be found in the Far East. A reflection of this construction of Jewishness in the East may be perceived in Matisse's remarkable painting *L'Asie* (1946). A partly naked woman swathed in beads, lengths of printed cotton and gossamer-thin silk stands against a red background looking down inscrutably on the observer: while she is supposed to be some sort of Asiatic she has nonetheless the air of a Sephardi Jewess. These constructions and inventions were to continue into the modern period with some remarkable results.

For centuries speculation had persisted that the Lost Tribes were to be found in the East. We have already seen that in the seventeenth century there were those who thought 'that famous civil (though idolatrous) nation of China are Hebrewes',[1] and we have also seen that Menasseh ben Israel was of the firm conviction that the land of Sinim mentioned in the book of Isaiah (49:12) from where some of the Lost Tribes were supposed to eventually return was none other than China. Indeed a theory had developed that American Indians were descended in very ancient times from Chinese Jews. A nineteenth-century Russian churchman even suggested that the Jews arrived in China before the birth of Moses.[2] This discourse existed elsewhere too: when the redoubtable Joseph Wolff was in central Asia in the 1840s he was told that the Jews of Samarkand had a tradition that the Lost Tribes were to be found in Chinese territory.[3]

Western Christians, perhaps most acutely British and American evangelicals, were prone to see traces of the Bible everywhere. As missionaries and others encountered exotic peoples, a discourse was frequently created which potentially served white, Western interests in a variety of ways. One way was to single out a particular minority from the mass, to argue that this group was in some way connected with the Israelites of old and to attribute to this minority moral characteristics that were close to the self-image held by Englishmen at the time. The supposed moral kinship of the English and the Jews has a long history and the projection of Israelite identities all over the world is in part a celebration of this perceived affinity. In evangelical circles particularly, a kind of philo-Semitism allied with a fulsome self-regard created the type of idea expressed by James Finn (1806–72), who was a famous British consul in Jerusalem from 1845–62. 'From the effect of their domestic morality,' he wrote, 'and family affections, these [the Jews] were the people who could best afford to look an Englishman straight in the face.'[4] Some Jews and other minorities exhibiting these admirable traits would then be targeted by missionaries and sometimes given educational help. These people, at least in principle, could be used in the struggle to dominate the majority. Such a projection clearly implies the construction and invention of an identity for these minorities from a barely apprehended aspect of the British colonial self.[5]

Throughout the world Western travellers, colonists, missionaries and others found similarities between remote people and the Jews. In the context of China the fabrication and elaboration of such similarities was common enough. When I was in Singapore in the 1980s I was struck by the comparisons that Jews and Chinese so frequently made with each other: respect for ancestors, a good business sense, a shared respect for education and so on.[6] Points of comparison like these had been made regularly over a long period of time. In 1921 *Israel's Messenger*, a Jewish paper in Shanghai, reported on a lecture by a certain Mr G. E. Sokolsky at a meeting of the literary circle of the Shanghai Zionist Association on the similarities between the Jews and the Chinese. Among other things, the speaker wondered 'what influence the Jews exerted on the Chinese in the old days when the Jew carried cotton from Egypt to China and the Chinese transported silk from their country to the Jews?'[7] This was no doubt a reasonable question and indeed certain similarities between the Jews and the Chinese may be said to exist. Some, however, took these ideas much further.

Missionaries active in western China at the beginning of the last century not only perceived certain similarities between the Jews and the Chinese – they actually saw all manner of traces of the Jewish people, and particularly of the Lost Tribes of Israel, among Chinese populations. One of them observed that several missionaries had a 'rigorous training in Bible studies, and lack of knowledge about social customs among other peoples, [which] led them to imagine that they had found in western China significant survivals of the biblical traditions that occupied so much of their thinking'. Particularly there was 'a missionary in Kweichow who believed he had found some old Hebrew practices among the Nosu and he also cited another one who claimed to have found among the Miao people an ancient song which described the Flood, the building of the Tower of Babel and the ensuing confusion of tongues and then went on to state their racial origin'.[8]

On 18 January 1923, a devout Scots missionary, the Reverend Thomas Torrance,[9] read a paper to the northern China branch of the Royal Asiatic Society in Shanghai in which he described the beliefs of the Ch'iang people among whom he had been working.[10] Torrance had first come across the Ch'iang in 1918. In 1920 he wrote his first article about them, 'The History, Customs and Religion of the Ch'iang, an aboriginal People of West China', which was published by the *Shanghai Mercury*. I have not been able to find a copy of this but it may be assumed that the basic ideas are those found in his lecture. His lecture described the time he had spent in a remote part of western China between the province of Szechuan and Tibet working among 'a number of tribes who are little known to the outside world. These are the great Rong with their five states, the wild Goloks, the sleek Sifan, the cross-bred Bolotsze, the thieving Hehshui people, the warlike Nosu or Lolos and the sturdy Ch'iang.'[11]

The sturdy Ch'iang, judging by this opening description already his favourite group, were described by Torrance as

> pastoral, farming folk, the remnant of a once great nation ... they live in flat roofed, biblical looking stone houses ... the most wonderful thing about the Ch'iang, next to their long existence as a separate people, is their religion. It is purely monotheistic and has remained so from time immemorial, in spite of the oppressions and contemptuous treatment of their idolatrous neighbours. This purity of religious belief forms at once a strong link of sympathy between us and them ... we view with a profound feeling of respect such manly qualities of character as have made them stand so well the test of time and we come to the study of their religious customs with an

> unequalled earnestness, because here we see them come down to us from the earliest antiquity. No Pharaoh's tomb, no cuneiform library, and no foundation of Judean city are more curious or fascinating than this hoary ritual of these simple highlanders ... The fact of finding monotheists in China is in itself a remarkable thing in a country that has gone wholly over to idolatry. The early though qualified monotheism of the Chinese pales beside it in interest. Despised, persecuted, broken, here are the residue of a race who have never bowed the knee to Baal, or forsaken the faith of their fathers.

The difference between the Chinese and the Ch'iang, claimed Torrance, is 'subtle but real'. It might be compared with the difference of 'spiritual conception' that separated 'Esau from Jacob, King Saul from King David'.

In addition to being 'manly', the Ch'iang were described as 'cautious' responding to kindness, 'clean', 'moral', 'strong' and 'free'. But even more significantly the colour white imbued them with a sense of awe. 'White,' Torrance noted, 'is regarded as significant of good and black of evil. A white man is their synonym for one who is just and upright; a black man literally denotes a blackguard. Accordingly, their mode of worshipping God, they call THE WHITE RELIGION' (capitals in original).

His description of Ch'iang rituals, of the ritual sacrifice of animals 'without spot and blemish', of the sanctification of the lamb, of white sacrificial robes, sacred groves, purification rituals, moon festivals, of days of sacrifice 'reckoned Sabbaths', scapegoat ceremonies (for scapegoat he uses the Hebrew term *azazel*), the use of unleavened bread, are all redolent of the Bible and of the religious practices of the ancient Israelites. Somewhat inconveniently the Ch'iang neither abstained from pork and other non-kosher foods nor did they circumcise their young. 'Yet,' proclaimed Torrance, 'their own judicial regulations often correspond to those in the Old Testament.' Needless to say, 'The first question asked by those who hear of their monotheistic faith and sacrificial customs is: are they not part of the Lost Ten Tribes of Israel? When this is denied the second follows hard on it: are they then not Jewish proselytes? The points of likeness between the Ch'iang religion and the Jewish are so many and intimate that the questions are natural.' However Torrance's conclusions at the time of this Shanghai lecture are somewhat different. Clearly he admires the Ch'iang ('the soul of the man is dead,' he wrote, 'who cannot love them') and thinks of them as special. He knows that they are a people with an ancient lineage. He concludes therefore not that the Ch'iang have derived their religion from the Jews but that the Jews have derived their religion in remote times from the Ch'iang: in other words that the fountainhead of Western religion was to be found in Torrance's own parish.

Such an empowering view was not entirely consistent. Even at this stage in the development of his ideas on the subject, the Ch'iang were practically Jewish. Firm in his Christian belief that the Gospel should be brought 'to the Jew first and then to the Gentile', he concludes that 'because of their resemblance to the former [they] have a strong claim to missionary priority. Some time ago the writer felt this so strongly that he sent an evangelist among them. Now there are two, both supported by Christians at home.' It is worth noting that Torrance made his views clear to the Ch'iang themselves. One observer who spent years in the area noted, 'This fiction created by Mr Torrance and his aides only helped increase the rebellious spirit of the Ch'iang converts, which led to even more ruthless oppression by the Chinese a few years later.'[12] And indeed the Ch'iang villages and churches established by Torrance were destroyed during the revolution.

In the vast sea of Chinese the Reverend Torrance had found common cause with a people professing 'the white religion', the forebears in his view of the religion of whites in his day. In 1934 he gave a similar lecture on the Ch'iang for the West China Border Research Society which appeared in its journal and advanced somewhat similar views.[13] But with the publication of his book *China's First Missionaries: Ancient Israelites* (London, 1937) he took the view – one that he had skirted around in China – that the Ch'iang were actually descended from the Jews. His book would, he wrote, 'describe the customs and religious observances of a colony of people descended from the Israelitish settlers who came to the Western borderlands of China'. In subsequent lectures he developed the idea further: the Jews had been appointed by the Almighty as missionaries to teach the world monotheism and those that got as far as China became the Ch'iang. In his last article the Ch'iang had become quite literally 'West China Jews', photographs purported to show their Semitic features and a photograph of a Ch'iang village is captioned, 'A typical Jewish village.'

Torrance's 1937 book made quite a splash. It was hailed as 'the greatest missionary book of the century' by the *Scottish Geographical Magazine* while *The English Churchman and St James' Chronicle* opined, 'these twentieth-century tribes are perpetuating today the actual customs of the Israelites who were contemporary with Elijah, Amos and Hosea ... How strange that we should have to go to the Chinese-Tibet borderland for the latest confirmation of the Divine Book.' The *Times Literary Supplement* observed somewhat chillingly in view of the fact that this was, after all, 1937, 'A close study of their rites and customs has enabled Mr Torrance to establish the identity of the Chiang people and to trace their history ... Mr Torrance's conclusions are confirmed by the illustrations to the text which show convincingly Jewish types.'

A similar discourse existed on the island of Taiwan, formerly Formosa, which today (along with the Pescadores, Matsu and Quemoy) is known as the Republic of China. The island was reached by the Portuguese in 1590, later held by the Dutch and Chinese and was occupied by Japan in the first Sino-Japanese War (1894–5). It was held by the Japanese until 1945. The majority of the population of Taiwan are ethnic (Han) Chinese who began to emigrate to Taiwan in the fifteenth century. There is also a small aboriginal population that today numbers perhaps 250,000. For centuries it had appeared to Europeans that there was something rather strange about this part of the population of Formosa. An account of the island's people by a Dutch clergyman, George Candidus, suggested links with the Indian population of the Americas, and indeed these had been noted by Father Lafitau early in the eighteenth century.[14] In 1904 *Israel's Messenger* reported an ironical article published in the *Jewish Chronicle*, by Albert Hyamson (1875–1954) the English civil servant and Jewish historian:

> The southernmost island of Japan proper is connected with Formosa, the latest acquisition to the empire, by a long and straggling chain of small islands known as the Loo Choo groups. These islands are inhabited by two races, the Japanese in the northern portion of the group, and the Loo Choans proper, the Aborigines, in all the islands. Of these latter, as of most the races, an Israelitish descent has been given but the 'proofs' on this occasion differ widely from, and are far more worthy of consideration than the fantastic legends in which rafts and fugitive kings and prophets take a leading part, that have been attached to the history of the Japanese nation in order to connect it with the Israelitish fugitives from the Holy Land ... Half a century ago a European Jew lived in one of the little-known centres of the Loo Choo group of islands. Apparently he combined the professions of merchant and physician, for he used to complain that

> the natives, when ill, refused to accept alleviation for their sufferings at his hands, but preferred to remain in pain since their own medicine men were unable to give them relief. Of the country itself he had a very unappreciative opinion. From his description in an early number of the *Jewish Chronicle* it seemed most unattractive and extremely poor in vegetation, in fauna and in every other detail. Passing rapidly from the country, this Jewish settler in a little known land turned to its inhabitants. Their appearance struck him as being essentially Jewish. The convexity of the noses of the natives and their partiality for long beards have been noted by all students of the Loo Choans. These features the writer emphasised in his account. In another direction the natives showed a remarkable resemblance to the Jews. The members of both races surpass all others in their longing for male offspring. The Loo Chooan Calendar included many strict fasts that resembled in most details those of the writer's own race, and he at the same time hinted at considerable agreement between the dates on which the two sets of holidays fell. The Loo Chooan betrothal rites constituted a strong link in the chain of proof that this Jewish settler in the Farthest East was spinning. 'The transaction takes place chiefly among the parents of the parties intended to be united in matrimony' . . . Similarities were pointed out between Hebrew and the native tongue. Of course in accordance with the precedents invariably followed when Lost Tribes theories are being evolved, resemblances were found between the nomenclature of the population and that of biblical personages . . . the theory, however, found its strongest supports in Holy Writ. 'I will send those that escape of them unto the nations, to Tarshish, Pul and Lud, that draw the bow, to Tubal and Javan. To the isles afar off, that have not heard my fame, neither have seen my glory; and they shall declare my glory among the Gentiles . . .' One further proof of the Israelitish ancestry of the natives of the Loo Choo Archipelago was produced and this was certainly expected to convince the most hardened sceptic. The natives suffered from exactly the diseases and plagues foretold for the Israelites in Deuteronomy. The sceptic read the statement and his scepticism survived.[15]

Let us return to the Chi'ang. The discourse surrounding them did what discourses do best: it kept moving. In our own times the case of the Chi'ang has been linked with other Judaising movements in the East. Indeed the speculations of Christian missionaries have been substantially adopted by Jews eager to find the remnants of Israel. Specifically, the ideas of Torrance – but not those of others who have worked on the religious ideas of the Ch'iang and quite discredited Torrance[16] – have been taken up by some Jews, notably by Rabbi Eliyahu Avichail and Amishav (My People Returns), the Israeli organisation dedicated to the finding and rehabilitation of the Lost Tribes and remote, dispersed remnants of Israel. Rabbi Avichail has known about the Ch'iang for some time. In 1985, an article in the *Hong Kong Jewish Chronicle* entitled 'The Lost Tribes – Found in Asia' presented the possibility that the Ch'iang are descendants of the Lost Tribes and mentioned Amishav's interest in them and the possibility of mounting an expedition to visit them.[17] Finally he was able to do so in 1998. He now believes that the Ch'iang are not only of Jewish origin but the source of other Jewish-seeming groups in the East. 'The Ch'iang also have a tradition of sacrificial offerings in purity, levirate marriage, etc. During the sacrificial offering they mounted twelve flags beside the altar representing their national forefathers (tribes of Israel?). In times of trouble they called on a god named Yahve.'[18] According to Avichail several hundred years ago the Ch'iang, with their Jewish customs and their undoubtedly Hebraic godhead, fled to Burma where these Jewish practices took root among the Karen people there, subsequently spreading to other Burmese ethnic entities. As we examine the evolution of the discourse in Burma it will be seen that a similar phenomenon occurs: a Christian missionary and colonial debate is taken up in its entirety by Jewish organisations and individuals.

The first 'authentic' Jew to spend any time in Burma, as far as I know, was a certain Shlomo Reinmann, a native of Galicia, who arrived in Rangoon in 1852 with the British army. Within five years, however, there were sufficient Jews – Baghdadi and Bene Israel Jews served there[19] – to warrant the construction of a small synagogue in the city, the Matzmiah Yeshurun.[20] But long before this actual Jewish presence had been established Western missionaries active in the country had formed the view that the Karen ethnic group was itself of Jewish extraction. This view is still held by some people and, as will be shown, has a bearing on the claims to Jewishness of many thousands of people on the Burmese–Indian border, some of whom have already emigrated to Israel.

Rabbi Avichail considers the Karen people to be descendants of the Ch'iang.[21] Why were they supposed by missionaries and others to have anything to do with Jews? Part of the answer, no doubt, has to do with the mechanics of colonisation, mentioned above. In much the same way as we have seen in the case of the Ch'iang, a particular, often 'loyal', minority was picked out and perceived to have strikingly superior characteristics. A way of explaining the group's unexpectedly 'superior' ability was to imagine their origins outside the locus of the inferior majority and to place it in some sense within the sacred history of the colonial power.

Thus it was that 'the loyal Karens of Burma', as one British official of the Bengal Civil Service called them in a book of the same name, achieved a special status in British eyes. According to an Indian journalist writing several decades later and no doubt imbued with the ethos of the Raj, they had proved their loyalty most conclusively when they had contributed proportionately more troops to British forces during the First World War than any other group in Burma. Later, too, their irregulars were particularly active in the suppression of the Burmese rebellion in 1931–2.[22] Such loyalty was mixed with nothing less than reverence for the white colonists. As the first Karen convert to Christianity put it, 'Through the goodness of God, my nation, sons of the forest and children of poverty, ought to praise thy nation, the white foreigners, exceedingly; and we ought to obey your orders . . .'[23]

This favoured group, as our Bengali civil servant expressed it, was not of indigenous stock. 'The skin is naturally fair, like that of the Chinese; and the features of those of pure blood are Caucasian in type – a characteristic which has been deemed by some to support their claim to have been one of the Lost Tribes of Israel.'[24]

The Karen were not only perceived as being racially superior, their very traditions seemed almost British in nature. Their religious practices were considered so akin to British ones that they 'could be recited with propriety in any Christian church in England'. Their culture, too, was reminiscent of British culture, 'their music is nearly all wild and plaintive like that of the Scottish and Welsh highlanders'.[25]

The Karens' account of their origins – that they were from River of Running Sand – no doubt served as a springboard for all sorts of speculation. This was a people with a mysterious past. Quite clearly there were striking and seductive similarities between their legends and those of the Jewish scriptures: an example was the Karen story of creation which 'was almost parallel to the Mosaic account in Genesis'. These similarities were not evident however to the first Christian missionaries active in Burma. This was perhaps because the Catholics who were the first to arrive paid little or no attention to them. Indeed it appears that the first mention of the Karen in any missionary literature was only in 1827.[26] As Dr Francis Mason, missionary and translator, laments, from Francis Xavier to William Carey the great missionaries who had passed this way had all been ignorant of this people. The first to observe the Karen and to note their similarities to the Israelites were the Baptist missionaries who had been forced to move to the coastal province of Tenasserim with the outbreak of the first Anglo-Burmese War (1824–6).

The British Baptist Missionary Society had been active briefly in Burma from about 1807 to 1813, but subsequently its work was handed over to the American Baptists. Francis Mason of the American Baptist Foreign Mission Society arrived in Burma in 1814 and in time became convinced that the Karen were part of the Lost Tribes of Israel. He had certainly reached this conclusion by 1833: on 6 December of that year he announced from his headquarters in the 'head waters of the Tenasserim' to Mr Maingy the British Civil Commissioner, who had requested a report on the Karen, 'the discovery of a fragment of the descendants of the Hebrews'. 'I sit down in the midst of the Karen jungle,' he wrote, 'to redeem my pledge and give you some account of the traditions existing among the Tavoy Karens.' In a passionate letter Mason listed the traits that proved their distinguished lineage: the nature of their god Pu or Yuwah, their belief in angels and Satan, the fall of man, the dispersion at Babel, the future destruction of the world, their love of God, their tradition of being a wandering people, their freedom from idolatry and so on. Mason opined, 'There can scarcely be a rational doubt that the Yuwah of the Karens is the Jehovah of the Hebrews . . . from the foregoing I am constrained to believe the Karens to be descendants of the Hebrews. Look at them, sir; is not the Jew written in their countenance?'[27]

It was splendid to have discovered a remnant of the Hebrews in this unpromising jungle but even more splendid that they had proved so wonderfully receptive to the Gospel. 'The history of modern missions,' he noted, 'has no parallel with the success that has attended the annunciation of the Gospel among the Karens. "Who hath heard such a thing? Who hath seen such a thing?" '[28] The opening words of the book Mason wrote describing his missionary endeavours among the Karen stressed his surprise that in this remote place such promising candidates for conversion should be found. 'Often perhaps had the Christian voyager gazed on the rocky promontories of Burmah, crowned with their whitened pagodas, that glow amid the eternal verdure of tropical climes; but he little thought that "the misty mountain tops" in the distance, threw their shadow over the dwellings of a people that generation after generation had charged their posterity never to worship idols.'[29]

If the Karens' scorn for idols was balm to a missionary, so was their legend of a lost written language and a lost book. What could this lost book be but the Bible? As Smeaton told the story in 1887, 'They believed that God, who had cursed the Karen for losing the written Word, would certainly call upon them some day – near or distant, they knew not – to say how much they remembered of it; and that the blessing to each would be apportioned according to the care with which its words and truths had been treasured up.'[30] 'And where was this remarkable body of tradition from?' asked Harry Ignatious Marshall, another American Baptist missionary. 'Was it their independent possession from the beginning of time, their only relic from a more vigorous and highly civilized past when as they explained, they had not yet lost their book? Or had it been borrowed from another people whom they had met in the course of their wanderings from their northern birthplace to their present home? Some of the early missionaries including Dr Mason, thought that the Karen might be found to be the Lost Tribes of Israel or, if not actually descended from Abraham, that they had received instruction from colonies of Jews, who were supposed to have spread to the East in ancient times.'

Marshall went on in his book, *The Karen People of Burma*, to discuss where this Jewish influence could have come from, 'The story of the creation among these people has such marked parallelism with the Hebraic story that, even though its origin has not been traced, we find it difficult to avoid the suspicion that it came from an Hebraic source, being carried by some wandering story-teller or unknown missionary only to become incorporated into the tribal belief of the Karen along with their own primitive mythology.'[31]

Above all, it was the cult of the high god Yuwah or Ywa, reminiscent of the Hebrew YHWH, which excited Christians and later Jews and inspired them with the certainty that here must be some long-lost relic of the ancient religion of the Hebrews.[32] Marshall found particular significance in the fact that the Karen prophets of Yuwah were 'at enmity with' the other Karen priests who dealt with the spirits. In 1847 a Catholic priest, Father Plaisant, described one of these Yuwah cults. The Karen priest, he asserted, was associated with an old woman of remarkable piety, 'both wore white garments and dwelt in the temple, *bu do*, where at new and full moon they led public rites before an altar. Asperging the congregation with holy water before they entered, the ... priest offered rice, water, betel leaf, and areca nut and chanted invocations to Ywa.'[33]

According to Father Plaisant, the early Baptist missionaries had got it about right: Yuwah created the earth, he made man and all living creatures, he was omniscient, omnipotent, perfect and eternal. According to the priest, in the days after the creation Yuwah set aside the 'book of gold' for the Karen, who failed to come and get it. It was therefore entrusted to his younger 'white brother'. 'Thereafter ... the latter obligingly built a boat for Ywa and transported him across the ocean, whence Ywa ascended to heaven. In their sacred songs, the Karen look forward to the return of the White Brother and their book, as well as to the advent of Ywa ...'[34]

Theodore Stern notes that this general characterisation of Yuwah is no doubt the product of a Christian reading of the Yuwah traditions. It is interesting to note that the Baptists projected the idea of the god as YHWH or Jehovah, while the Catholic Plaisant introduced a reflection of the Virgin Mary into the frame by giving Yuwah a wife and subsequently a son. It is the son who takes on the character of the Saviour, dying and coming back to life. The perception of the Karens as people within the colonists' own field of ethnic and sacred history spread beyond missionary circles. In *The Karens of the Golden Chersonese* (1876) Lieutenant Colonel A. R. McMahon of the Madras Staff Corps and Deputy Commissioner in British Burma followed Mason in pointing out that occasionally a Karen could be found with rather European features: in support of this he quoted a British doctor who had published an article in the *Journal of Indian Archeology* that pointed to their long Caucasian faces and straight noses. McMahon viewed their religion as 'Noachic' – a primitive form of monotheism – and stressed their belief in 'the existence of a Supreme Being, God eternal, the creator of heaven and earth and all things'.[35]

According to Stern their identification as Israelites lent a certain stature to the Karen in their own eyes: they could now claim to be part of the sacred history of some of the great nations of the world.[36]

As far as I can judge the first time the identification of the Karens as Israelites was given serious attention by Jews was in the 1930s. In a Bombay Jewish journal, *The Jewish Tribune*, of April 1934 appeared the first of a series of articles written by J. E. Joshua, a member of the Bene Israel. Joshua, who was based in Rangoon, entitled his article 'The Lost Jews of Burma'. 'They live in forests and villages and hills,' he wrote. 'They hunt animals, grow paddy and keep elephants . . . In fact, the Chinese Jews, who originally migrated from Persia to China, are today within the confines of the land of golden pagodas, spirits and white elephants but known as Karens.'[37]

Joshua also connected the Yuwah traditions with the Hebrew YHWH. He quotes Karen poetry in support of the essential monotheism of the Karen religion:

God is unchangeable, eternal
He was in the beginning of the world
God is endless and eternal
He existed at the beginning of the world
God is truly unchangeable and eternal
He existed in ancient time at the beginning of the world
The life of God is endless

As Joshua put it, among the traditions of the Karens may be found 'all the familiar accounts of the creation of the world, the first earthly couple, the temptation and fall, the deluge, the dispersal of mankind after the building of the Tower of Babel'.[38] He insisted that 'there is nothing extant to show that these traditions may have been introduced from an outside agency, particularly a Hebraic source. The only Jews then occupying a neighbouring country were the Chinese Jews who were greatly assimilated.' It had been suggested that the Portuguese may have introduced some of these ideas but Joshua dismissed this on the grounds that they limited their brief stay in the sixteenth century to Rangoon. When Christian missionaries arrived in Burma the Karens knew nothing of Christianity so, as Joshua notes, it could not have been their influence. In addition, the more remote the Karen communities were from Rangoon and its ports, the greater their knowledge of these traditions.

Joshua highlights too, 'it is not without significance that the holy task of returning the Lost Book, the treasure and hope of the Karens, was entrusted to the white man. It obviously made a subtle distinction for not entrusting this task to their darker neighbours, the Burmese, the Talaings, the Chinese and the Indians.'

The tradition goes that:

With buffalo horn Ywa sounds the note;
A white man steers the golden boat;
Father call with trumpet tone
Of itself the boat comes on.

The ivory trumpet Ywa will blow;
Hearing, following, noon, night, go
When Ywa blows the horn, obey
Noon or night make no delay.

Although used as a bulwark against the attractions of Buddhism, this and other traditions were not so useful against the Christian missionaries, who had no qualms about presenting one of their number as the long expected 'white brother' to gain new adherents to Christianity. The simple Karens of the villages and hills received this momentous news with great excitement. Ko Tha Byn, the first Karen convert to Christianity, conveyed the message that the long-awaited 'white brother' had actually returned and that in fact he was none other than the Baptist missionary, the Reverend Boardman. The Karen sent their elders to greet this messenger from Yuwah.[39]

Joshua's enthusiastic account of the Karen's history and religion was identical to that found in missionary sources. Indeed most of it was lifted directly from them. His view of the Karens' human qualities is also identical. They were loyal and 'honest, fair and unobtrusive; quiet, reserved and simple in habits and manners'. Joshua's conclusions, however, are in some ways quite different. The Karens' extraordinary beliefs and their fine qualities made them ideal subjects for conversion not to Christianity, but to mainstream Judaism. Joshua was aware of the difficulties this posed within Judaism but as he saw it the dreadful circumstances in which Jews found themselves in the world in the 1930s certainly justified a new policy on what might constitute Jewishness. Joshua had come to similar conclusions as the groups advocating a kind of universal Judaism in Palestine and elsewhere, without, to my knowledge, having any link with them. As he put it, 'Without denying that ... Judaism frowns at conversion ... yet in modern times a relaxation of this rule became unavoidable in respect of the Marranos of Spain and the dark Jews of Abyssinia. The Karens by nature of their Jewish origin, rightly belong to this family of neo-Jews . . .'[40]

What of the impact of all this on the Karen themselves? Theodore Stern has rightly shown that pre-colonial Karen religion was highly charged with its own millenarian expectation and that the Messianic character of early nineteenth-century Baptist belief played to that expectation. He also notes that the Karen, as simple hill people, were not alone in casting envious glances at the rich civilisations of the plains and, 'viewing their humble condition against the splendour of their lowland neighbours they have nourished legends of past glory, when they too dwelt in walled cities and possessed writing'.[41] Today there are few echoes of specifically Judaic Messianism among the Karen but in Burma, and particularly in the region of Tiddim, such ideas are alive and well. As this book is being written a new Jewish interpretation of Karen traditions espoused particularly by Rabbi Avichail, Amishav and the American organisation Kulanu (meaning 'all of us'), is being used to prove that such traditions are connected with the aspirations of a quite different group – the Shinlung – to be considered a Lost Tribe of Israel. Their Jewish-seeming traditions have thus taken on a new importance in the context of India.[42]

Chapter Seven

THE LAND OF HARD BONDAGE: THE LOST TRIBES IN INDIA

The people of Judea and those who dwell in the remotest Countries of the Indies agree very well in their Temper, their Customs and Manner of Governing.

M. de la Créquinière

Today the population of India is around one billion. After China it is the second most populous nation on earth. The Jewish population of India reached perhaps thirty or forty thousand after the Second World War[1] but today is much less. In other words Jews count for a minuscule fraction of Indians. Why then in *The Moor's Last Sigh*, a novel set mainly in Bombay, should Salman Rushdie use as a figure of baroque, incarnate evil a Jew from Kerala? Why in *In an Antique Land* should the equally gifted Amitav Ghosh be fascinated by a twelfth-century Jewish merchant, Abraham ben Yiju of Mangalore? A surprising number of other Indian literary works deal with Jews and there is still an interest in comparing the religious systems of India with Judaism.[2] India has a dazzling array of problems, real and imagined. It is difficult to imagine that the Jews figure prominently among them. And yet they seem to.[3]

Did Westerners impose a Judaic identity on Indians as they did so frequently elsewhere? At the outset it must be said that for many Western travellers the multitudes of India did not immediately evoke the suggestion of a monolithic Judaic ancestry. However, comparisons between Indians and Jews were made with astonishing regularity. As early as the seventeenth century François Bernier, the scholar and traveller, who was in India from 1656–68, was asked by Melchissedec Thevenot (1620–92), a traveller and publisher, to discover if Jews had long been resident in Kashmir. Bernier reported that Jews had once lived there, but that they had converted to Islam. Nonetheless, as he put it:

> there are many signs of Judaism to be found in this country. On entering the kingdom after crossing the Pire-penjale mountains the

> inhabitants in the frontier villages struck me as resembling Jews. Their countenance and manner and that indescribable peculiarity which enables a traveller to distinguish the inhabitants of different nations all seemed to belong to that ancient people. You are not to ascribe what I say to mere fancy, the *Jewish* appearance of these villagers having been remarked by our Jesuit Fathers and by several other Europeans, long before I visited Kachemire. A second sign is the prevalence of the name of Mousa, which means Moses, among the inhabitants of this city, notwithstanding they are Mahometans. A third is the tradition that Solomon visited this country and that it was he who opened a passage for the waters by cutting the mountain of Baramoulé. A fourth, the belief that Moses died in the city of Kachemire, and that his tomb is within a league of it. And a fifth may be found in the generally received opinion that the small and extremely ancient edifice seen on one of the high hills was built by Solomon; and it is therefore called the *throne of Solomon* to this day.[4]

One of the most striking of the early works devoted to comparisons between Jews and Indians was M. de la Créquinière's *Conformité des coutumes des Indiens orientaux, avec des Juifs et des autres Peuples de l'Antiquité*, which was published in Brussels in 1704 and the following year in London, translated by John Toland, the well-known historian of philosophy and religion.[5] De la Créquinière had spent a number of years in India and paid particular attention to the inland peoples whose traditions had not been overtly affected by contacts with outsiders. His intention was not to throw any particular light on Indian society but rather to 'clarify Antiquity' and especially to cast light on the Bible.[6] In other words he wanted to hold up to the mirror of India Europe's own religious legacy to see what was reflected in it. A number of Jewish customs were much discussed at the time in intellectual circles in France: one of these was circumcision, and de la Créquinière wrote at length on this subject in the context of India.[7] In addition to circumcision de la Créquinière enumerated many other similarities between the Israelites and the Indians: their 'enchantments', funerals, public buildings, their way of eating locusts, their esteem for the arts, their aversion to wine, their ointments, their sweet-scented waters, their way of fighting, their shared love of washing and extreme cleanliness. In this latter point the Indians 'may dispute with the most scrupulous Pharisees with whom they agree in many things beside'.[8] He concluded:

> The Indians agreed with the Ancients and particularly with the Jews; but one that would Reason like a Pagan would find a far greater Resemblance between these two Nations . . . the people of Judea and those who dwell in the remotest Countries of the Indies agree very well in their Temper, their Customs and Manner of Governing. First, both of them Lived in Hard Bondage, to which they were so much the more subject, because they lov'd it and even ador'd their Captivity; I mean that of the Law which was the hardest slavery . . . the learning of both consists only in getting by heart what they say the Gods have done for them; besides, the Books of Morality whose precepts they take care to learn . . . The Jews and Indians have preserved at least in a great measure the Simplicity of the Primitive Ages of the World; which they make appear in the food, their Cloaths; and their Pleasures; wherein they always seek after that which is most Natural; for they love that most which most readily offers itself to their thoughts and most Naturally gratifies their Fancy . . . They practise very punctually all the *Rules* which the *Religion* they profess prescribes; and considering that no Man can live independently, but is in a manner born for Subjection, they love rather to serve their Gods and submit blindly to their Law than to be Slaves to Caprice and Ambition . . . they never trouble their heads about Novelties but follow their *Traffick* or exercise themselves in that *Trade* which they have learn'd from their Fathers.[9]

This passage then suggests that the passivity, the closeness to nature of Indians, their learning by rote, their lack of ambition, their 'Simplicity of the Primitive Ages of the World' were similar to characteristics perceived in Jews and that both possessed something close to a natural religion.

In 1792 the scholarly Catholic missionary, the Abbé Dubois, arrived in India, where he was first attached to the Pondicherry mission before going to work in the Dekhan and the Madras Presidency until 1823, when he returned to France. The bearded abbé, who travelled around in native dress, knew classical and colloquial Tamil and spent his years in India studying the lives and customs of the Hindus. His research was written up and in 1806 his manuscript was handed to an English officer. It remained unpublished until 1816 when it appeared in London under the title *Description of the Character, Manners and Customs of the People of India and of their Institutions Religious and Civil.* Whereas the abbé did not believe that Hinduism derived from Judaism, like de la Créquinière he noted, 'Many passages in the Hindu sacred writings recall the rules which the law of Moses laid down for the children of Israel concerning the various kinds of defilements, real and technical ... It is in fact impossible to deny that there are many striking points of resemblance between Jewish and Hindu customs.'[10]

Such comparisons continued. C. T. E. Rhenius, for instance, who was sent by the English Church Missionary Society to South India in 1813, noted that 'the Vishnu and Siva sects and religious worship exhibit a strong likeness to the Jewish dispensation'.[11] Similarly the Brahmin caste was perceived by many as having specifically Jewish attributes. As R. Lovett wrote of the Brahmins in his *History of the London Missionary Society 1795–1895*, 'Each is an infallible pope in his own sphere. The Brahman is the exclusive and Pharisaic Jew of India.'[12]

Explanations of the origin of the Brahmins often followed this path. According to some, high-caste Hindus were actually Scythians and as such probable descendants of the Lost Tribes of Israel. One English writer, G. Moore, the author of a book on the Lost Tribes which was published in 1861, 'transcribed' Indian inscriptions into Hebrew in order to prove this contention. According to Moore Buddhism was a fraudulent development of Judaism which had been brought to India intact by the Lost Tribes.[13] Claudius Buchanan, one-time vice-provost of the college of Fort William in Bengal and a member of the Asiatic Society, like others before him was inclined to the fairly popular view that Hinduism had borrowed substantially from Judaism in ancient times: he dismissed furiously suggestions that the opposite might be the case.[14] He held fairly sober views on the issue of the Lost Tribes. For instance he maintained that 'the greater part of the Ten Tribes which *now* exist are to be found in the countries of their first captivity'. Nonetheless he too believed that many of the populations in Afghanistan, Bokhara and Kashmir were of Jewish descent.[15]

A key thinker in the evolution of the discourse which linked Jews and India was Godfrey Higgins (1772–1833), whose chief works were *Horae Sabbaticae* (London, 1826), which examined the origins of the Sabbath; *An Apology for the Life and Character of Mahommed* (London, 1829); *The Celtic Druids or An Attempt to show that The Druids were the Priests of Oriental Colonies Who Emigrated from India and were the Introducers of the First or Cadmean System of Letters, and the Builders of Stonehenge, of Carnac, and of Other Cyclopean Works, in Asia and Europe* (London, 1827); and *Anacalypsis – an Attempt to Draw Aside the Veil of the Saitic*

Isis; or an Inquiry into the Origin of Languages, Nations and Religions (London, 1833–36).[16] Higgins, a contemporary of Lord Kingsborough, was a quite remarkable man and is still evoked regularly by Theosophists, seekers of the Holy Grail, Lost Tribes enthusiasts, Afro-centrists, Hebrew Israelites and various esoteric sects.

Higgins studied law at Cambridge, before joining the Volunteer Corps when it seemed that Napoleon would invade England. He was promoted to major in the Third West York Militia in 1808. Appointed Justice of the Peace in the West Riding of Yorkshire he used his position to expose the appalling treatment of 'pauper lunatics'. At the same time he campaigned for the reform of Parliament, was opposed to excessive taxation, resisted the Corn Laws and fought against the exploitation of child labour. But it was as a religious thinker and student of comparative religion that he was to make his greatest mark. He became a member of the Society of Arts, the British Association for the Advancement of Science and other learned bodies, and devoted himself wholeheartedly to the origin of religious phenomena. In the preface to the 1829 edition of his book on the Druids, he stated that he was preparing a new work that would review 'all the ancient Mythologies of the world, which, however varied, and corrupted in recent times, were originally one, and that one founded on principles sublime, beautiful, and true'. He posited that there were ancient civilisations that had acquired superior religious knowledge, much of which has since been lost, and that all religions have an universal origin. He was struck by the 'absolute ignorance displayed in the writings of the ancients, of the true nature of their history, their religious mythology, and, in short of every thing relating to their antiquities'. He, by contrast, was convinced that 'there was a secret science possessed somewhere, which must have been guarded by the most solemn oaths. And though I may be laughed at by those who inquire not deeply into the origin of things for saying it, yet I cannot help suspecting that there is still a secret doctrine known only in the deep recesses, the crypts, of Thibet, St Peter's and the Cremlin.'[17]

Convinced that Hebrew place names were to be found all over India, Higgins ridiculed the idea 'that the old Jewish names of places have been given by the modern Saracens or Turks'.[18] In proof of this he observed that when the first Muslim conquerors arrived at Lahore they found that the name of the Hindu prince defending the city was already 'Daood or David'.[19] However the great cities of India, 'Agra, Delhi,

Oude, Mundore, etc., which have many of them been much larger than London', can hardly have been built, all of them, by 'the little Jewish mountain tribe (the "Lost Tribes")'. The only way of accounting for them and other features of India was 'the supposition that there was in very ancient times one universal superstition, which was carried all over the world by emigrating tribes, and that they were originally from Upper India'.[20] The Jews, specifically the tribe of Judah, thus originated in India, '... the natives of Cashmere as well as those of Afghanistan, pretending to be descended from the Jews, give pedigrees of their kings reigning in their present country up to the sun and the moon, and along with this, they shew you the Temples still standing, built by Solomon, statues of Noah, and other Jewish Patriarchs ... the traditions of the Afghans tell them, that they are descended from the tribe of Ioudi or Yuda, and in this they are right, for it is the tribe of Joudi noticed by Eusebius to have existed before the Son of Jacob in Western Syria was born, the Joudi of Oude, and from which tribe the Western Jews with the Brahmin (Abraham) descended and migrated.'[21] Similarly, 'in the valley of Cashmere, on a hill close to the lake, are the ruins of a temple of Solomon. The history states that Solomon, finding the valley all covered with water except this hill, which was an island, opened the passage in the mountains and let most of it out, thus giving to Cashmere its beautiful plains. The temple which is built on the hill is called Tucht Suliman ... Afterwards Forster says, "Previously to the Mahometan conquest of India, Cashmere was celebrated for the learning of the Brahmins and the magnificent construction of its temple." Now what am I to make of this? Were these Brahmins Jews, or the Jews Brahmins?'[22]

India and the surrounding countries thus became a rich hunting ground for remote Jewish communities, and continue so to be. Behind most speculation on the subject lurks the old idea that the Lost Tribes may have reached India in remote times. This discourse is clearly rooted in mediaeval thought on the subject. As we have seen, Mandeville, for one, claimed that the Lost Tribes were to be found in mountain valleys in a distant land beyond Cathay, 'toward the high Ind and toward Bacharia'.[23] Specific Lost Tribes were supposed to have spread throughout the surrounding area as well. Allen Godbey mentions the Kerala tradition that the tribe of Manasseh was sent east by Nebuchadnezzar and that many of them spread through India and the surrounding countries.[24]

Afghanistan was one of the favoured supposed homes of the Lost Tribes. According to Afghani belief the Afghan people were banished by Nebuchadnezzar into the mountains of Ghur where they maintained a relationship with the Jews of Arabia. When some of the Arabian Jews converted to Islam, one of their number – a certain Khaled – wrote to the Afghans and invited them to do so too. A number of Afghan notables arrived in Arabia under a leader who traced his descent back forty-six generations to King Saul. Muhammad greeted him with the deferential title *malik* – king. At the end of the nineteenth century the leading families of Afghanistan still claimed descent from the man so honoured by the prophet and the Afghanis' claim to be of Israelite descent is accepted by the majority of Muslim writers, as well as by many others.[25] Buchanan noted, 'the tribes of the Affghan race are very numerous, and of different castes; and it is probable, that the proportion which is of Jewish descent is not great. The Affghan nations extend on both sides of the India ... some tribes have the countenance of the Persian, and some of the Hindoo; and some tribes are evidently of Jewish extraction.' In the case of Bokhara, Buchanan seemed to think there was firmer ground for speculation. With Giles Fletcher's well-known book *The Tartars Or, Ten Tribes* (London, 1609–11) in mind, he observed, 'This is the country which Dr Giles Fletcher who was Envoy of Queen Elizabeth at the Court of Muscovy assigned as the principal residence of the descendants of the Ten Tribes. He argues from their place, from the name of their cities, from their language, which contains Hebrew and Chaldaic words, and from their peculiar rites which are Jewish. Their principal city Samarkand is pronounced Samarchian, which Dr Fletcher thinks, might be a name given by the Israelites after their own Samaria in Palestine.' It is worth noting that this is apparently what the Bukharan Jews thought too: Joseph Wolff, the Lost Tribes hunter already mentioned, reported, 'the Jews in Bokhara are 10,000 in number. The Chief Rabbi assured me that Bokhara is the Habor, and Balkh the Halah of II Kings: 17:6.' Wolff was also told that in the heights of the Hindu Kush the tribes of Naphtali, Dan, Zebulun and Asher were still to be found and that they still knew the *Shema Yisrael*.[26] Wolff also found traces of the Lost Tribes in Afghanistan. 'Some Affghauns,' he wrote, 'claim a descent from Israel. According to them, Affghaun was the nephew of Asaph, the son of Berachia, who built the

Temple of Solomon. The descendants of this Affghaun, being Jews, were carried into Babylon by Nebuchadnezzar, from whence they were removed to the mountains of Ghoree in Affghanistan, but in the time of Mohammed turned Mohammedan.'[27] And local experts supported him: a certain Captain Riley, according to Wolff, 'the best Arabic scholar in India . . . looked on the Affghauns as of Jewish descent'.[28] In Peshawar Wolff found traces of Israelite descent among the 'Kaffre Seeah Poosh' and, as he noted, 'some of the learned Jews of Samarkand are of my opinion'.[29]

By the end of the eighteenth century this view was widespread. In 1799 Charles Crawford also located some of the Lost Tribes in Afghanistan. According to 'the best Persian historians', some lived among the Tartars, 'who boast of their descent from the Jews' ('the Tartars have a town called Jericho') while the name Samarkand, in the vicinity of which town were to be found a Mount Zion and a River Jordan, he too took to be a corruption of Samaria. Missionaries had reported back that not only were the inhabitants of these areas Jews but that in Tartary there were to be found people who spoke a language similar to that of some American Indians – of course also Lost Tribes.[30]

John Chamberlain, a Baptist missionary in India in the second decade of the nineteenth century, was quite convinced the Ten Tribes were to be found in the vicinity of Afghanistan. He noted, 'I find there are many of the Ten Tribes towards Candahar. Many of the Afghans are undoubtedly of the race of Abraham. One person I saw at Delhi had all the appearance of an Israelite, and on asking him whether he was not a son of Israel he confessed, "I am." They are now become Musulmans; but have not forgotten that their progenitors were the sons of Israel . . .'[31] In fact throughout the nineteenth century the idea that the Afghans were of Jewish descent was commonplace in Christian circles: the missionaries William Carey and Joshua Marshman, Sir Alexander Barnes and Sir William Jones, the Sanskrit scholar and member of the Asiatic Society of Bengal, are all mentioned as espousing this view,[32] which in turn gave further credence to the idea.[33]

Some of these Indian and central Asian Lost Tribes were spotted in Europe. In 1833 the *Anglo-Germanic Advertiser* reported that 'the Lost Ten Tribes of the Jews have been found in Li Bucharia, some of them attending the last Leipsic fair as shawl manufacturers. They speak in Thibet the Hebrew language, are Idolaters, but believe in the Messiah, and their restoration to Jerusalem; they are supposed to consist of ten millions, keep the Kipour, and do not like white Jews, and call out like the other tribes, "Hear, O God of Israel, there is but one God", are circumcised, and have a Reader and Elders.' And in 1840 in a long pamphlet entitled *An Appeal on Behalf of the Jews Scattered in India, Persia and Arabia* the missionary J. Samuel, a Jewish convert to Christianity, announced that in the area of Afghanistan there was a 'population of many hundred thousand Jews, descendants of the Twelve Tribes, just waiting to be converted'.[34]

The notion that the Afghans were of Jewish extraction became even more widespread and is still popular. In 1928, as the *Boston Herald* (27 April 1928) noted, a controversy was caused by 'the visit of the King and Queen of Afghanistan to England, over the so-called Jewish origin of the Afghan people ... as to the Afghans quite a number of British officers well acquainted with them are said to be strong believers in the Hebrew theory. And what of the evidence in its favour? One thing which travellers sometimes tell us after investigation on the spot is that nearly all the Afghan women and many of the men are "of a distinctly Jewish cast of countenance" and that a large number of them have Jewish-Christian names, such as Ibrahim for Abraham, Ayub for Job, Daoud for David, Ismail for Ishmael, Ishak for Isaac, Yohia for John, Yakub for Jacob and Suleiman for Solomon. The Afghans, moreover, are known to recognise a common code of unwritten law which appears to resemble the old Hebraic law, though it has been modified by Mohammedan ordinances ... And eager as are the subjects of the King of Afghanistan to claim Hebrew descent there is little likelihood of them joining the Zionist movement or swelling the twentieth-century migration to the Holy Land.'[35] Rabbi Abraham Hacohen, formerly the head of the Jewish community in the Afghan city of Harath, has recalled hearing the former Afghani king Habib Allah proclaim that he was derived from the Israelite tribe of Benjamin. An Afghani Jewish immigrant to Israel similarly remembered King Habib Allah riding around Harath on horseback. When he was greeted by representatives of the Jewish community of the city the king asked the Jews to which tribe of Israel *they* belonged. Abashed they answered that they did not remember. Habib replied, 'Well we *do* know. We, the Mahmad Zei family, are all descendants of the tribe of Benjamin from the seed of King Saul, from the sons of Yonatan Afghan and Pithon.' This is the claim of many Pashtun elders to this day: they are descended, they say, from Pithon of the tribe of Benjamin, a great-grandson of King Saul, who is mentioned among a list of hundreds of names chronicling the descendants of the Twelve Tribes (I Chronicles 8:35). We know no more of him.

Support for the identification of the Pathans as Israelites in Afghanistan and elsewhere was also given by Isaac ben Zvi, the second president of the State of Israel. Among other things he noted that all Pathans acknowledge an oral constitution known as *Pushtun-Wally*, which he claimed closely resembles Hebrew law.[36]

Today the Pathans of north-western Pakistan and south-eastern Afghanistan are widely believed to be of Israelite extraction, especially since the showing of a television documentary by the Emmy award-winning film-maker Simcha Jacobovici in the United States in the spring of 2000. In 1993 the *Jerusalem Report*, a relatively sober Israeli periodical, noted that in many respects the Pathans are among the more serious of Lost Tribes claimants. 'Numbering at least fifteen million, the Sunni Muslim Pathans live on both sides of the Afghan–Pakistan border (and as far east as Indian Kashmir) where part of the Ten Tribes are believed to have settled. Indeed, the names of Pathan sub-tribes seem to echo those of the Israelite tribes: Rabani (Reuven), Shinwari (Shimon), Daftani (Naftali), Ashuri (Asher), Yusuf-sai (sons of Yosef). The mostly illiterate Pathans have a centuries-old tradition of Israelite ancestry, and some still call themselves "*Bani* Israel", the children of Israel. A retired Pathan diplomat living in the US is translating a book on basic Judaism into Pashtu, the Pathan language, which the Amishav group plans to distribute among educated Pathans . . .'

With the terrorist attacks of 11 September 2001, interest in the Pathans increased overnight. A virulent, mediaeval hatred of Israel and more widely of Jews underlay a good deal of the resentments of Osama bin Laden and al-Qaeda's ideologues. It was somewhat paradoxical then that the sixteen-million-strong Pathans so long suspected of being Jewish themselves were the great supporters of al-Qaeda. According to the Pathans *they* are the real Afghanis: the others – particularly the Uzbeks and Tajiks – are rank outsiders who have perfectly good homelands elsewhere. The Pathans, who are to be found in Pakistan as well as Afghanistan, see themselves as a superior group: and one of the things that sets them apart is their belief that they are descended from the Jews of old. Pashtun separatists aspiring to an independent

Pushtunistan (otherwise called Pakhtunistan or Pakhtoonistan), who have been active for the last fifty years, make particular play of their proud descent from Abraham and Isaac.

The Kulanu list-serve carried many communications on the Pathans, most of them sympathetic. In the charged climate after the attacks many feared for the safety of the Pathans and expressed a kind of fraternal solidarity with them. The president of Kulanu, Jack Zeller, observed, 'I would hope that a Kulanu inclination would be to greet every Pathan with sincere warmth, if only to make up for neglect and denial that is not without pain.' Another contributor observed, 'In spite of the fact that the Pathans are not Jewish in the modern sense of the term, we are still their brothers, and it hurts me deeply that they have joined our most bitter and implacable enemies.' The suggestion that the Pathans are of Jewish origin may have had some impact on recent events. It has been suggested for instance that because of this ancient tradition the mainly Pashtun Taliban were not as opposed to Israel as other Islamists and that in this respect a rift existed between the Pathans and their Arab 'guests'.[37] The supposed Israelite origins of the Pathans were well known in the area. A Northern Alliance commander quoted recently in the New York Russian-language newspaper *Novoye Russkoye Slovo*, spoke of the Pathans in the crudest anti-Semitic terms. And other voices were raised against the 'Jewish' Pathans in which anti-Semitic rhetoric was present. As one Muslim contributor to an internet site has put it, 'May Allah ruin the homes of the Pathans and their Punjabi masters because I know from experience that the Pathan race is wretched in its entirety. They are a cursed, Jewish-natured lot. Point out one good Pathan out of the more than eleven million of the *Khar* population that resides in North-West Frontier Province and Baluchistan. They are all traitors ... They are either servants of the Punjabis or they are Kafir and anti-Islam ... When Afghans find the opportunity, they should slit the throat of every Pathan they can lay their hands on. A good Pathan is a dead Pathan. Let Allah sort out the good from the bad.' One Jewish response to this was that 'the Israelite Pathans need our help in the face of hostile anti-Semitic opposition to their own self-identity. They have tried a couple times to break free of Pakistan ... but this has not yet come to fruition.'[38]

It may be added that in Pakistan there is a virulent strain of anti-Jewish and anti-Zionist sentiment. In some cases India is perceived as being in direct collaboration with Israel, to the detriment of Pakistanis and Muslims throughout the world.[39] One Pakistani author concludes a political pamphlet with the ringing denunciation, 'The mentality of leaders in both countries [India and Israel] is the same. Having studied the mental make-up of the leaders in India and Israel one starts wondering if "Aryan Brahmins" now ruling India are not one of the "Lost Tribes" of the Jews.'[40]

Amishav arranged an expedition to visit the Pathans and the Kashmiris in 1982. One of the delegates was a young rabbinical student called Henry Noach, a descendant of the illustrious Manuel Noah (1785–1851), who had been such a strong supporter of the theory of the Israelites in America.[41] According to the *Jerusalem Report*, 'While visiting the Kashmiri national museum, Noach met its director, Prof. F. M. Hassnain, who asked the young tourist where he was from. Noach ... replied that he'd come from Jerusalem looking for traces of the ten tribes. Hassnain became visibly excited. "I've waited for you for thirty years!" he said, explaining that he'd written a book tracing the Israelite origins of the five million Kashmiri Sunni Muslims.' And indeed the claim to be of Israelite extraction is widespread among Kashmiris, who point to the similarity of place names which appear to reflect biblical names like Mamre, Pisgah and Mount Nevo. The internet is full of web pages that purport to show historical connections between India and the Jews, India and Jesus, who is alleged to have gone there, the identical nature of Hebrew and Sanskrit and so forth.

On one such website a certain Gene D. Matlock unwittingly follows in the path of Daniel Defoe, who had claimed a connection between Hebrew and the languages of the 'Subjects of the Great Mogul, that is to say, in that Part of the World we call more properly India'.[42] Matlock more specifically believes that Sanskrit is Hebrew and quotes 'part of his complete manuscript showing the global influence of ancient India's culture and language'. He shows that Judaism started in India and points to the presence of a vast number of Hebrew and biblical place names scattered throughout India. These include, 'ancient Seuna-Desa (Zion Land) in what is now Maharashtra ... the city of Paithan, on the banks of the river Godivari ... the Indo-Hebrews named the part of the river passing through Paithan's territory Paithan (Pison, Phison) the city of Satana ... According to the legends of the Yadavas (Indo-Hebrews), Satana would have made the folks in Sodom and Gomorah envious.' Matlock concludes, 'The truth about the origins of the Hebrews has been screaming in our faces for thousands of years, but our benumbed minds have chosen not to hear it.'

Jews were not immune to Lost Tribes enthusiasms on the subcontinent. In 1883 a young Sephardi Jew, Isaac Hayyim Barukh, armed with a letter to the sons of Moses (like so many of his predecessors) set off from Tiberias and in 1886 arrived in Calcutta. In an article in a Jewish Judeo-Arabic paper called *Ha-Perah*, a publication of the Indian Baghdadi community, he explained that he was an emissary from the Holy Land and that he was seeking the sons of Moses who lived beyond the Sambatyon. In the same year he published a further announcement in the paper, namely that in Tibet and on the way to Tibet he had discovered traces of the sons of Moses. In 1885 he was in Bombay where he founded the Society of the Founders of the Flag of Israel, and a couple of short-lived journals. The society helped to fund a further mission to find the sons of Moses, but unfortunately the Jew from Tiberias was stopped by the British on the borders of India and was forced to return to Bombay. In a farewell article in *Ha-Perah* he denounced the British authorities, who he said had deliberately aborted his mission because, for their own inscrutable reasons, they wanted 'to put off the Redemption of Israel'.[43]

Tibet continued to offer scope for speculation. A further theory noted in 1904 by *Israel's Messenger*, and first put forward by the American J. D. Eisenstein, had it that the Luz of the book of Judges was none other than the Tibetan capital Lhasa. The newspaper commented, 'Mr Eisenstein quotes the Talmud to the following effect: It is the same Luz where Sennacherib ascended but could not disturb it nor could Nebuchadnezzar destroy it. It is the same Luz where the Angel of Death never predominated. "What did they do with the aged? They took them outside of the city walls, where they died." The city was therefore distinguished for its impregnability and for the longevity, or, rather immortality, of its inhabitants. The former qualification is undoubtedly descriptive of the city of the Dalai Lama.'[44]

The Bene Israel community of western India shared many of these ideas. A Bombay Jewish journal noted in 1898 that the discoveries of a Hungarian Jew, a certain Dr Stein, an Orientalist who for some time occupied the chair in Sanskrit at the University of Budapest, would 'finally settle the descent of the Afghans from the Ten Tribes. The Afghans themselves believe in the Israelite descent and call themselves

Bene Israel. Circumcision is said to have existed among the Afghans before their conversion to Mahomedanism in the first century of the Mahomedan era, and they still maintain the old customs prevalent in Israel of yore, such as the punishment of stoning and the obligation of marrying a deceased brother's widow. There are many inscriptions in Afghanistan and the surrounding country in the so-called Arian or Bactrian language which, when transliterated into the Hebrew language, make good sense and defy interpretation otherwise.'[45] This notion had become sufficiently anchored in Jewish thought that by 1926 Jacques Faitlovitch, the activist for the so-called Black Jews of Ethiopia, the Falashas, had tried to persuade the American Pro-Falasha Committee to send a mission to Afghanistan to study the Jewish element in its population.[46]

One of the most obvious candidates for membership of the Lost Tribes was the community of Bene Israel itself. Israel ben Joseph Benjamin (1818–64), the Romanian Jewish traveller otherwise known as Benjamin the Second (a somewhat self-serving nod in the direction of Benjamin of Tudela, the great twelfth-century Jewish traveller) left a rather confused account of the Lost Tribes in India in his well-known book *Eight Years in Asia and Africa from 1846–1855*. The Bene Israel – otherwise, according to him, known as the White Jews – lived in the 'East Indies since the remotest ages. I have the firm belief and do not consider it difficult to prove, that the Bene Israel are not only real Jews, but are likewise lineal descendants of the Ten Tribes, who in the time of Hoshea, the last king of Israel, were carried into exile by the Assyrians to Halah, Nabor, the shores of the Ganges, and the cities of the Medes ... The river Gozen, mentioned in the Bible, is according to the assertions of the Bene Israel, no other than the Ganges which flows through India, on the shores of which this tribe dwells in great numbers. The Indian word "Ganges" contains all the letters of the Hebrew word "Goshen" ... it is known that the Ganges has its rise in Upper Thibet, a country bordering on the kingdom of Cabul ... The Jews who travelled through the desert, have as it were, left a trace of their passage behind them; for several brethren remained there, whose descendants exist to the present day.' According to Benjamin the Second the Bene Israel once owned a chronicle which covered their history until the time of their arrival in India. However, on account of 'the many wars they had with Europeans, with regard to their occupation of the country, this chronicle was lost, the Bene Israel being forced always to flee from one province to another'. Benjamin also brings the famous Cochin Jewish community into his record of the Lost Tribes in India, although he gives no evidence for their origin, and the Canarinz of the Malabar coast who, says Benjamin, 'appropriated to themselves a great many Jewish practices'.[47] In the same vein an article in 1899 from the *Jewish Chronicle* quoted in *The Bene Israelite* (a Bene Israel newspaper in Bombay) noted that in general the Bene Israel indignantly reject the title of 'Jew'. The article observed that the German-Jewish orientalist, Dr Gustav Oppert (1836–1906), who held the chair in Sanskrit at the University of Madras before taking up a teaching post in Berlin in 1894, 'is of opinion that they are survivors of the Lost Ten Tribes, that were made Assyrian captives. Other reasons in support of this belief are the absence till recently of the Torah from their ritual, and that they did not possess the later books of the Hebrew canon.'[48] In India today there are still a number of groups who claim descent from the Lost Tribes of Israel or from some other distant and venerable Jewish community. There are small and ancient Muslim communities throughout India and Pakistan who call themselves *Banu Israil* – children of Israel – and claim descent from the ancient Jewish communities of Medina. There is a Christian community called the Kenanaya, centred in Kottayam in Kerala which claims descent from Jews: one or two members of the community have even converted to Judaism in recent times. And in Andhra Pradesh there are two small Telugo-speaking communities together numbering five or six hundred members who believe that they are the remnant of the Lost Tribe of Ephraim, learn Hebrew and practise a sort of Judaism. None of these groups has attracted much, if any, international attention. The Bene Israel community of western India, who at one time attracted a good deal of attention, are no longer the focus of international interest as likely claimants to the mantle of the Lost Tribes of Israel. That has passed to another, much larger group, on the other side of India in the states on the Burma frontier.

Chapter Eight

THE BURMESE FRONTIER: THE LAND OF STRANGERS

We the children of Manasia are coming.

A Shinlung song

The development on the India–Burma frontier of a new Lost Tribes discourse has produced one of the most remarkable Judaising movements of recent times, which involves a number of groups of people from north-east India, Burma and mainly from Assam, Mizoram and Manipur. The group includes Chins, Lushais, Kukis and Mizos. Some have recently found their way to a Jewish identity and indeed several hundred have formally converted to Orthodox Judaism.[1] Many thousand more quite clearly practise an Orthodox type of Judaism: this is to say they practise a religion which, while not being accepted by Orthodox Jews as Judaism, has essential features in common with it and aspirations to belong to the mainstream of Jewish life and practice. In these areas those who have moved towards this Israelite identity and an identification with Judaism are often referred to as Shinlung and I shall use this term for them here. For the most part the Shinlung do not see themselves as converts in the usual sense of the term. They believe that they are historically of Jewish descent, like other such groups – one might cite the Telugu-speaking Jews of Andhra Pradesh, who believe themselves to be descended from the tribe of Ephraim.[2]

Until recently there was very limited contact between the Shinlung and the other Jewish communities of India. When I first came across them in 1985 there was a small number of their young people studying in Bombay at the ORT school,[3] where they had contact with Bene Israel and other Indian Jews. At the time, and no doubt still today, the Bene Israel and other Indian Jews were pretty sceptical about their claims.

★

It seems altogether likely that in this area, as elsewhere, the enthusiastic identification of the Shinlung with Judaism owes much to the activity of missionaries in the region as two researchers, Weil and Samra, have already suggested. In 1813 William Carey of the British Serampore Baptist Mission went to Assam with the intention of converting the Assamese to Christianity. He succeeded in converting a few Khasi in the Shella district of the Khasi Hills and a few more in the Brahmaputra Valley where the Mission established a church.[4] In 1819 Carey translated the New Testament into Assamese and by 1833 had completed the translation of the whole Bible, although both translations were more or less unintelligible to the Assamese. The Serampore Mission had the support of David Scott, the Commissioner of Assam, but despite this advantage was forced to abandon its work in 1836. American Baptists took over the mission for a while, but it was taken under the wing of the Welsh Mission in 1841. Until 1874, when Assam (including Manipur) achieved provincial status, it was administered by the British as part of Bengal. The Brahmaputra Valley was basically Hindu, however the Khasi Hills were the preserve of the hill tribes who were gradually brought under British control from 1823.[5] In 1890 Manipur was brought under British paramountcy as a result of the Chin-Lushai expedition and the Anglo-Manipur War, and Christian missions began to operate fully in the territory of present-day Mizoram and Manipur. The missions who were principally active in the area were English and Welsh Methodists, Welsh Presbyterians, and English and American Baptists.[6] The missions here were massively successful: by 1951 there were almost 180,000 converts to Christianity in Mizoram and almost 100,000 in Manipur. According to a 1981 census, eighty-three per cent of the population of Mizoram – some 400,000 people – and thirty per cent of the population of Manipur had by then converted to a form of Christianity.[7] This census also revealed that there were 2,581,000 Christians in the entire region of north-east India.[8] By and large these converts were drawn from the so-called tribal class, which eventually became predominantly Christian.

The Protestant evangelical Christianity that penetrated these areas has been perceived as a particularly effective tool in the cultural and religious context of the area. It has been argued that the Lushai were especially susceptible to this prophetic, ecstatic, revivalist, speaking-in-tongues kind of missionary effort, but it appears to have been pretty effective throughout the area.[9] No doubt the success of the missionaries may be attributed in some measure to the inroads of modernity into the area in the wake of the British conquest. The old autonomous self-sufficient village culture gradually disintegrated throughout the nineteenth century under the impact of the outside world and Christianity was embraced in much the same spirit and for the same reasons as other features of British modernity.[10]

The missions were successful in almost completely eradicating the traditions of the tribals: my late colleague Christoph von Fürer-Haimendorf recalled the concern of an elderly Naga villager, 'the Christians say all of us who worship our gods will go to hell . . . I had a wife who was so good. She died some time ago. Has she been put to fire?'[11] The message of the Gospel – the universal love of God – seemed to be a preferable ideology to that of Hinduism which, if it incorporated tribals at all, would have done so at the lower end of the caste system. The fact that the British overlords also subscribed to this religion gave it added lustre. As Samra points out, the efforts of the missionaries to create written languages with a Roman script from the languages and dialects of the region further alienated the local population from the surrounding cultures, while the educational opportunities provided by the missions proved a conduit to increased identification with the West. Turning their backs on their own culture the first native Christians soon started to denigrate tribal traditions – indeed to recall them with disgust. On the other hand the spread of the Christian faith generated the spread of new religious movements, which have been described as 'products of Christianity'. Some of them invoked and elaborated the religious traditions of the past: as Samra notes, 'Groups which identify the ancestors of the Chin, Kuki and Mizo tribes with the Lost Tribes of Israel fall within this category. While they retain the biblical world view learned through the missionaries, these groups manage to restore some dignity to their ancestors. Rather than viewing their forebears as "head-hunting savages" such groups find that their ancestors displayed many admirable qualities and values similar to those taught by the missionaries.'[12]

Weil has commented that the relative ease which marked the transference from traditional religion to Christianity also marked for many of the same people what she calls the 'double conversion' to Judaism: 'In the past forty years groups of people in Mizoram, Manipur and Tiddim have started observing Judaic practices in the belief that Jewish customs and the Jewish faith are compatible with – indeed are one and the same – as indigenous tribal religion. Their link to Judaism is through a lost Israelite claim associated with millenarian beliefs which, ironically, may have been introduced to them through Christianity.'[13] There is no real irony here however. The world of the Bible had been introduced into this area by missionaries since the beginning of the nineteenth century and local people made of it what they did. That the idea of an Israelite identity was the direct result of missionary and colonial intervention in the area is entirely beyond any question. One of the ways in which the idea might first have been introduced is through British Israelism: the widespread notion that the British themselves were of Jewish ancestry. In 1936 J. B. Smart of Bangalore reported to the Indian–Jewish journal *The Jewish Tribune* that 'many Protestant ministers are now preaching that the British are the Lost Ten Tribes – it is a fact'.[14]

By whatever mechanism, it seems entirely clear that in the case of the Shinlung the idea they had traits in common with the Israelites of old was one that, as elsewhere, was suggested by missionaries. If one is seeking irony it can be found in the fact that some of the Shinlung now say that it was the Baptist missionaries and particularly William Pettigrew (1869–1943) who, having spent some forty years in Manipur, succeeded in *eradicating* their 'Judaism'. Subsequently, 'American missionaries began arriving . . . and added to the difficulty the remaining Jews faced in maintaining their identity'.[15] In fact the missionaries *created* this identity. No doubt the Shinlung were receptive to the missionaries' suggestions because of the respect they already had for the Israelite history and institutions that they had been taught. One early missionary among the Shinlung is quoted as having said, 'You look like the descendants of the Jews . . . But your faces are not like the Jews, you look a bit different. But you have the same way of doing things . . . You are nearer to them than we white people . . .' The same missionary noted, 'Your way of living, custom, culture are like it is said in the Bible. In the Bible it's written – do this, don't do this. These are already taught by your ancestors. There are no other people like you in the world.'[16]

By 1936 the revivalist Saichhunga had internalised this message. No doubt Israelite tribal society had a particular appeal to the tribal society of the area and Saichhunga was soon claiming that the Mizos were 'the lost tribals of Israel'.[17] But in the early 1950s the movement gained much greater impetus. In 1951 Challianthanga,[18] the head deacon of the United Pentecostal Church in Buallawn, a village some hundred miles north of the Mizoram state capital of Aizawl, had a vision in which it was revealed to him that the Mizos were one of the Lost Tribes of Israel and that consequently if they were to avoid destruction in the impending End of Days they would have to follow the biblical laws applying to the Israelites and make their way to Israel.[19]

Levy Benjamin, General Secretary of the Manasseh people of Shinlung-Israel, north-east India, Mizoram noted in a letter of 1984 to the Chief Rabbinical Council in Israel, 'In the year 1936 the word of the spirit of our Lord came to Pu Kapa and Pu Saichhuma, telling them that we are Israel. Also in 1946 the same message was received by Pu Chala of Buallawn village.'[20] In due course a memorial stone was erected outside Buallawn with the English words 'Memory of Israel' carved in the stone. The Mizo text read, 'For He who is mighty has done great things for me and holy is His name. And His mercy is on them that fear Him from generation to generation . . . and has raised up a horn of salvation for us in the house of His servant David'. Samra, who has seen the monument, points out that the quotation is taken from the New Testament (Luke 1:49–50, from the prayer of thanksgiving of Mary when she discovers she is with child) and sees the stone as a symbol of a people 'who have come to regard themselves as Israelites and have deemed it imperative to observe the laws applicable in the Bible to Israelites – *because* they believe in Jesus'.[21] No doubt the genesis of this new identification is to be found in Christian faith and praxis: however increasingly in some cases the effect has been the abandonment of Christianity and Jesus. So the stone outside Buallawn may suggest a signpost to what appears to us (but perhaps not to them) as a radically new identity. In other cases local Christianity, in *opposition* to the Christianity of the missionaries, has spawned new religious movements – essentially Christian – which depend on an Israelite identity and which attempt to fuse the laws of the Old Testament with the theology of the New.[22] The origins of the movement have been connected, among other things, with a Christian Messianic movement of the Lushai which preached the imminent return of the Messiah: a part of the argument insisted that all Jews had to immediately return to the Promised Land and the Lushai, or some of them, took that to refer to themselves.[23] This fusion includes a number of Judaic practices including the maintenance of the Sabbath, the refusal to eat pork and circumcision.

When I first came across the Shinlung in the ORT school in Bombay in 1985, I was told that a Judaising movement had started in the early 1950s when a local Mizo-speaking Hmar Messianic Christian pastor called the Reverend H. Thangruma, who had been settled in Churachandpur and then moved to Aizawl, had warned his neighbours that if they did not revert to their ancient faith – in other words Judaism – they would be destroyed. He claimed that Mizos were of either the Lost Tribe of Ephraim or Manasseh. He foretold that they would be restored to Israel.[24] He had been in contact with a Jewish Christian group in Jerusalem called the Zion Church of God, which drew its inspiration from Judaism as well as Messianic Christianity. Thangruma's movement, which was similarly inspired, started in Churachandpur in south-western Manipur and has since spread over a very wide area. Although it was essentially Christian, Jewish feasts such as Sukkot and Shavuot were observed and there was a strict prohibition on the eating of pork – a Mizo staple. In about 1976 some of Thangruma's followers abandoned him and set up a movement of their own which still retained some vestigial Christianity but was more unambiguously Jewish. It has been suggested that this was a result of the contacts the Shinlung had already had with the ORT School in Bombay, where some of them had studied mainstream Jewish practice. This group was the forerunner of the Judaising movement of today, which seeks inspiration and help from Israel.[25] Other Israelite groups have sought help from the Christian world. As Samra has remarked, particular outside influences are two American-Christian churches – Bet HaShem from New Haven, Indiana and the Assembly of Yahweh from Holt, Michigan, which stress adherence to the laws of the Old Testament while accepting the divinity of Jesus.[26] To this one could add the American Church of God which started a school and a church in Churachandpur, Manipur in 1971, in which Judaising practices such as the celebration of the Jewish feast of Sukkoth were encouraged.

The period of insurrection known as the 'Mizo Unrest' (1966–86) convinced many people in north-east India, Christians and Judaisers, that the End of Days was approaching and this in turn sharpened the Judaisers' desire to be restored to the land of Israel. As *Time* magazine reported in 1987, 'Jewish sects . . . continue to spring up in the hills of Mizoram. One is called Enoka Thlah – descendants of Enoch – whose members claim that God has been speaking to them through a teenage boy since 1985 when the youth relayed God's message that the Mizos were really a Lost Tribe of Israel. More recently the messages have ordered them to celebrate the Sabbath on Saturday and to stop eating pork.'

By about 1972 the generalised notion that the Shinlung were descended from the Lost Tribes had sharpened into the belief that they were descended from one specific tribe of Israel connected with the name of a Shinlung ancestor which has a number of quite similar forms somewhat akin to the name Manasseh. As one Shinlung noted, 'in many of the chants used in various sacrifices and in other sacred matters the name of Manasia or Manase is used'. One example is provided by Samra, 'At Kawngpui Sial (a pre-Christian sacrifice for success in hunting) the priest, followed by his party, chants:

Those above and those below,
go away, flee,
We the children of Manasia are coming.'[27]

Another song, which I noted in 1985, describes how Manmasi went into exile:

Manmasi, you came crossing seas and rivers.
You came through hills and mountains.
You came through all this
To the Land of Strangers.

Yet another I came across in the same year apparently described how Manmasi brought his people across the Red Sea after the tribulations of Israel in Egypt:

We observed the Sipkui feast
Crossing over the Red Sea, running dry before us.
And the walking enemies of mine,
The riding foes of mine
Were swallowed by the sea in their thousands.
We were led by the fire at night
And by cloud in the day.

So this remote ancestor was taken to be none other than Manasseh, the elder of the two sons of Joseph and Asenath and progenitor of the tribe of Manasseh. This has led to the group adopting the name Benei Menashe – the sons of Manasseh (although Weil believes it was Rabbi Eliyahu Avichail who suggested this name to them).[28] According to the

Shinlung, then, their ancestors were the Israelites exiled by Shalmanezer, King of Assyria, in 722 BC. They settled in Persia, from where they were driven to Afghanistan, they crossed the Hindu Kush and finally arrived in China. They came into contact with the Jewish community in Kaifeng but were enslaved during the reign of the Chinese emperor who instituted the Great Wall of China, Qin Shihuangdi – the first emperor of the Qin dynasty. Escaping the Chinese they took refuge in caves: the Shinlung share the tradition that their ancestors came from *sinlung* – the Chin-Kuki word for cave – although some of them explained to me that *sinlung* in fact means closed valley.[29] They claim to have had a parchment 'book' which may have been eaten by a dog. These beliefs seem to reflect other traditions which were collected in Godbey's great work, a copy of which is owned by Rabbi Avichail. Godbey cites, for instance, an old tradition of Cranganore in Kerala that Jews of the tribe of Manasseh were placed in the Far East by Nebuchadnezzar, many of whom finished up in India. Others have cited the belief that Manasseh 'was on the borders of China and Tartary and in five centuries had spread Judaism through all central and eastern Asia'. Godbey noted, 'With this must be grouped the statement of Dr Wolff that Genghis Khan had a corps of Jewish troops and was even taken by some to be a Jew.'[30]

The Shinlung as they were first observed were able to find a number of somewhat loose parallels between their ancient beliefs and traditions and the religion of Israel: from their High God – Pathian – to a variety of Shinlung festivals which they claimed mirror their Jewish equivalents. As Weil has noted, particular play was made of the apparent resemblance between the Shinlung Chapcharkur Festival and the Feast of Passover.[31] My informants in 1985 offered me a number of rather vague parallels: belief in a sort of heaven and hell; the practice of animal sacrifice; something similar to a day of atonement, which had traditionally been observed and so on. But between 1985 and 2001 something radical had happened to their collective memory. Informants consulted in 2001 gave much more detailed descriptions of ancient festivals that were similar, if not identical, to Jewish holidays; they claimed that their original tribal traditions included much more in the way of specifically Jewish customs, rituals (including circumcision and the ritual slaughter of animals) and songs and legends with an unmistakably Jewish flavour. Rabbi Avichail had admitted that when he first encountered the Benei Menashe he had his doubts about their claims. 'On my first visit to

India I was in doubt if we could even be fifty per cent certain . . . The important thing is that their motivation is good and we are obligated to convert them and bring them to Israel. Who can know if they are from the tribe of Manasseh?' After his visit to the area in June 1998, where again he listened to their songs and legends, he was finally convinced that the Mizos are indeed 'from the Ten Lost Tribes. It was very, very clear.'[32]

Over the last twenty years the links between the Benei Menashe and the Jewish world have become very much stronger. With the development of information technology the Shinlung find themselves in daily contact by email with Jews elsewhere. There is now a Benei Menashe website with a quantity of articles about the genesis of the Shinlung's 'Judaism', most of them written by Western Jews, which some of the Shinlung can access. Comments by outsiders on tribal traditions thus contribute to and fortify a particular version of tribal memory. One such article even suggests that women's shawls derive from Jewish prayer shawls as they allegedly have 'stripes and tassels'. The mass of supposed similarities constructed in this process of identity-building has been enough to convince educated insiders as well as outsiders. Zaithanchhungi, a local anthropologist, is convinced that here we have much more than a happy coincidence.[33]

It is not only Judaisers in the strict sense of the term, or Messianic Christians wanting to follow the Bible to the letter, who have been affected by the development of an Israelite identity. There is a general and quite widely held belief among the people of the area that prior to the coming of the missionaries they practised a form of Judaism. This belief is enshrined in a number of official government publications. The relationships between these three groups – Messianic Christians, observant Judaisers and those who cling to an Israelite identity without it necessarily affecting their religious life – are quite fluid, and individuals move from one to another without difficulty. But the disparate movements, at any rate the 'Christians' and the 'Jews', are increasingly at loggerheads with each other.[34]

With the development of the Judaising movements, a great interest was soon shown in the State of Israel. In 1959 some of the early Judaisers found an address in Israel to which they could write. According to one of them, 'they sent a letter to that address and sealed it with their tears'. They subsequently discovered that the Prime Minister of Israel had opened their letter before the Knesset. 'As soon as he opened that letter ... they said the Parliament building was shaking, as if there had been an earthquake. So members ran out of the Knesset, but outside there was no shaking. It just occurred inside the Knesset, so that it was some sort of miracle by God.' A reply to the letter was apparently received, which led to some sort of contacts being made with the Israeli consulate in Calcutta.[35] Petitions started arriving at the consular offices of the State of Israel. Weil cites a pamphlet sent to Prime Minister Golda Meir in 1974 in which the Mizos (an acronym, it was explained, for the Mizoram Israel Zionist Organisation!) requested her 'sympathetic consideration ... in order that we may all return to Zion, our ancestral homeland'.[36] Since then the Shinlungs' attempts to emigrate to Israel have been taken up by a number of not negligible advocates, notably Rabbi Avichail and Amishav, and Kulanu.

Amishav was born in 1975 and may be perceived as a part of the Messianic fervour ignited in Israel by the victories of the Six Day War and the Greater Israel Movement. The spark that led to the founding of Amishav is said to have been a lecture given by Rabbi Avichail on the Lost Tribes of Israel at the religious seminary Yeshivat Mercaz ha-Rav in Jerusalem. It was held in the presence of Rabbi Zvi Yehuda Kook, the charismatic man who played such a seminal role in the creation of the Gush Emunim (Block of the Faithful) movement and the growth of nationalist, Messianic fundamentalism in Israel.[37] Subsequently in 1979 Avichail received a letter from a group calling itself 'Jews of North-East India' asking for his assistance. The following year he asked the Shinlung to nominate two individuals to study Judaism in Israel. Two men – Gideon Rei and Shimon Gin – arrived and studied at Machon Meir and the Kever Yosef rabbinical seminary. For those left behind the desire to go to Israel was becoming ever more fervent: in 1984 a submission from a Mizo named Levy Benjamin to the Israel Chief Rabbinate stressed that from the time of Challianthanga, Mizos had wanted to emigrate to Israel, 'From every part of Mizoram we cried longing for our homeland Israel and searched every possible way for contacting [it].'[38] In 1985 some thirty young Benei Menashe were converted by the Chief Rabbi of Netanya in Bombay or Calcutta. Three years later twenty-four more Shinlung were converted in Bombay by a *beit din* (rabbinical court) presided over by Rabbi Yaakov Neuman of the South African *beit din*. A year later this group emigrated to Israel. In 1991 Avichail went to visit the Benei Menashe *in situ*: he was given what amounted to a royal reception and no doubt his presence further encouraged the Judaising movements in Manipur and Mizoram. In the same year the Indian census reported that in Manipur and Mizoram respectively there were 792 and 373 people who had recorded themselves as Jews. Another 570 in Mizoram had declared themselves to be Messianic Jews and another 497 put themselves down as Enoka Israel. An ORT-sponsored book written by two Indians (one of them a Bene Israel Jew) observed that with these three groups the total Jewish population of India in 1991 stood at 6,338.[39] In 1993 a new factor came into play: Avichail had received a number of demands from farmers and others in the Gush Katif Jewish settlements in the Gaza Strip to supply Benei Menashe labourers to replace the Palestinian workers, who were increasingly considered to be a security risk. In general it is clear that for the Gush Emunim settler movement the Benei Menashe were a godsend – front-line troops for Israel's demographic war with the Palestinians. Subsequently the community has settled mainly in right-wing settlements – Kiryat Arba, Ofra, Beit El and Elon Moreh. Dr Irving Moskowitz, a wealthy Florida businessman whose charitable foundation had previously supported extreme right-wing causes in Israel (such as *Ateret Cohanim*, which helps Jews buy Arab property in the old City of Jerusalem), was willing to cover the costs of this immigration. As he has put it, 'Yes I helped the Shinlung. I helped them with my time, my energy, and my money. People always ask why . . . I believe that the Shinlung are one of the Lost Tribes of Israel . . . How can I not help them?'[40]

A group of forty-one Shinlung arrived in Israel in 1993 on a work-study programme: they were greeted with flowers and new skull caps at Ben-Gurion Airport by members of the board of Amishav and representatives of the Gan Or settlement, which was to house them. Avichail observed that hitherto there had been immigration into Israel from the two tribes of Judah and Benjamin, but now the situation had changed. As he put it, 'there now appears to be the beginning of a stirring among the dispersed of the Ten Lost Tribes of Israel, as it is written: "And he will gather the dispersed of Israel and assemble the scattered of Judah" (Isaiah 11:12).'[41]

In 1994–5 another 110 arrived, their expenses borne, as before, by Dr Moskowitz. In February 1996 the Sephardic Chief Rabbi of Israel, Rabbi Bakshi Doron, agreed to the conversion in India of the parents of the young unmarried Benei Menashe in Israel at the rate of forty every six months. These candidates were prepared for conversion to Judaism partly by an emissary sent from Israel. In addition to the work of conversion, efforts have been made to assist the Benei Menashe in India in the construction of synagogues, community centres and even a seminary and a kind of kibbutz. It is clear that the Shinlung make every effort to acquire the necessary items for the practice of orthodox Judaism: books, *haggadot* (the text of the Exodus from Egypt recited at Passover), *sifrei torah* (Scrolls of the Pentateuch), *siddurim* (the weekday and Sabbath prayerbook) and *mahzorim* (Festival prayer book) are in great demand and are supplied by Kulanu and Amishav. To help raise funds for their cause the Benei Menashe sew prayer shawls and prayer shawl bags, which are then marketed by Kulanu in the United States and elsewhere. Kulanu itself has made substantial contributions towards the costs of the immigration process. Moreover the cause of the Shinlung has been taken up by Kulanu in a fairly major way. Thanks in no small part to the efforts of the organisation there are now a considerable number of Benei Menashe in Israel: according to one account there are 10,000 'actively Jewish' Benei Menashe in thirteen towns in India, and of these 3,500 have formally converted to Orthodox Judaism. There are several hundred of them in Israel.[42]

On a research trip to Israel and India in January 2001 it was apparent to me that the sincerity and Jewish 'orthodoxy' of the converts was very pronounced. One of my informants had spent some years in Israel, had served in the army and studied at a *yeshivah*. When I met him he was on his way back to Mizoram to visit his parents. He was deeply concerned by the problems that would confront him in his former homeland. His grandparents, he admitted shamefacedly, had been Christians. But his parents had been practising a variety of Judaism since his birth and perhaps before. However, he confided to me, 'they are not halakhically Jewish'. Which is to say that they were not Jewish according to Orthodox Jewish law, or halakhah. He was worried that he would not even be able to eat with them. It was, he told me, impossible to get kosher meat as there was no halakhically fit slaughterer, or *shohet*, in Mizoram. Any meat consumed by the sons of Manasseh, no matter what they had done to it or not done to it, could not properly be considered kosher and therefore he could not eat it. In addition, his father was in the habit of performing *kiddush* – a ceremony and prayer marking the holiness of Sabbath and festivals – but as his father was not a halakhic Jew his *kiddush* was not permissible. Should he insist on doing the *kiddush* himself, at the risk of humiliating his father? Should he tell his mother, who prided herself on her good kosher cooking, that in fact it was not kosher at all and that he, her son, could not and would not eat it?

When I first came across members of the Judaising Shinlung in 1985, claims of 'normative' Jewish origin were already being made with conviction and growing stridency. An article in a 1986 issue of *India Today*, an English-language Indian magazine, quoted L. S. Thangjom, the director of tourism in Manipur and a prominent member of the 'Jewish' community, as saying, 'If there can be black Jews in Ethiopia and Mongoloid Jews in China, what is so surprising about our ancestry?'[43] This is increasingly the discourse in the parts of the Jewish world that have an inclusive view of Judaism. The name of the Benei Menashe now occurs regularly in discussions of 'marginal' groups and, despite the occasional articles in the Israeli press warning that millions of Indians are just waiting for the opportunity to emigrate to Israel, it is probable that in time the Benei Menashe will establish themselves in Israel like a number of analogous groups in the past.

We have seen here how an essentially Christian and colonial discourse drawing on evangelical hopes and expectations whose roots are to be found in mediaeval views of the unknown world of Asia as well as in British Imperial needs and attitudes has been developed in Burma and the Eastern Indian states of Manipur and Mizoram. This discourse, generated substantially by Christian missionaries in the past, has served in the manufacture of a new agenda dedicated to encouraging the 'Lost Tribes of Israel' wherever they may be to look upon the State of Israel as their state while urging the Jewish State to welcome these neo-Jews as citizens.

Chapter Nine

DOOMED TO WANDER: LOST TRIBES IN THE PACIFIC AND NEW ZEALAND

> The many points of resemblance in feature, general customs and manners may enable us to discover in the widely spread Polynesian race, a remnant of the long-lost tribes of Israel.
>
> Richard Taylor, *Te Ika a Maui, or New Zealand and Its Inhabitants* (1855)

Inevitably the sudden confrontation of isolated societies with the modern world led to a long period of confusion. This was in part because European society was itself chaotic and confused, with multiple and conflicting strata that gave out quite different messages. Traditional societies absorbed these conflicts and contradictions and made of them what they could. One of the features of this confrontation, both in the East and in Africa, was the imposition of an Israelite identity upon indigenous peoples, which was in some cases to have a profound effect upon their future development.

The exploration and colonisation of the Pacific was attended by lively speculation about long-lost Jewish communities and the likely existence of the Lost Tribes in these remote islands. In the second half of the sixteenth century a number of Spanish explorers, principally Alvaro de Mandaña and the pilot Pedro Fernandez de Quiros, set out into the Pacific from the Peruvian port of Callao. De Mandaña had been stimulated by stories of previous Inca explorers who had supposedly found rich islands some six hundred leagues to the west. For some these represented the fabulous Ophir of King Solomon, although on Benedictus Arias Montanus' world map of 1571 Ophir was marked on the west coast of South America, somewhere in Peru, perhaps in the vicinity of Callao. In any event, when a group of islands was finally discovered, they were called the Solomon Islands.[1]

In the seventeenth century the idea of a Pacific Ophir gave way to rumours that there was a large island in the Pacific rich in gold and inhabited by Jews. This was a time when speculation about the Lost Tribes and their role in the End of Days was approaching fever pitch in England and Holland. But the association of Jews and gold suggests a projection of anti-Semitic stereotypes and colonial fantasies about unknown regions. The Dutch East Indian Company sent Abel Janszoon Tasman (1603–*c.* 1659) to investigate these rumours and to discover the 'Great South Land'. With the experienced hydrographer Franz Jacobszoon Visscher as pilot, Tasman set off with a convoy of two ships: his flagship, *Heemskerck*, and an armed transport ship, *Zeehaen*. His voyage failed to cast light on the matter but he did discover Tasmania and, at noon on 13 December 1642, a 'large land, uplifted high', which was the first sighting of the Southern Alps of New Zealand between present day Hokitika and Abut Head. In time the long-sought Pacific Jews were imagined into existence by the British in New Zealand in the form of the Maoris.[2]

British and French exploration of the Pacific was coloured by speculation about Jews and the Lost Tribes from the beginning. Captain Edward Davis, skipper of the *Bachelor's Delight*, claimed to have discovered a fabulously wealthy island. This was taken to be 'the coast of *terra australis incognita*', which by this time had been endowed in the imagination of many people with incredible wealth. Subsequent attempts to retrace Davis's route to the wonderful island were frustrated by a lack of more precise information, although some people thought that the island of Tahiti was Davis's island and that here a white-skinned people would be found.[3] George Robertson, master of the *Dolphin*, noted that 'this race of white people in my opinion has a great resemblance to the Jews, which are scattered through all the knowen parts of the Earth'.[4]

This rumour soon spread: in 1767 Jean-François-Marie de Surville set off from Port-Louis in Brittany and arrived the following year at the mouth of the Ganges. His initial plan was to trade between the French settlements in India and China. But then the rumour struck that a fabulously wealthy island had been discovered. As one French observer put it, 'I was in Pondicherry in August 1767 when the rumour spread that an English vessel had found in the South Sea a very rich island where among other peculiarities a colony of Jews had been settled.'[5]

As the young Thomas Macaulay (1800–1859) was gloomily speculating on England's future, he imagined a time when 'some traveller from New Zealand shall, in the midst of a vast solitude, take his stand on a broken arch of London Bridge to sketch the ruins of St Paul's . . .'

At the time nowhere on earth was considered more remote, and thus further from future cataclysms, than New Zealand. And yet there, too, the idea that the local population was descended from the Lost Tribes of Israel was mooted shortly after the settlement of the colony.

When Captain James Cook arrived in New Zealand in 1769, there were around a hundred thousand Maoris living there. An agricultural Polynesian people, they are thought to have arrived on the islands from the central Pacific in about AD 1000.[6] Linked by a common language, customs and inter-marriage, and toughened by a history of incessant tribal warfare, they presented a united front against the European foe and in the process discovered a new, common identity in the face of the outside threat. This is reflected in the name 'Maori', which means ordinary or normal, and which came into use at this time as a way of distinguishing themselves from the 'abnormal' represented by the settlers.

The convict settlers of Australia who made the onward journey to New Zealand and were among the first Europeans to permanently settle there were not, it may be imagined, the gentlest of men, and by the 1830s there were some two to three thousand of them making sufficient mischief for the British Government to want to take measures to establish order. As far as the settlers were concerned the Maoris presented a problem. In Australia, as in parts of South Africa, murdering local people was considered not much more of a crime than hunting down wild animals. In 1838, to the general surprise of many Australians, Governor George Gipps made it clear that murdering the local Aborigines was broadly unacceptable: indeed it would be punishable by death. The same restrictions were to apply in New Zealand. But here the situation was rather different. From the outset the Maoris presented a much more co-ordinated resistance than the native people of Australia had been able to muster. Indeed in the course of the years they had managed to inflict a number of crushing blows on British troops and had it not been for their logistical weakness and the practical difficulties of keeping a permanent army in the field, they may well ultimately have driven off the invaders. So how was it that these unkempt savages, clearly inferior in every way, had on occasion been able to keep eighteen thousand well-trained, well-armed British troops at bay?

It was clearly necessary in these circumstances to understand this formidable enemy. Sir George Grey (1812–98), as colonial governor of

New Zealand, supervised the first collection of Maori traditions and myths.[7] One way to explain the Maoris' temporary success was to argue that in fact the tribe did have certain rather impressive innate, inherited racial characteristics after all. This discourse has produced many theories over the years, including ones that traced the descent of the Maoris to the Aryans in India, or to the peoples of South America. But perhaps the most popular and certainly the most influential of such theories was to suggest that they were descended from the Ten Lost Tribes of Israel. Some of the great British explorers, not least Cook, had prepared the way for this idea. The discovery of the Baring Straits – 'about twice the breadth of the Straits of Dover' – showed that people had commonly passed from Asia to the Americas. This, in turn, supported the popular view that the American Indians were Jews and that Jews might have spread out into the Pacific from the Americas.[8]

An early champion of the theory of Israelites in New Zealand was the Anglican clergyman Samuel Marsden (1765–1838). Like many British missionaries in the nineteenth century he was of humble origins. Son of a Yorkshire blacksmith, he had come under the influence of William Wilberforce, the Christian campaigner against the slave trade (1759–1883). As early as 1819, after his second visit to New Zealand, Marsden declared that the Maoris had an Israelite lineage. His comparative study of the Maoris and the Jews suggested to him certain striking similarities derived in some cases from a pretty negative view of both peoples. He found a shared trading prowess – the Maoris, like the Jews, would 'buy and sell anything'; Maori priests would exhort war parties 'in a similar language to that of the Jewish High Priest of old'; a Maori chief would decapitate an opposing chief who was killed in battle 'as David did to the head of Goliath'; even cannibalism was evoked – on the grounds that Jesus had told the Jews 'he that eateth my flesh and drinketh my blood dwelleth in me and I in him'. Marsden's somewhat inchoate views became widely known and soon other missionaries were listing dozens of points at which Jewish and Maori practice coincided – from menstruation-related ritual to burial practice.[9] No doubt the reason for these efforts was to place the unfamiliar Maoris within the familiar context of Christian knowledge: to replace the unknown 'other' with the known. Attempts to re-type them took in features other than their religion. The very social structure of the Maoris was seen as reflecting the tribal structure of ancient Israel. Arthur Thomson (1816–60), appointed assistant army surgeon in 1838, was convinced by his experience with them that the Maoris had Jewish physical characteristics – specifically 'Jewish noses'.[10] The idea was soon advanced that the Maoris' languages too were derived from Semitic sources, perhaps from traders in the Malay peninsula, and various supposed lexical similarities were found.[11] The general idea was further promoted in *Te Ika a Maui, or New Zealand and Its Inhabitants*, by the missionary Richard Taylor (1805–73). Taylor compared the Maoris with a number of other groups, including the Japanese, Polynesians and Malays, and concluded:

> that the many points of resemblance in feature, general customs and manners may enable us to discover in the widely spread Polynesian race, a remnant of the long-lost tribes of Israel and when the time arrives for their restoration from all countries in which they have been dispersed from 'Hamath and the isles of the sea' that, in that day, it will be found, even to these ends of the world, the fearful denunciation of Divine wrath has driven his apostate people, who forsaking the true light given them and preferring heathen darkness, here to be suffered to dwell in that darkness, until they had fulfilled their appointed times. We have no reason to suppose that when the ten tribes were carried captive by Assyria that they were all placed in the same spot . . . on the contrary we have the denunciation that they should be scattered . . . and we cannot suppose that the mere taking them out of their own land was the termination of their punishment but that it was only the commencement of it.

According to Taylor the Lost Tribes would undoubtedly have sought:

> the grand marts of commerce, no longer possessing fixed homes, they became merchants, as a matter or course, and those who still continued to love war and independence, or a pastoral life, would retire before their enemies, and thus, should it be proved that the Afghans are Jews, we see how they would reach that country. Whilst some, perhaps those from Babylon, remained in India, as the Black Jews state they have done, some would pass on thence and people the Indian isles as the Malays. From the Caspian many may have followed the caravans across Central Asia, Thibet and Tartary, until they reached the Eastern Coast, and thence from island to island, this race doomed to wander, may have done so, either intentionally or otherwise, as ships are constantly picking up large canoes, which have drifted away from their island home . . . Doubtless this has ever been

> the case and whilst numbers have thus miserably perished, some few have escaped and become the inhabitants of many a lone island of the Pacific Ocean.[12]

The theological implications of all this were clear for Taylor: the Maoris were one of 'the lost tribes of Israel which with its fellows having abandoned the service of the true God and cast aside his word, fell step by step in the scale of civilisation; deprived of a fixed home, became nomad wanderers over the steps of Asia – a bye-word and a reproach among the nations and gradually retreated until in the lapse of ages they reached the sea, and thence, still preserving their wandering character, from island to island driven by winds and currents and various causes until they reached New Zealand and there fallen to their lowest state of degradation, given up to the fiercest passions, consumed and being consumed, they are enabled to reflect, repent and amend and resolve to arise and go to their father.'[13]

Taylor found supplementary proofs for his grand theory in the supposed similarity of a number of Hebrew words with Maori: *pardes* – orchard – he compared with the Maori *paral* – a small plain enclosed by a forest; *kara* – cry out – with the Maori *karanga*; the Hebrew *mot* – death – with the Maori *mate*, and so forth. Taylor's ideas are of course part of a much wider discourse. It is of interest that, as he put it, 'Maori has precisely the same meaning as the word "Moor".'[14]

Taylor's analysis implies the crucial need for the Maori to be brought to Christ. Equating them with wandering nomads or Moors 'fallen to the lowest state of degradation', and as low as could be in the 'scale of civilisation', deprived them of all legitimacy. They had no vestiges of a settled, civilised people. They had no hope spiritually, no rights politically, and no legal tenure of their land. They were thus fair game both for the missions, the settlers and the colonial authorities.

Needless to say Taylor's and other missionaries' theories had an impact upon the way the Maoris saw themselves. Deeply impressed with what they had read in the white man's Bible, they drew sustenance and inspiration from it – perhaps not exactly in the way the missionaries might have hoped. The great stories of bloodshed, war and heroism of the Old Testament appealed to a people with such war-like traditions, and increasingly the Maoris began to see themselves as the children of Israel, enslaved in a white man's bondage and bound to resist by what ever means they could, as had the Israelites of old. The biblical stories provided them with a manifesto of resistance. The myth of the Lost Tribes was used as a means of restructuring their own Maori identity in the cause of this resistance and of enriching their own past with a myth that carried with it clouds of glory in the eyes of their all-powerful conquerors.

By the middle of the nineteenth century many Maoris had internalised the colonial fantasies about them and started declaring themselves to be Israelites. In 1833 a movement started in the North Island led by Papahurihia, who is said to have been on a number of voyages with a Jewish sea captain from whom he may have learned something about Judaism, as well as various magic tricks and the art of ventriloquism. Armed with this unusual amalgam of knowledge he tried to start a new religion. Basing it principally on what the Maoris had learned from the missionaries, he placed particular emphasis on their supposed descent from the Lost Tribes of Israel. Papahurihia claimed that the god of the Jews appeared to him at night in the form of a serpent – Nakahi (the similarity with the Hebrew word for serpent – *nakhash* – did not go unnoticed in this discourse). Calling themselves Jews, Papahurihia and his disciples insisted that Saturday was the true Sabbath. The warrior-priest Te Atua Wera was the Messiah of this religion – he was believed to be able to make stones, trees and houses speak.

Another tribal warrior, Te Ua Horopapera Haumene, who fought against the British with distinction in the mid-century land wars, came to the conclusion, in a trance, that he was Moses and subsequently went by the name of Te Ua Jew Ua. The Archangel Gabriel initiated him into sacred lore, which included magic chants and signs that had one signal property: they would give the Maoris immunity against the white man's bullets. He also founded a new religion called Hau Hau, again predicated upon the belief that the Maoris were of Israelite extraction.

It would be interesting to know if there was any Jewish influence on these new nineteenth-century religious movements. Certainly there were some Jews in the country from the early period of settlement. One of the first writers to describe New Zealand was a Jew – Joel Samuel Polack – who travelled there between 1831–7.[15] Subsequently there were English Jews on the first immigrant ships in 1840. The Hau Haus' sense of Jewish solidarity led them to spare any Jews they came across in the settler towns they captured. In March 1871 the schooner

Eclipse berthed in Opotiki, on the north-east coast of the North Island. Some of the passengers, including the Reverend Carl Sylvius Volkner (1819–65) and the Reverend T. S. Grace, were captured by the Hau Hau under the command of their arch-priest Kereopa. The owner and captain of the *Eclipse* was a Jersey-born Jew, Captain M. Levy (1821–1901). Both he and his brother, as Jews and thus 'akin to the Hau Hau', were freed. On 2 March 1864, however, Volkner was taken into the local church of St Stephen's, stripped of his clothes (the best garments were taken by the leader of the Hau Hau party) and allowed to pray in front of the altar before being hanged. An hour later he was decapitated and the Hau Hau allegedly crowded around the altar to drink his blood from the communion cup while Kereopa recited the prayer, 'Hear O Israel, this is the word of God, of Abraham, Isaac and Jacob. We are the Jews who were lost and have been persecuted!' Kereopa then gouged out Volkner's eyes and gave orders that his head be smoke-cured.

Another Maori figure who considered himself to be Jewish was Te Kooti Rikirangi, formerly a member of the Hau Hau who was deported in 1860, along with other Hau Hau, from the east coast to the remote Chatham islands, some five hundred miles east of New Zealand. Only twenty-five years before, the peace-loving hunter-gatherer people of the Chathams – the Moriori – had suffered a terrible fate. On 19 November 1835 a ship bearing five hundred Maoris had arrived on the island. The Moriori, who had a tradition of solving disputes peacefully, put up no resistance and were largely exterminated and in many cases eaten. In the following years the island remained particularly bleak and under-developed. During this harsh period of exile, in what for Te Kooti and his followers was the land of their bondage, Te Kooti studied the biblical texts. Fired by the verse from Joshua 23:5–6, 'And the Lord your God, he shall expel them before you – and ye shall possess the land', in 1868 Te Kooti escaped from the Chathams on the schooner *Rifleman* and later landed at Whareongaonga where, along with his followers, he was involved in many bloody incidents. The religion he founded was known as Ringatu – meaning the upraised hand – the reference being to the Jewish sacerdotal blessing. Worshippers met together on the twelfth day of each month, which has been taken as a 'nod in the direction of the Twelve Tribes'.[16] Having successfully avoided arrest Te Kooti finally settled in Tokangamutu where he established himself as a preacher and faith healer. Pardoned by the

British authorities in 1883 he died, mourned by his followers, a decade later. On his death bed he prophesied that 'in twice seven years a man shall arise in the mountains to succeed me. He shall be the new prophet of the people'.

A follower of Te Kooti, Rua Kenana Hepetipa (1869–1937), a Tuhoe prophet born in the Ureweras, started having visions which revealed to him that he was this new prophet. Assuming the title Te Mihaie Hou – the New Messiah – Rua Kenana declared himself to be the brother of Christ and the son of the Holy Ghost.[17] Like Te Kooti before him he had a formidable reputation as a healer and was sought out by whites as well as by Maoris. In 1906 he went to Gisborne carrying a large black box on a packhorse. At night the box was laid to rest in a specially erected tent. This he proclaimed was the Ark of Covenant – the symbol of God's eternal covenant with Israel. As the Israelites had carried the Ark with them to Jerusalem so, he declared, he would take the Ark to Maungapohatu where he would build the House of the Covenant. Rua's Tuhoe people were gradually being wiped out by European diseases, among other things. His plan was in part an attempt to cut off the Tuhoe from any contact with Europeans. In this desolate and remote place, a town in the heart of the Ureweras, the area of his birth, Rua and his followers had to contend with terrible privations. Yet it was here in Maungapohatu that he set about building the new Jerusalem.

Within two years they had constructed a remarkable complex constructed along biblical lines. First to be built was Hiruharama Hou – the House of the Lord. Then came the Hiona – the Court House. It was from the Hiona that Rua ruled: it was a splendid two-storey building, painted in the white and blue livery of Israel. Within three years of his arrival he had attracted more than a thousand Maori 'Israelites' to the banner of his faith. Disliked and feared by the British – not least for the isolation in which he chose to live – in 1916 Rua was sentenced to twelve months' hard labour and eighteen months' probationary treatment, after he was convicted of 'sly-grogging', resisting arrest and treason. The Maoris claim to this day that during the gun-point arrest, his son was killed and his daughter raped. The trial brought him financial ruin, he was imprisoned, and his standing dropped among his disciples. The beautiful Hiona was demolished, although a small temple was established with some of the materials. But Rua, abandoned by the majority of his followers, remained faithful to his vision and until his death in 1937 led a smaller group of Israelites known as Iharaia.[18]

What explanation may be enlisted for these religious manifestations? In another context Robert Levi has written about the ambivalence felt in Tahiti towards 'collective ancestors'. As he put it, 'they are ashamed of the primitiveness and heathenism of their past, from which Christianity had rescued them, as generations of pastors have reminded them'. Some sense of shame may be responsible for the Maoris' and other peoples' identification with Jews – the authors after all of the West's religious traditions.[19]

In 1906, the year Rua was attempting to build a new Jerusalem in Maungapohatu, *The Messenger* – a bi-monthly publication of the New Zealand Mission of the Church of Jesus Christ of Latter-Day Saints – asked in its front-page editorial, 'Are the Maoris of Israelitish origin?' In *The Book of Mormon* three migrations are recorded from Asia to the Western world. The first of these took place at the time of the Tower of Babel and the latter two in 600 and 588 BC during the reign of Zedekiah. These émigrés were to populate North and South America. Some of them, according to *The Book of Mormon*, left the west coast of America in about 55 BC but never returned. *The Messenger* argued, 'it was some of these, we submit, that after spending some time in Hawaii resumed their journeyings and eventually landed on the islands of New Zealand ... as early as 1843, only thirteen years after its humble beginning, the Church of Jesus Christ of Latter-Day Saints, sent its missionaries to the Polynesians, believing them to be of Israelitish origin and descendants of the people of whom *The Book of Mormon* is a history'. In the following pages fifty separate similarities are listed, from the common use of fringes to the veneration of sacred trees to demonstrate the Israelite origins of the Maoris.[20] These attempts to enlist the Maoris in Mormon sacred history have no doubt left their traces in the collective imagination of the native peoples of New Zealand.[21] It must also be noted that the idea that British people in general were descended from the Israelites became particularly popular in New Zealand in the first decades of the twentieth century.[22]

The development of similar ideas may be observed elsewhere in the Pacific. In the last two decades of the seventeenth century the great English explorer and adventurer William Dampier (1652–1715) crossed the Pacific twice. According to John Campbell's map of Dampier's discoveries there was thought to exist a race of Jews in New Guinea 'suspected to be a remnant of the Ten Tribes of Israel'.[23] This idea resurfaced in 1904 when Mr Oliver Bainbridge reported to the *Cape Times* that he had discovered a race of 'strange people in Central New Guinea'. He referred to them as 'Black Jews'. A year later he gave a talk illustrated by 'a magnificent series of magic-lantern pictures' at the Lyceum theatre in Shanghai, on his discoveries 'in the Land of the Black Jews'. Bainbridge, dressed for the occasion in:

> grey serge tunic and riding-breeches and leather gaiters at once proceeded with his lecture, which with the pictures, which were projected on a screen suspended behind the lecturer, from a lantern operated by his assistants in the stalls, occupied two hours in the delivery. Mr Bainbridge has a splendid ringing voice, which could easily fill a building of four times the size of the Lyceum, and, succeeding at once and with a facility which evinced ripe experience on the platform, in capturing the attention and sympathy of his audience, he held it to the finish, never pausing in his discourse . . . His overall thesis was the 'ethnological unity of mankind'. At one point a really remarkable picture was projected on the screen, showing in profile the head of a black New Guinea Jew, and the lecturer pointed out in convincing and eloquent terms how the subject of the picture differed from the ordinary inhabitants of the country, in his prominent Hebraic nose – a very well-marked feature – high, bold, intellectual forehead and 'Kinky' hair. He told of the temples these people have on the island of Kwei . . . and about a strange hieroglyph . . . painted in black on the white bark of a tree in the country, and which no one had yet succeeded in deciphering, though its distinct resemblance to an ancient Hebrew character was well marked. Mr Bainbridge had many pictures to show of the these strange and interesting people, all of the same distinctively Jewish type and much to tell of their superiority in intelligence to the ordinary Papuans, their abstention from pork, scaleless fish and other articles of diet forbidden by the Law of Moses.[24]

He stressed the similarities of customs, religions as well as physical appearance, 'the likeness of the white Hebrew race is remarkable, the one great difference being that the New Guinea specimens of the twelve tribes are black. Among them are to be found many Albinos.' As *Israel's Messenger*, the Shanghai Jewish newspaper, reported it, 'Asked if they were intelligent, Mr Bainbridge replied that they were but the only sign of an educational system he observed was tablets used in religious observances.'[25]

It is interesting to note that today in Papua New Guinea echoes of such ideas are still prevalent. In a private communication Almut Schneider (EHESS, École des Hautes Études des Sciences Sociales, Paris) observed:

> During my fieldwork (1997–99) I occasionally heard people in Western Highlands Province, PNG (Tambul/Nebilyer and Mt Hagen town), referring to themselves as 'the last tribe' or 'the lost tribe'. What they meant was the last of the 'twelve tribes of Israel'. People (and not necessarily only the very religious ones!) consider themselves to be the thirteenth tribe, that was lost (or not known about) for a long time and had been 'found' when the Europeans and Australians entered Papua New Guinea. (The notions of 'lost' or 'last' are either applied simultaneously, or alternatively.) People were very keen on 'verifying' and always asked me, if I knew about that thirteenth tribe, if I had read about it in the Bible (and I found that difficult to answer . . .). I suppose it has in a way to do with a local evangelical church called the 'Papua New Guinea Bible Church'. Since they consider themselves to be genuinely a 'national church' (in contrast to the Catholic or Lutheran Church which stress the universal aspect of their denomination) the idea of forming a separate, defined part (as a 'thirteenth tribe') of an encompassing whole (Christianity) would fit into their 'politics'.

According to Schneider very many people in Papua New Guinea, including people of different denominations and those with no religious affiliations at all, are proclaiming their Israelite identity as members of the Thirteenth Tribe of Israel.

Chapter Ten

OUR OWN PEOPLE OF JOSEPH'S SEED: JAPAN

Our Nippon is the branch of your kingdom of Israel as well.

A Japanese writing from Manchuria in 1922

In early mediaeval times Jews from Europe and the Middle East may have been involved in trade with Japan through their connection with the silk route. Later, during Japan's so-called 'Christian Century' (1542–1639), some Jews participated in the limited trade initiated by the Portuguese and the Dutch. But it was not until after 1853, when Commodore Perry of the United States Navy arrived in Japan and initiated the process that was to re-open Japan to outside influences, that Jews started to settle in the country. Alexander Marks, who arrived in Yokohama in 1861, was the first Jewish resident of modern Japan; by the end of the 1860s, the city had fifty Jewish families from Poland, the United States and England. During the next few decades Jewish communities established themselves in Nagasaki, where they were primarily involved in the import-export trade, and subsequently in Kobe and Tokyo. Today there are still no more than a thousand 'authentic' Jews in the country.

The first actual encounter between a Jew and Japan to have a discernible impact on the place came in 1904. After enthusiastically engaging the Russian troops in the Russo-Japanese War Japan got to the point where it could no longer sustain the financial burden of fighting such a powerful opponent. The vice-governor of the Bank of Japan was sent to London to raise a loan. He had little initial success until, by chance, he met up with the American-Jewish financier, Jacob Schiff. In the wake of the infamous 1903 pogrom in Kishinev Schiff was only too happy to help: he raised a bond issue of $200 million which enabled Japan to go on to win the war. Subsequently Schiff became something of a national hero in Japan and the Emperor Meiji invited him to the Imperial Palace for lunch. Schiff was the first foreigner to be thus honoured. This incident established in the Japanese mind the idea that Jews had unlimited access to money and that they were all-powerful. Such a stereotypical perspective was shored up when the *Protocols of the Learned Elders of Zion*, an anti-Semitic forgery by the Tsarist secret police, the Okhrana, was published in a Japanese translation after the First World War.

After the Russian revolutions of 1905 and 1917 quite a number of Jews made for the West, where they found havens, particularly in Great Britain and the United States. But some took the long overland route eastwards and found sanctuary in Manchuria, China and Japan. During the 1930s and the early years of the Second World War, notwithstanding the close ties Japan enjoyed with Hitler's Germany, thousands of Jewish refugees from Nazism found temporary shelter in Japan before being relocated. This was partly the result of Japan's 'Jewish policy', which was an important element in Japanese foreign policy considerations before and during the war. The backbone of today's Jewish community still consists of Russian émigrés, but the majority of Jews now living in the country are temporarily based American businessmen and their families.

In view of these tiny numbers and the minuscule impact that Jews, Judaism or Jewish history and concerns have had on Japan, it is difficult to understand the influence of the image of the Jews on the contemporary Japanese *imaginaire.* Perhaps some superficial similarities between Japan and Israel, or even Japan and the Jews may, in part, account for it. As the Israeli scholar of Japan Professor Ben-Ami Shillony has observed, 'Today the Japanese and the Jews are the two most modern and Westernized non-Christian peoples ... both view themselves as unique and totally different from the rest of the world. To the Japanese anyone else is a *gaijin*; to the Jews he is a *goy* ... these two peoples seemed to have swapped their historical roles. The Japanese long known as fierce warriors have become shrewd and pacifist merchants; while the Jews long famous as shrewd and pacifist merchants have turned into fierce warriors ...'[1]

It is in fact in Japan that we can trace the most remarkable evolution in the Pacific of an imagined Judaic past. As elsewhere in the world, the theory that aspects of the country were to be explained via an Israelite model was introduced by Western agents and almost immediately found fertile soil. Soil so fertile that within a remarkably short period a host of notions were advanced by the Japanese themselves claiming that they had a direct common ancestry with the Jews, or at the very least that there were links between them. King Solomon's Mines were said to have been discovered at Mount Tsurugi on the island of Shikoku. The village of Shingo in the Aomori prefecture has been identified as the grave of Jesus, who travelled to Japan after his brother James was crucified in his place, and the people of the Shiga prefecture north-east of Osaka, noted for their frugality, have been awarded Jewish ancestry. The Japanese royal family, like the British one, has been accorded an Israelite pedigree and the Samurai, as well as a number of other groups, have been dubbed descendants of the Lost Tribes of Israel. In March 1987 a semi-popular monthly, *History Reader*, with a circulation of 180,000, devoted some ninety pages to the question of Japan's supposedly Jewish roots, and nine pages of photographs depicted ancient 'Jewish' settlements throughout Japan.[2] But perhaps the most striking outcome of the Japanese fascination with Judaism has been the establishment of religious sects, with tens of thousands of adherents, notably the Makuya and Beit Shalom, whose rituals and beliefs have a preponderance of Jewish and Israeli characteristics.

The identification of Japan or the Japanese with the Jews goes back at least to the seventeenth century. We have noted the passage that claims, 'we may . . . say that fruitful India are *Hebrewes*, so *Japonia* . . .'[3] And in *The Last Trumpet and the Flying Angel* (London, 1849) John Finlayson, friend and supporter of Richard Brothers, claimed that 'even in China, Japan and Ethiopia . . . are the descendants of the Hebrews'. But the first full-blown development of the theory was put forward by Norman McLeod, a Scot who started his career in the herring industry before he ended up in Japan as a missionary. In the preface to his *Epitome of the Ancient History of Japan*, first published in 1875, he noted that he had arrived in Japan in 1867 – the last year of the Tokugawa regime – and that he had intended to write a multi-volume work on the country, which among other things would furnish the reader with 'a more detailed account of the origins of the Japanese with a description of their Jewish belongings'.[4] McLeod remarked that the 'Japanese Samurai have an ancient tradition that they come from a far country situated in the west of Asia and that they called a counsel of war and agreed amongst themselves that they would proceed to the East and seek out and conquer some unknown country'. It was clear from a variety of sources that this western Asian country was the land of Israel. As he noted, somewhat breathlessly, 'The passage in II Kings 17 and 19 would lead us to believe "and they built the high places in all their cities from the tower of the watchmen to the fenced city". I have visited nearly all the most ancient castles in Japan and I found the high places similarly situated ... the so-called Shinto temples are the ancient high places of Israel defamed.' Among other things he pointed out that the first known king of Japan was Osee, crowned in 730 BC, that the last king of Israel was Hosea who died in 722 BC, and that there are similarities in the construction of Japanese temples and the Jerusalem Temple, in the clothes and instruments used by their respective priesthoods, and so on.[5]

McLeod's ideas reached a wide international audience, including a Jewish one, and no doubt had an impact on Japanese thinking. Within a couple of decades of their publication they formed part of a half-serious discourse which circulated throughout the Western Jewish press and elsewhere. By the time of the Russo-Japanese War of 1904 the Shanghai-based newspaper *Israel's Messenger* reported a German humourist, Julius Stettenheim, who had recently found some remarkable grounds for believing that the Japanese were indeed the descendants of the Lost Tribes:

1. The Russians have noted that they are beaten on almost all days except Saturday, and have also been informed that the Japanese are not allowed to do any work on the seventh, except to pursue the enemy when there is danger that they might escape.
2. Hogs are raised by the Japanese merely to feed foreigners and not for their own use.
3. The name of the capital is derived from the Hebrew 'Tekio gedaulo' which denotes that the city was undoubtedly founded after some great victory.
4. The name Wei-hai-wei is based on the often-heard and well known Jewish expression 'Eiweh' and denotes that the Japanese suffered many hardships before the city was constructed. (For a similar case of etymology compare the name 'Weimar'.)
5. The mutual hatred between Japan and Russia.
6. The official Japanese organ is called 'Tschuwo' which is a good Hebrew word meaning 'answer' or 'repentance'.[6]

Two scholars who have delved into the intriguing topic of the Japanese perspective on the Jews, David Goodman and Masanori Miyazawa, believe that the multitude of theories generated in Japan linking the two peoples – the so-called 'common origin' theories – were broadly 'products of the ... English tradition of speculation on the fate of the Ten Lost Tribes of Israel'. No doubt this is the case insofar as the missionary who introduced them was British. However alongside the speculation of early Western visitors, and particularly McLeod, the local reading of the Christian Bible also played an important if perhaps secondary role in the spread of the fantasy of Israelite origin which, as we have seen elsewhere and as we shall see perhaps most powerfully in the next chapter, forms a consistent feature of the Western colonial enterprise.

In Japan one of the first Japanese to propose a common ancestry for the Jews and his own people was Saeki Yoshiro (1871–1965), who published his theory as an appendix to an academic work on Nestorian Christianity in 1908. Saeki was a serious scholar of Christianity in China. He came to the view that the Hada clan – a continental group supposed to have arrived in Japan in the fifth century and to be found to the west of Kyoto in a village called Uzumasa – was Jewish. He adduced in favour of this proposition a range of fairly puerile philological arguments from which Goodman and Miyazawa selected the following: *uzu*, he reasoned, is a corrupt form of *ishu* or Jesus; *masa* is the Hebrew form of Messiah; as well as others of a similar nature. Notwithstanding the less than compelling nature of this evidence the Uzumasa connection was not only the linchpin of Saeki's argument, but has become the basis of a great deal of subsequent common-origin theorising.[7]

Foreigners continued to find traces of Jews in Japan. In 1908 *Israel's Messenger* reported that there were not only 'Jews with pigtails' in China, and in Abyssinia 'Jews whose skin is dark' but also Jews in Japan. Called 'Ety' these Jews lived in a self-imposed ghetto, worked as shoemakers and ate meat. As the paper enthused, 'the fact that the "Ety" make shoes out of leather is also quoted by those who believe them to be Jews as an argument in favour of this theory'. The religion of these carnivorous cobblers 'resembled worship in a synagogue rather than that of a Buddhist temple' and the 'Ety' women, much prized by the Japanese, were 'of the Semitic type rather than the Mongoloid.' 'In the ghetto of Nagasaki', the report continued, 'the "Ety" observe the Sabbath very religiously'. The piece was based on a published report by a Russian traveller and writer called Vassili Nemirovitch-Dantchenko who had recently travelled throughout Japan and had concluded that the 'Ety' must be Jews who had been so long in Japan that they had assimilated almost completely to Japanese norms.[8]

In 1929 Oyabe Zen'ichiro (1867–1941), a Yale-educated Christian minister who had worked as a missionary in Hawaii, published his *Origin of Japan and the Japanese People*, where he continued the arguments of Saeki. He elaborated on the contention that the Japanese emperors were also of Israelite descent. He observed, 'It is well-known to Biblical scholars in the West and the world over that proximately three hundred years before the enthronement of the Emperor Jimmu (in 660 BCE), two tribes of the Hebrews – Gad the most valiant and Manasseh, who were descended from the eldest son of the patriarch – fled eastward carrying the Hebrews' sacred treasures and to this day their whereabouts remain unknown. A close study of the ancient Hebrews as they are described in the Jewish scriptures reveals an extraordinary number of similarities between our two peoples. The Japanese and the Hebrews are virtually identical. These exact correspondences convince me that we are in fact one race.' Underlying Oyabe's thesis was his belief that Christianity and Shinto were much the same thing and that for Shinto to serve the Japanese nation better it would do well to adapt more explicitly Christian features, including a direct line of descent, from Jewish thought. Another common-origin theorist was Kawamorita Eiji (1891–1960). Kawamorita, a Presbyterian minister, spent most of his life in the United States and produced a large two-volume work in Japanese – *Study of Japanese Hebrew Songs* – which argued that in Japanese folk songs were to be found traces of a Hebrew that had otherwise disappeared from Japan some thirteen hundred years before. This work continues to sustain Japanese Lost Tribes enthusiasts. Kawamorita's central view was that Japan is a holy nation, that God is the source of all holiness and that therefore Japan's holiness must originate from God. Consequently Japan's divine emperor could only have descended from Israel – the chosen people of God. Kawamorita was led to the belief 'that our Emperor is the undisputed successor to the eternal throne of the Great King David of Israel and that without the Emperor system Japan will lose its reason to exist'. Goodman and Miyazawa came to the conclusion in this section of their work that as the three common-origin theorists were Christians, educated first in Christian schools and later in the United States, they were therefore alienated from the mainstream of Japanese life and their nationalism, based on the principle of a holy Japan enjoying a sanctifying commonality with the Jews, 'was an attempt to reconcile their Christianity with their Japanese identity'.[9]

Elsewhere the same or similar ideas were being harnessed to a quite different cause. After the Anglo-Japanese alliance of 1905 a British-Israelite pamphlet appeared arguing that Japan, not America, was the true Manasseh and this idea was to persist in British-Israelite literature for several decades to come.[10] Thus in 1921 E. A. Gordon, a British-Israelite with the usual British-Israelite love of capital letters, wrote from Kyoto in *Israel's Messenger*, 'I hope you will not think it a mere fancy that the coming friendship of this crown prince from the Sunrise Land with our Prince "David" of Wales (whom his great-grandmother Victoria was convinced would lead his people back to the Land) may be the fulfilment of the prophet's visions of the "Two sticks", "Judah and Ephraim", becoming one (Ezekiel 37:16). With the New Nehemiah at Jerusalem and the New Daniel over India – it all looks like it!'[11] And in the *Heritage of the Anglo-Saxon Race* (1941) there is a further and spirited application of British-Israelite theory to Japan (as with practically all British-Israelite literature there is an embarrassing surfeit of finger-wagging, as well as of capitals). Racist, bigoted and full of references to *Lebensraum*, it is not difficult to see where the sympathies of the writer lay. The author notes that the tribe of Manasseh was split into two: one part settled east and one part settled west of the Jordan. 'Eastern Manasseh with Reuben and Gad went into Exile first, about 750 BC. From tombstone inscriptions in the Crimea and elsewhere we trace that they were in part scattered "as far East as China". Ancient maps made before the time of Christ show us the Sacae or Saccasennae out on the sea of Japan before Jesus Christ came to earth. Many names in Japan are purely Hebrew in sound and meaning. THE RULING FAMILIES OF THE WHITE JAPANESE, THE SAMURAI, ARE OUR OWN PEOPLE OF JOSEPH'S SEED, WHO TOOK THEIR NAME SAMURAI FROM SAMARIA THE CAPITAL OF THE TEN TRIBES, built in 924 BC by King Omri ... If the Samurai of Japan are of Israel from Samaria, they like Ephraim and Manasseh, are of Joseph's seed to whom were given the material blessings and the material wealth AND THE COMMISSION TO SETTLE THE WASTE PLACES OF THE EARTH ... These were to be scattered among all the nations and if Japan be of Israel stock ROOM MUST BE FOUND FOR HER, for God's purpose cannot be defeated. All sections of Israel must have room to bloom and grow properly ... In the time of the world's greatest need Japan did not treat her engagements as "scraps of paper". She came to the world's assistance. She did everything she was asked to do, did it surprisingly well and was willing to do more (surely an evidence of WHO they are).'[12] Of course the book was written (AND PROBABLY PUBLISHED) before Pearl Harbour (7 December 1941).

The ideas of McLeod, Saeki and others duly passed into Jewish circles as well. Right at the beginning of the twentieth century a dialogue opened up in the Shanghai Zionist Association's *Israel's Messenger* between those Japanese taken by these ideas and Jews. In October 1904 the Nagasaki correspondent of *Israel's Messenger* wrote, 'In view of the recent publicity you have given to ... a Japanese gentleman having embraced Judaism, it may, I think, interest your readers to know that I have lately received a letter from a wealthy Japanese gentleman, Mr Moissa, who is living in a village called Oshima, in which he states he claims descent from one of the Jewish Lost Tribes. I may also add that I have received from him a book with a history of our forefathers written in the native language ...'[13]

In the next issue a reader commented, 'A picture in the Gihon mansion at Kyoto represents King Solomon receiving the gifts of the Queen of Sheba. Almost everywhere in Japan there are seen drawings and sketches of the temple of Solomon and his throne, just as they are described in the Bible. The unicorn, the fantastic animal dear to Israel, is also very often found ... In the mausolea of the Emperors and in the oldest graveyards of Japan, we find all the shapes of the old graves of Palestine, the Jewish instruments of music, the cornet, the psalter, the harp of ten strings, the drum, the flute ...'

In 1922 the same journal reported a Japanese correspondent who was urging from Manchuria that a 'Judeo-Japan Society be organised in the near future'. His reasons for this were in part his belief that, 'Our Nippon is the branch of your kingdom of Israel as well, as we are the people chosen of God ... The God of Nippon is Jehovah and its shrine is the same style as the Tabernacle of yours. The most precious and necessary treasure for the Imperial House is the Ark which keeps those we call "Three Divine Vessels" ... Some years ago Professor P. Y. Saeki of Tokyo drew attention to the traces of Ancient Israel found in Japan –

the "David's Shrine". Also the celebration of a "Viceroy over the river" at midnight, resembling the Hebrew Passover where Mochi (Hebrew Motzah) is annually eaten; and in its near vicinity two ancient stone well-heads inscribed in Chinese characters with the magic word "Yisrael!", the name of the district being Uzumasa, which is the "ya-t-sin" used at Sianfu in China for Syria. This erudite scholar further found villages named "Gose" and "Manasse".'[14]

The most recent Jewish version of the idea, as far as I am aware, is by an Israeli – Joseph Eidelberg. Eidelberg's book, *The Japanese and the Ten Tribes of Israel* (Givatayim, 1980), compares the historical accounts of the Hebrew Bible with Japanese dynastic histories and concludes that Japanese history suggests to him that there are similarities between Hebrew and Japanese and that the Taika reforms of 645 (thought by all serious historians to be the result of Chinese T'ang influence) in fact 'bear a striking resemblance to the Hebrew laws of the Old Testament and particularly to the body of laws set forth in the Book of Deuteronomy'.[15]

A quite common view, known as the 'reverse theory of common origin' (reminiscent of similar theories with respect to India), has it that Moses did not receive the Torah at Mount Sinai but travelled to Japan, where he was instructed in the Shinto faith which he brought back in a modified form to the people of Israel.[16]

Israelite theories have had a really striking impact on Japanese society and no doubt have contributed to the totally bizarre Jewish discourse in Japan. The general perspective on Jews is more or less anti-Semitic but intensely vague. For instance the definition of the word 'Jew' in Sanseido's *New Crown English-Japanese Dictionary* (Tokyo, 1964) is as follows: 'Jews covet money – consequently there are many Jewish millionaires. The word can be used in lieu of the following: "avaricious", "miser" and "rich".' Jewish conspiracy theories based largely on Western anti-Semitic ideas are rife and books peddling such ideas have achieved staggering sales. These days many Japanese bookstores have what they call a 'Jewish corner', where titles such as *The Jewish Plot to Control the World, The Secret of Jewish Power that Moves the World*, and so on, are displayed.[17] This interest in Jews has been present in Japan for years. In 1970 a book entitled *Nihonjin to Yudayajin* – The Japanese and the Jews – won one of Japan's most coveted literary prizes and sold well over a million copies (by 1987 it had sold three million copies). Sales of a similar order have since been achieved by *If You*

Understand Judea you understand Japan; *The Jewish Way of Blowing a Millionaire's Bugle*; *If You Understand the Jews You Understand the World: 1990 Scenario for the Final Economic War*; *Miracles of the Torah which Controls the World* and others besides.[18] The mass media frequently carry sensational stories along the same lines. A more general Japanese interest in things Jewish or Israeli is quite apparent. From the amazing popularity of *The Diary of Anne Frank* to the unprecedented commercial success of the musical *Fiddler on the Roof*, a Jewish seam appears to run through Japanese society. There is a large literature in Japanese devoted to the kibbutz and there is even a Japanese Kibbutz Association, some 30,000 strong, which was founded in 1963 by Tezuka Nobuyoshi and has established a kibbutz in Akan, Eastern Hokkaido.[19] The fascination with Israel and Jews seems endless. When I was in Japan in the 1980s I was shown a letter that seemed typical from a man from Yamato City in the Kanagawa prefecture. The letter concluded, 'I am afraid of the God of Abraham. I am sure that only the God of Abraham is God. I think that Jews are lucky because they are descendants of Abraham. I heard that anti-Messiah may come out of the tribe of Dan. I want to know the reason. Would you tell me the reason? Sixty yen stamp is put on this letter.'[20] The combination of fear, admiration and even envy is palpable.

After the Second World War it was already evident that there was a keen interest in Judaism in Japan. At the time there was a growing proselytising trend in Israel and the United States which led to 'outreach' activity being initiated in Japan. Since the 1920s Jacques Faitlovitch, the 'father' of the Falashas of Ethiopia,[21] had been interested in the possibilities presented for Jewish missionary endeavour in Japan. In 1954 Faitlovitch set off in order to set up a Jewish 'outreach' centre.[22] Behind this move lurked the sense that the Japanese were thinking of converting to Judaism *en masse*. This entire discourse of imagining the Japanese into an Israelite mould, including the Jewish desire to convert the Japanese, derives ultimately from the Christian missions.

In Japan today perhaps the most apparent legacy of the ideas of the Scottish missionary McLeod is to be found in the Makuya and Beit Shalom sects.[23] Although both of them are essentially Christian sects accepting the divinity of Christ, their 'Jewishness' is very visible. Over the years thousands of Makuya have gone to Israel where many of them have learned Hebrew: indeed just a few days before writing these lines, as I waited in queue at Lod International Airport, I encountered a large group of Makuya students wearing *happi* coats with the Jewish menorah emblazoned upon them and carrying Israeli flags. They were delighted to be able to converse in Hebrew. Indeed, as I discovered in the 1980s, it is possible to travel throughout Japan and find Hebrew-speaking members of the movement, which is now 60,000 strong, in most of the major towns. I am told this is even more true today. The importance of a good knowledge of Hebrew for the Makuya can be judged by the fact that they have brought out a beautifully produced Japanese–Hebrew dictionary, the first ever.

Whenever the Makuya get together they sing secular and religious Hebrew songs, many of them the songs of modern Israel. They adopt Hebrew names, observe the Sabbath and keep a form of Kashrut: they light candles on Friday evening, break *hallah* and read from the Jewish prayer book – the siddur. Their view of the world is informed by a profound admiration for Israel and the Jewish people. This love for Israel often finds practical expression: a Makuya volunteer was wounded in the 1967 war and in the wake of the Israeli victory a Makuya 'pilgrimage' marched through Jerusalem carrying a banner proclaiming 'congratulations on the Greater Jerusalem'. To some extent their admiration for Jews derives from the Christian part of their ideology. But, in addition, it springs from the national nature of Judaism – the idea that it is the religion of the Jewish people, and from Zionism.[24] The Makuya are intensely nationalistic and, in some ways, are looking towards the redemption of the Japanese nation, which will be modelled upon the redemption of Israel.

Makuya was founded – as they stress – at about the same time as the State of Israel.[25] The founder of Makuya, Abraham Ikuro Teshima (1910–73) met Martin Buber, the Jewish philosopher, on a number of occasions. According to Teshima's account Buber told him, 'The religion of the Bible not only saves individuals but also redeems whole nations: it has never been an individualist religion. If ever the Japanese mind is poisoned by so-called Western Christianity, which lays its basis on the individual's expression of faith, then I am afraid that the Japanese nation will collapse. God's concern is with the redemption of people.' Teshima's fear was that the Japanese, unlike the Jews, who never lost their sense of being the people of Israel, had begun to view themselves increasingly as individuals. Teshima argued, 'In post-war Japan, individualism and egoism, resulting from the prevailing, misinterpreted ideas of democracy, are gnawing at all aspects of national life ... What has made Japan such a pitiful country? It is the result of the wrong school education under the control of the communistic *Nikkyoso* (Japanese Schoolteachers' Union) which regards patriotism as the residue of the pre-war indoctrination of militaristic totalitarianism and hence shuns teaching "the pride of a nation" such as expounded in the Bible.' Whereas Teshima felt that because the Jews had the Bible, they could bring about what he regarded as the greatest miracle of the twentieth century – the re-establishment of the Jewish State.[26]

With the death of Makuya's founder the spiritual guidance of the movement fell to Dr Akiva Jindo. When I met Jindo in Tokyo he was an engaging man with a quick smile. He entered the room quietly, bowed deeply, and shook hands with me very firmly, in the manner of evangelical Christians. His own background was not unlike other Japanese Lost Tribes enthusiasts of an earlier generation, such as Oyabe Zen'ichiro and Kawamorita Eiji. After completing his Japanese high school, Jindo had gone to study in the United States. He had been awarded a scholarship at Swarthmore College, Pennsylvania, a Quaker foundation, where he studied chemistry. He then did a doctorate at the University of California at Berkeley. During one summer vacation he was invited to attend a Makuya meeting in Tokyo. During the prayer-meeting the founder of the movement, Teshima, now an old man, was approached by a stream of sick and crippled people. 'The professor', in Jindo's words, 'grabbed a polio child by the limp legs and stared up to heaven with eyes closed. During that breath-taking moment all eyes were on him. And, look! The crooked legs became straight. The power had entered into the numb legs and hands. And then a blind man was restored his sight. After each miracle hand-clapping burst from the audience and the voice of prayer became more intense.' Immediately Jindo became an enthusiastic member of Makuya. After completing his doctoral work he started working in the research division of the Hitachi Company. But his real interests lay with Makuya and, when Hitachi refused to give him leave to join the seventh Makuya 'pilgrimage' to Israel, to the consternation of friends and family he decided to do something that is quite unheard of in Japan – quit the company.

Jindo and I sat cross-legged on the *tatami* mats around a low table. As tea and rice cakes were served by a young Hebrew-speaking and kimono-clad Japanese woman, I asked him why there was no cross in the building, whereas it was full of Jewish emblems. Gently he replied, 'Makuya is a Japanese Jewish religion. Most of our members were formerly Buddhist or Shinto and now they have become firm believers in the God of the Bible. But we are not following a Western religion and we do not need Western symbols. For us the cross is associated with "Western" Christianity. We feel that we are members of a Jewish faith, but we still retain our Japanese customs. We go to the Buddhist temple to visit the graves of our ancestors and parents and for national reasons. Like the Zen master we meditate upon the *tatami* mat . . . So, you see, we Japanese Makuya are interested in our Jewish roots. Through the line of the tribe of Zebulun we *are* Jewish. And that means that we are passionately interested in Israel and support the State as much as we can . . . Our Japanese background is part of our Jewishness because our culture owes a lot to Judaism. The structure of the Shinto shrine, for example, is very much like the structure of the Second Temple. Shinto also has the idea of the invisible godhead. And once a year the Emperor, dressed in white garments, went into the Holy of Holies, in his capacity as high priest, and asked forgiveness for the sins of his people. Very much like the Day of Atonement. As you know, there are various theories about the origin of the Japanese people. It is said that some came from the south-east Asian islands and some from northern Asia. But the most important element, we believe, consisted of groups of Semitic people, particularly the tribe of Hada, whose origins are directly traceable to the land of Israel. Their original worship was the religion of Israel. There are traces of their ancient Hebrew songs in a number of folk songs sung in Japan to this day. In the area of the great Shinto shrine of Ise people sing a song called Ise Ondo.' He sang some unintelligible words. 'It's the song of Miriam from Exodus 15. Can't you recognise it?' he asked excitedly. I had to confess that I could not. 'It was brought to Japan by the tribe of Hada, and their descendants have kept the tradition for around 1,500 years.' Jindo talked earnestly for some time about the tribe of Hada.

According to his version of Japan's early history this tribe was to be identified with the Lost Tribe of Zebulun. The family crests of the Hada tribe showed sailboats similar to depictions found at archaeological sites in Israel. The Hada brought with them the knowledge of silk weaving and they soon became the industrial leaders of the country, while their sound financial instincts enabled them to serve the Imperial Court as economic advisers. Zebulun/Hada called their god Ogami or Yahada (which Jindo explained as the god of Hada) and their faith was gradually taken over by Japan's warrior class – the Samurai. The fact that their god Yahada was adopted by the royal family suggested a special relationship between the Jews and the royal family. Jindo explained that one member, Prince Mikasa, had made a detailed study of the gold mirror that forms part of the royal regalia of the imperial family. According to Japanese legend the sun goddess Amaterasu Omikami had been frightened by her brother Susano No Mikoto and had taken shelter in a cave, thereby plunging the world into total darkness. In order to entice the sun goddess out of the cave, the god Amano Koyane No Mikoto hung a golden mirror encrusted with gems outside the goddess's hiding place and started to recite a specially composed prayer. Amaterasu finally emerged and light was returned to the world. 'When Mikasa examined the mirror,' said Jindo solemnly, 'he found a Hebrew letter in each corner which together make up the divine name of Jehovah . . . If you look closely at the features of the imperial family, you can see that they look quite different from the ordinary Japanese. The late Premier of Japan, Prince Ayamaro Konoe, looked exactly like a European Jew and the same can be said of Prince Mikasa. It is quite likely that the royal family themselves are descended from the Lost Tribe of Zebulun!'[27]

The book to which Jindo referred was entitled *The Ancient Jewish Diaspora in Japan: the Tribe of Hada – Their Religious and Cultural Influence* (Tokyo, 1976), by Ikuro Teshima. Glancing through the book I noticed a photograph of the Great Wall of China captioned, 'Architectural masterpiece by the hands of the Jewish Diaspora.' It is possible that at this point my face started to betray signs of scepticism. In any event Jindo stopped smiling and rather abruptly turned on a video of a Makuya conference which had been held the year before on the higher slopes of Mount Myoko. It was extraordinary.

The first part of the film showed Makuya members, some of them in their teens, undergoing *hiwatari*: the ritual of walking barefoot over beds of burning coals. 'This,' said Jindo, 'is one of the Japanese sides of our faith. It comes from Buddhism, of course. It is the expression of our total dedication to the God of the Bible. Of course, those who believe they will not get burned, by the power of faith do not get burned.' The young initiates approached the fire fearfully; many of them completed the ordeal sobbing with pain. Obviously they had not believed enough. There were others who crossed in a sort of ecstasy, smiling and singing Hebrew *Palmach* songs from the Israeli War of Independence as they kept their eyes fixed on a giant menorah, which had been placed on a prominent mount near the site of *hiwatari*. I felt sure that the Israelites of old would have felt comfortable here on this high place with the smell of burning flesh in their nostrils. 'Does this not remind you of the story of my namesake Rabbi Akiva?' asked Jindo. 'When he was being tortured to death by Roman soldiers he started to laugh. When they asked him what he was laughing about, he replied that he had never fully understood what it meant "to love God with all your heart and with all your soul", but now that he was able to praise God even during this torture he finally understood the biblical text.' Jindo explained the reason the Makuya were singing *Palmach* songs during their ordeal was because *hiwatari* was testing their mettle as 'soldiers of Israel'.

Later in the film, crowds of Makuya could be seen whirling in ecstasy, carrying velvet-covered Torah scrolls high above their heads in imitation of the Jewish feast of *Simhat* Torah, which marks the completion of the year's synagogue reading of the Pentateuch. The scrolls had been donated to the Makuya by the Israeli Egged bus company after four hundred Makuya members had toured Israel in Egged buses. This part of the ceremony, Jindo told me, was called *Simhat* Makuya. The film went on to show Makuya members saying fervent Hebrew prayers standing under freezing waterfalls, following the Japanese tradition of *misogi*, the spiritual exercise of waterfall purification.

Some time later I accompanied Jindo to a Makuya prayer meeting. Behind the podium the entire wall was covered by the white background and red sun of the Japanese national flag. To my right Jindo whispered to me, 'You know that Japan is called the "Land of the Rising Sun", which is the meaning of the word *nihon*. But for us the word has another meaning: the Hebrew root *nahah* means to follow, and the word *hon* in Japanese means book, so the word *nihon* means the followers of the book, which is to say the Jews. So the flag of Japan is also the flag of Makuya.' The speaker led the Makuya in prayer and then read, first in Hebrew and then in Japanese, from Psalm 137, 'By the rivers of Babylon, there we sat down, yea, we wept, when we remembered Zion.' In the background a Yamaha organ softly played 'Jerusalem the Golden', a popular song associated with the Six Day War and around me, the men and women of Makuya, the exiled tribe of Zebulun, the spiritual children of a Scottish missionary called Norman McLeod (formerly a worker in the herring industry) wept in longing for their lost land.

Chapter Eleven

AFRICA: ABRAHAM'S SEED

At this day also . . . there inhabiteth a most populous nation of the Jewish stock under a mightie king.

John Pory, 1600

In the study of my summer home in the Languedoc I have a nineteenth century print of a 'savage'. Its lips are thick and protruding, its forehead meagre, its hairy body naked but for the animal skin hung round its neck. Its skin is distinctly dusky, perhaps black. Its toes are furrily prehensile and its legs have a goat-like hairiness. Although there is no real suggestion of a sexual organ of any sort, the belly hair is profuse and somehow ominous. It is human, sure enough, because it carries a crudely wrought axe. But the fearful glance over its shoulder towards the open spaces, as he (it clearly is a male although I have hitherto unconsciously used the pronoun 'it') turns into an area of forests and caverns, suggests clearly that this is a creature of the forest – a savage. This print portrays the weight of the word 'savage' as it hung in the imagination of the nineteenth century and it incorporates much of the word's range, as well as its etymology. It has interested me not least because one is aware that such a depiction in prose or art today would be unlikely, politically incorrect, contrary to the Zeitgeist. For much of the last century, at least, we were aware that the savage is somehow within us and not just a crude caricature of the 'other', or more genuinely, not just the 'other' itself. So when George Santayana writes in *Dialogues in Limbo*, 'the young man who has not wept is a savage', we instinctively approve. The evolution of the word and what it signifies, in the English language at least, is instructive: a sense in the seventeenth century that the natural savage state of freedom as Dryden put it, 'when wild in woods the noble savage ran', was desirable gives way by the nineteenth to a meaning close to the antithesis of civilised.

The notion that someone not sharing your own cultural and ethnic attributes is by definition 'barbaric' or 'savage' is hardly recent. In ancient Mesopotamia the divide essentially followed urban–nomad lines. For people living in lower Mesopotamia, it was the tent-dwelling, raw-flesh-eating, ungodly nomad from the semi-desert who epitomised the savage. People from the Zagros Mountains were also, but less emblematically, considered to be savages and there is a reference to mountain dwellers' language as the 'twittering of birds'.[1] Greek and Greco-Roman civilisations dismissed outsiders as 'barbarians', which term is also said to derive from the cacophony of birds as opposed to the speech of civilised humanity. 'Savagery' as a close synonym of 'barbarian' has a similarly bucolic etymology and is connected with the closed and unknown world of the forests, the world of the savage who hangs on my wall. The first European impressions of the languages of southern Africa were expressed in similar terms. In 1614 John Milward claimed that the language of the Hottentots was 'a chattering rather than a language'; in 1649 Jean-Baptiste Tavernier wrote, 'when they speak they fart with their tongues in their mouths'.[2]

These antecedents suggest that the borders between the civilised 'I' and the savage or barbarian 'other' were initially drawn at the limits of the known world. The town dweller knows nothing of the desert. The plainsman is ignorant of the mountains and forests. A few years after John Milward was writing, John Milton dismissed the riches of the great Persian and Indian courts as no more than 'barbaric Pearl; and Gold'. Such magnificence was quite simply beyond his Puritan ken.[3] This dialectic of 'self' and 'other' has required constant modification. With the rise of universal ideological systems such as Christianity, traditional ways of understanding the 'other' were faced with a particularly vexatious challenge. How could the 'other' be a true savage if he too were a child of God? In *The Universal Prayer* Alexander Pope noted, 'Father of all! In every age, in ev'ry clime adored, by saint, by savage, and by sage, Jehovah, Jove or Lord.' The origin of the word cretin exemplifies the problem: the Swiss used the word to describe the hopelessly degenerate and loathsome creatures that lived beyond and above their valley systems. Notwithstanding their utter marginality they were nonetheless Christians (*crétins*). But still, as Chaudhuri perceptively remarks, the dialectic of barbarian versus civilised came to the fore in Europe at the time of the Reformation as a useful concept in the war of abuse between Catholic and Protestant.[4] This ever-changing dialectic of 'us' and 'them' takes on a particular pungency in the attempt to incorporate parts of the savage world into the sacred history of Christendom.

It has already been remarked that the confrontation of particularly isolated societies with the modern world gave rise to certain tensions and confusions, and this was nowhere more true than in Africa. Europeans' views of Africans and their way of life, their religions and social mores were to have a profound impact upon the development of the African continent. Further confusion was to be generated by the amalgamation of traditional African and European or modern elements. These processes may be seen to have started from the outset of colonial intervention. One of the key areas of confusion was religion.

From mediaeval times until at least the seventeenth century the general assumption in Europe had been that there were four main world religions: Christianity, Islam, Judaism and Paganism.[5] In time the great text-based, priestly religions of India, Japan and China could be approximately accommodated into an extension of this scheme of things, as the parallels between them and the religions of the Judeo-Christian-Islamic tradition were so evident. Such religions may have been explained via Judaic models, and often were, but they were perceived as actual religions. The problem arose with the unknown religious systems of Africa, parts of the Americas or Australia where such evident parallels did not seem to exist. What happened in the case of Africa in the realm of religion was reflected elsewhere in the 'savage' world.

The 'savage' religious and philosophical systems of Africa were simply incomprehensible to the colonists, missionaries and others who observed them. They were beyond the limits of the known world and far beyond the limits of their own experience and imagination. As they were incomprehensible they were sometimes hardly perceived to exist at all. In the context of the Cape, which from the seventeenth century on was a relatively well-known part of Africa, the culture of the indigenous peoples was regularly described in negative terms: they had no laws, language, reason or religion. In 1634 one traveller noted that they are 'without any Religion, Lawe, Arte or Civility that we could see'.[6] This view remained more or less standard, at least for many Western travellers and, in white racist enclaves in southern Africa and elsewhere, is no doubt still cherished today.

The acute sense of difference traditionally felt by Europeans with respect to Africans may in part be explained by the fact that until the second half of the nineteenth century little was known of the great majority of the African interior, or indeed of swathes of the coastal area. A critical feature of Africans was, of course, that they were black, supposedly quite the opposite of white. Similar suppositions were made of black people as were made at much the same time of American Indians.[7] Were they really human? In 1520 the Swiss medical writer Paracelsus had argued that the black race was of a quite different origin. By the second half of the eighteenth century a full-scale debate emerged between monogenists, who claimed a common origin for the whole of humanity, and polygenists, who argued that Negroes were quite simply members of a radically different species.[8] Eventually the idea emerged that the Negroes were a separate species more or less intermediate between Europeans and the 'oran-outangs'.[9]

For centuries Europeans had lived in ignorance of Africa. In early mediaeval times the entire Eastern world beyond Islam was more or less unknown and from the time of the Muslim conquest of Egypt in 641, Africa and the Indian Ocean were effectively removed from the European sphere. Even in classical times Africa had been insulated from Greek, Roman and Egyptian influence by natural barriers. In time Muslims and particularly Arabs acquired a good deal of information about the African coasts, and no doubt more than we suspect of the interior, but Europeans had almost none. Even by the time of the Renaissance the Dark Continent was little more than a concept: parts of the littoral were known but the interior was a void which cartographers could decorate according to their fancy. Thus Swift's famous lines:

> So Geographers, in Afric maps,
> With savage-pictures fill their gaps;
> And o'er unhabitable downs
> Place elephants for want of towns.

Well into the Renaissance the main sources of information on Africa remained classical texts. Manuscripts and early printed versions of Ptolemy's *Geography*, whether in the original Greek or in Latin translation, normally reproduced four maps of (northern) Africa which illustrates how pre-Renaissance European knowledge about the continent was limited to the Mediterranean coast and the lower Nile. For mediaeval Europe the Bible and the classical texts, chiefly Homer,

Herodotus, Pliny and Ptolemy, were the principal sources of information on Africa. In book one of the *Odyssey* Homer had distinguished between two Ethiopias, one in the east and one in the west, at opposite ends of the earth. Aeschylus considered that eastern Ethiopia stretched as far as India, and this confusion was to continue until the mediaeval period. Such a polarised Africa was in time taken to represent the 'admirable Ethiopia' of the Nubian-Meroitic civilisation on the one hand, and the savage regions of sub-Sahara on the other. For Herodotus the men of Meroe were 'the tallest and most handsome in the world', whereas the sub-Saharan Negro population were 'dog-faced creatures and beasts without heads'.[10]

This division fed into a mediaeval discourse as alive in Islam as it was in Christendon, in which all sorts of expectations were centred on the *bon éthiopien.* Africa continued to be seen both as a terrestrial hell, and beyond the Mountains of the Moon described by Diogenes, a terrestrial paradise. There was some biblical support for these essentially classical ideas. The Nile was often taken to be the Gihon, one of the four rivers of Paradise, described in Genesis as the river 'which flows around the whole land of Cush, where there is gold, and the gold of that land is good' (the other three were the Pison, the Hiddekel and the Euphrates). Many fifteenth-century maps include the river Gihon, '*qui descendit de montibus paradisi*', and Paradise is often presented, as it is on the Munich portolan of 1502, as a walled mountain-top town in Africa. As against the African paradise there was the other Ethiopia – the successor to the terrestrial hell: the Africa of cannibalism and the slave trade, of unbearable heat and decimating disease, of foetid swamp and jungle – the white man's grave, the heart of darkness, what D. H. Lawrence called 'the continent of dark negation'. This ambiguous view achieved striking iconographic form in the famous Hereford *Mappa Mundi*, probably drawn by Richard de Bello in 1289. The map represents a symbolic world with Jerusalem at the centre, Paradise at the top, and damned souls being dismissed from the seat of judgement to join the bestial figures, which are trooping towards a crescent-shaped Africa that borders the edge of a flat, round world. Africa is divided roughly by an elongated Atlas range: on one side of it there are illustrations of biblical and classical stories and pious depictions of the lives of the saints; on the other side are deformed savages. Some have ocular irregularities, like the four-eyed maritime Ethiopians, or the Blemyes with eyes in their breasts, or the one-eyed panther-eating king of Ethiopia; then we see hermaphrodites, snake-eating troglodytes and humanoid creatures with mouths so small they are condemned to suck their food through straws. In short, the known side of Africa was more or less an extension of Christendom; the unknown the epitome of savagery, of barbarism.

The literature produced by the colonisation and exploration of Africa maintained this polarity of perception to a remarkable degree. J. C. Prichard, the eminent English ethnologist of the first half of the nineteenth century, maintained that the African 'races' with the most pronounced 'Negroid' traits, 'deformed countenances, projecting jaws, flat foreheads', were the most 'savage and morally degraded' of the African peoples. On the other hand those tribes with a 'nearly European countenance and a corresponding configuration of the head' were the most civilised and therefore the closest to Europeans.[11] In the course of the nineteenth century a myth known as the Hamitic hypothesis developed into the conventional wisdom of the time. This myth maintained that light-skinned peoples of Egyptian or Indo-European origin had in times past spread across Africa, where they still formed an elite in many societies. As they gradually interbred with subject peoples they themselves degenerated. This was the explanation put forward for the apparent decline of a number of African societies from Yorubaland to Benin or Great Zimbabwe. The view persisted well into the twentieth century. Its most forceful proponent was the British anthropologist Charles Seligman, whose widely admired and hugely influential *Races of Africa* (London, 1930) stated categorically that 'the civilisations of Africa are the civilisations of the Hamites'.[12] Such views were echoed by a number of Germans, notably Leo Frobenius, who was convinced that the Yoruba, for instance, came from Atlantis.

Let us now return to our Israelites. In mediaeval times, as we have seen, there was the notion that somewhere in Africa Jewish kingdoms were to be found. Eldad's famous book fed into this, as did countless other sources including Mandeville, who explored the parallel idea that a Christian kingdom existed, connected with the Lost Tribes as well as the Pygmies and the Amazonians. It stretched from East Africa to the Indus and across Africa as far as the Atlantic Ocean, and was ruled over by Prester John.[12] During the fifteenth century, under the influence of Prince Henry the Navigator (1394–1460), Portuguese seamen had been venturing down the West African coast until in 1487 Bartholomew Diaz was blown round the southern tip of Africa, holding out hopes of a sea-route to India, which was accomplished by Vasco da Gama in

1497–9. Until the Portuguese voyages of exploration brought the African coast within the European sphere Arab travellers, as we have seen, had much greater contact with Africa than did Europeans, producing works of geography and history that revealed some of the continent's mysteries. In the tenth century Abu'l Hassan al-Masudi noted that the mid-point of what is today Mozambique was the limit of Arab navigation at the time, and in about 1030 the polymath Abu Rayhan al-Biruni confirmed this. Further information was given by al-Idrisi in the twelfth century, followed by Abd al-Munim al-Himyari in the fifteenth.[13] Nonetheless, for the Arabs the distinction between the civilised races (such as themselves) and peoples such as those to be found in the interior of Africa – the despised *Zanj* – was clear as day. Ibn Khaldun observed of such folk that they were 'closer to dumb animals than to rational beings'.[14]

For Renaissance Europe the best known of the Arab historians and geographers of Africa was Leo Africanus (*c.* 1492–*c.* 1550). He was born of Arab Muslim parents in Granada and was originally called Hassan ibn Muhammad al-Wazzân al-Zayyâtî. After the Spanish conquest of Granada in 1492, his wealthy family moved to Morocco, and the young Hassan travelled widely in Africa, visiting Timbuktu and the sub-Saharan empires of Mali and Bornu. Captured by Italian pirates off the North African coast on a return trip from Mecca in 1518, Hassan was compelled to convert to Christianity and was baptised at St Peter's in Rome on 6 January 1520 as Giovanni Leo Africanus. His most important work was the remarkable *Description of Africa*,[15] which was written around 1528–9 and which was for many years the only source on sub-Saharan Africa (he also wrote an Arabic grammar and a manual of Arabic rhetoric).[16] *Description of Africa* at once became an essential part of the rapidly expanding body of sixteenth-century European geographical knowledge. Translated in 1556 into both Latin and French, it went through a number of editions in several European languages. An English translation by John Pory appeared in 1600 which was read by Ben Jonson and probably by Shakespeare and John Webster.[17] In the book there are frequent mentions of Jews in Africa: he notes that once upon a time Jewish law was widely observed, that there were warrior tribes in the Atlas claiming descent from King David, that the Canaanites travelled to Africa followed later by the Sabeans and that the ruler of Timbuktu could not stand the sight of Jews.[18] As the major modern source on Africa it carried great authority. In a postscript to the English edition entitled, 'A summaried discourse of the manifold religions professed in Africa', John Pory noted, 'At this day also the Abassins affirm that upon the Nilus towards the west there inhabiteth a most populous nation of the Jewish stock under a mightie king. And some of our modern cosmographers set down a province in those quarters which they call the land of the Hebrews, placed as it were under the equinoctial, in certain unknown mountains, between the confines of Abassin and Congo.'[19]

John Ogilby (1600–76), the translator and publisher whose work ranged from translations of Homer to his series of books on geography, gave further information about Jews on the continent in his *Africa* (London, 1670). He noted of the coast of Guinea, 'Many Jews also are scattered over this region; some Natives, boasting themselves of Abraham's seed, inhabiting both sides of the River Niger: others are Asian strangers, who fled hither either from the desolation of Jerusalem by Vespasian or from Judea wasted and depopulated by the Romans, Persians, Saracens and Christians ...' And Ogilby also included the suggestion by Leo Africanus that Jews were to be found in the inland areas.[20] In J.C. Wyld's *Chart of the World* (London, 1820) there are still echoes of this: almost in the centre of Africa Wyld indicates the presence of 'Lamelins (Jews)'.

As Europeans got to know Africa better, it became clear that a number of African societies were more refined than had been suspected. There appeared to be, as classical sources had suggested, 'good' Africans and 'bad' Africans. In some cases it was apparent from the outset that a given society did indeed have a religion and a culture and that it was necessary to understand them. The tension between 'primitive', on the one hand and 'refined' on the other, created the need for an extraneous explication for sophisticated features of African society. One explanation was the idea that all savage races were derived from earlier and more sophisticated ones. Thus in the mid-nineteenth century Richard Whately noted that all 'savages are degenerated remnants of more civilised races'.[21] Sophie Dulucq has shown how the mantle of specific ancient societies was carefully and systematically placed on the shoulders of the more 'advanced' groups: the reference to antiquity often conferred nobility and was often applied to conquerors rather than to the conquered, to nomads rather than to sedentary peoples.

In a parallel development the attempt to comprehend led to African religious systems frequently being compared to the religions mentioned in the Bible and the assumption was often made that such and such religion was derived from an Israelite model, from the worship of Baal mentioned in the Bible, or from the religions of ancient Egypt (also mentioned in the Bible). In some cases other classical models were called upon.[24]

The discourse, which permitted traces of the Hebrew people, their language and their religion to be found in every corner of the African continent was no doubt aided by the rise of evangelical Christianity. The humanitarianism of the evangelicals had never accepted the polygenist view. As far as they were concerned, 'God that made the world ... hath made of one blood all nations of men' (Acts 17:24–6). The evangelical revivals were responsible for stimulating missionary work in Africa in the first place. Protestant missions – the London Missionary Society (founded in 1795, it tellingly changed its name to The Church Society for Africa and the East in 1812), the Church Missionary Society (1799), the Wesleyan Methodist Missionary Society (1813) and the American Board of Commissioners for Foreign Missions (1810) all plunged into the African mission field.[25] The British and Foreign Bible Society was originally brought into existence to provide bibles in Welsh. At its first meeting in 1804, however, the founders resolved to promote 'the most extensive circulation of the Holy Scriptures both at home and abroad'. Africa was soon to be flooded with bibles.[26] Had the interests of the Society been restricted to the spiritual needs of the Welsh the future history of Africa might have been quite different.

What did these evangelical missionaries to Africa themselves think about Jews and why did Jews figure so immanently in their discourse of otherness? One nineteenth-century missionary to Uganda, Harry Nevinson, demonstrated the extent to which there had been an internalisation of British-Israelite discourse.[27] He observed, 'The strictly biblical education produced ... the illusion that both the promises and the threatenings of the Jewish lawgivers and prophets were specially designed for ourselves by a foreseeing Power. We never doubted that we English Evangelicals were the Chosen People and when every Sunday evening we sang the *Magnificat*, "As He promised to our forefathers, Abraham and his seed for ever", we gave no thought to the Jews; and when soon afterwards, we sang in the *Nunc Dimittis*, "To be a light to lighten the Gentiles, and to be the glory of Thy people Israel", we meant the Missionary societies would spread the light of the Gospel to Negroes, Chinese and Indians, while God's English people retained the glory.'[28] French rationalism also contributed to a more humane view of African society. For the *philosophes* all men were capable of developing into fully rational human beings.

Once colonists started the long process of making sense of the African interior the literature which already existed started to filter into the European collective consciousness and 'Jewish' constructs started to play a remarkable role in the decipherment of the continent. Even though different circumstances prevailed in each area the use of an Israelite model seems to have penetrated just about every corner of Africa. As is well understood the construction of the 'other' is regularly a reflection of the self. What frequently happened in the missionary situation was to impose upon others – radically different others – an aspect of the imagined identity of self. Perhaps the more radically different the 'other' was, the more necessary this mechanism became.

I have already mentioned the remarkable Yoruba people of West Africa. Already in the 1820s the English explorer Captain Hugh Clapperton observed that the Yoruba were thought to be of Canaanite extraction.[29] By the end of the century a Yoruba Christian, the Reverend Samuel Johnson, pastor of Oyo, wrote a history of his people more or less absorbing the idea of an Eastern origin. Dispatched to a British missionary society in 1899 the manuscript was 'lost'. The author died in 1901 and it was not until 1921 after many vicissitudes that the work, edited by Johnson's brother, saw the light of day. Johnson imagined that the Yoruba had come from Mecca from the line of Lamurudu – a king of Mecca – which name was perhaps a corruption of Nimrod, 'the mighty hunter' of the Bible. In any event according to him there could not be 'the slightest doubt' that they came from the East.[30] The idea of an extraneous origin for the Yoruba persisted among Africans. In 1955 S. O. Biobaku claimed that they came from the ancient kingdom of Meroe and Emmanuel Ughulu claimed a Jewish origin for the Esan tribe.[31] In the case of the Peul people of West Africa all sorts of more directly 'Israelite' theories were advanced by early anthropologists: were they a Lost Tribe of Israel, or were they rather descended from the Egyptians? Or had a Roman legion gone astray in the Sahara?[32] According to French colonial historians the mediaeval West African empires of Songhai and Ghana were founded by among others Jewish migrants from the Near East. In addition the ruling dynasty in Ghana was thought to be of Jewish origin and the burial mounds in the Niger delta were supposed to have been built by Jews. In 1939 one French historian – Robin – observed that there was a group, also in the Niger delta, that was white and ruled over black people with the assistance of *You Houzou* – the name of a supernatural creature of phenomenal strength which Robin construed to mean 'Jew'.[33]

One of the mechanisms in the colonial context that was productive of an imagined Israelite identity, as we have seen elsewhere in the case of the Karen or the Ch'iang, was the selection of a particular group supposed to have superior qualities and to have originated outside Africa. One such group was the Ashanti. By the British they were variously described as virile, courageous, patriotic, organised, constant, in short 'the most civil and well-bred people . . . in Africa'.[34] Friedrich Ratzel enthusiastically endorsed this view, 'in the judgment of Europeans they are among the best breeds of Guinea – intelligent, industrious and courageous'.[35] They were supposed therefore to be from elsewhere. Even though the Ashanti themselves made every effort to 'record their origin as being from Ashanti proper', Captain R. Sutherland Rattray, who had spent twenty years in West Africa and was 'without question the leading authority on all matters pertaining to the Ashanti', opined, 'I feel sure that they came from the North or North-West', adding somewhat lamely, 'they do not know this themselves'.[36] One of the first Europeans to spend much time with the Ashanti was Thomas Edward Bowdich (1791–1824) whose *Mission from Cape Coast Castle to Ashantee* was published in 1819 and formed part of the new descriptive literature, which included Sir Richard Burton on Dahomey (now Benin) and Eugène Casalis on the Sotho. Noting the 'Grecian features' and 'aquiline' faces of the Ashanti, Bowdich went on to write *Essay on the Superstitions, Customs and Acts Common to the ancient Egyptians, Abyssinians and Ashantees* (Paris, 1821), in which he argued that the Ashanti people derived from 'the civilised Ethiopians of Herodotus'.[37] The explorer Sir Henry Stanley (1841–1904), while working for the *New York Herald*, observed a striking similarity between an Ashanti stool and the depiction of a stool he had seen in Thebes in Egypt. Impressed by the workmanship of the said stool, he went on to enthuse about the excellence of Ashanti sandals, 'Sandals! At the very repetition of the word one's thoughts revert to the inhabitants of Egypt, Syria and Asia Minor.'[38] Anything fine in African culture regularly elicited the reaction that it must be from somewhere else – and the usual locus was Palestine or the Middle East. The so-called Benin bronzes were regularly attributed to lost Israelites, Egyptians or the men of Atlantis and many other African artistic traditions were explained away as deriving from the art of ancient Egypt.[39]

A full-blooded Israelite theory with respect to the Ashanti was presented in a detailed study published in 1930 by Joseph J. Williams, a Jesuit member of the Royal Geographical Society and the American Geographical Society, who found traces of Hebrew in the Ashanti language, 'not a few Hebrew words and possible certain distinctive Hebrew constructions have been grafted on the native languages of the Ashanti'. He took the name Ashanti to mean the sons of Ashan, which he declared to be a city in Judea. Jewish customs, too, were found aplenty in Ashanti rituals, from marriage rites to purification ceremonies and menstrual seclusion. He found 'certain cultural elements common to the Ashanti and the ancient Hebrews, such as the Ob cult, religious dances, use of "Amen", vowel value ... endogamy, cross-cousin marriages, familial names, exogamy'. Then there was the similarity between the 'Supreme Being' of the Ashanti and the Hebrew Deity and, remarkably, 'the survival of what has every appearance of being the breastplate and *misnefet* of the High Priest', complete with the insignia of the Lost Twelve Tribes of Israel. Finally Williams drew a somewhat desperate comparison between the famous golden stool of the Ashanti and the 'chair of Moses' in the synagogue in Kaifeng.[40] He reaches the final conclusion that 'the Supreme Being not only of the Ashanti and allied tribes, but most probably of the whole of Negro Land as well, is not the God of the Christians which, at a comparatively recent date, was superimposed on the various tribal beliefs by ministers of the Gospel: but the Yahweh of the Hebrews, and that too of the Hebrews of pre-exilic times.'[41]

In the Great Lakes area of East Africa there was a long-running discourse which placed the origin of some of the indigenous population outside the locus of the lakes and within some imagined biblical or quasi-biblical framework. With respect to Uganda Herman Norden noted that there was an ancient lineage of thirty-three kings 'that traces back to King David. It is a proud history. The legends tell of the Uganda people crossing the Nile centuries upon centuries ago and subduing all tribes whose country they traversed. They claim the highest native civilisation in Africa.'[42] Sir Harry Johnston, the first British administrator of the Uganda Protectorate, and one of the great proponents of the Hamitic myth, thought that Phoenecians or Canaanites had crossed into Africa at some time (here following Leo Africanus), mingled with Ethiopians and descended into East Africa.[43] In Uganda missionaries soon added to this discourse. One Church Missionary Society worker saw the religion practised in the kingdom of Buganda as a 'mixture of Gnosticism and ancient Egyptianism'.[44] The Jewish people soon entered the consciousness of the indigenous population via the missionaries. Another CMS missionary mentioned that at the Ganda court the idea was propagated that 'Jesus Christ was a Jew ... [and] we Europeans did not follow one of our race, we looked for the truth where it was to be found and we found it among the Jews'. In the confusing circumstances of the early colonial period in Uganda, with so many competing systems and ideologies, truth was at a premium. By the 1890s yet another CMS missionary observed that 'the customs and manners of the Jews' were of 'the greatest interest' in Uganda. Within a few years one of the most remarkable Ugandans of his generation, Samei Kakungulu or Kakunguru, who had come to fame as a talented military leader on the British side against the Muslims, had decided to be circumcised. By this time he was powerful in the land, having been rewarded by the colonial authorities with a post as a semi-autonomous administrator in a large area centred on Mbale in the eastern part of the country, although he was later suspected of trying to make himself *kabakai*, or king. In 1920 he declared of himself and his followers, 'We will be known as the Jews' and in 1922 published a book which was essentially a guide to Judaism.[45] He died a Jew (albeit one with some residual belief in Jesus) and, despite persecution under Idi Amin, his followers in Mbale, known as the Bayudaya, have maintained their Jewish practices and are now some six hundred strong. While not claiming any Israelite ancestry for themselves, the Bayudaya are some of the best known of the African Judaising communities. I visited them in 1996 with an Orthodox Jewish friend when they observed their own kind of unofficial Judaism.[46] He found no difference between their mode of practice and that which he was used to in his London synagogue. In August 2001 two formal conversions to halakhic Judaism were carried out in the community and a mass conversion took place there in February 2002, conducted by four Conservative rabbis from the United States and one from Israel.

★

Many indigenous African peoples simply reminded Europeans of Jews or some other Middle Eastern people physically. Sidney Mendelssohn, a Jewish mining magnate in South Africa, observed on one occasion that when he looked at a crowd of black men at the mines certain faces stood out as being so indubitably 'Jewish' that he was tempted to greet them as brothers in this foreign land.[47] Writing of Ankole, south-east of Lake Albert, T. Broadway Johnson observed:

> The Banyankole, as the people of Ankole are called are an exceedingly interesting race, the purest, least mixed branch of the great Baima stock which constitutes the ruling caste in all the kingdoms around. In figure they are tall and lithe, and their long thin faces, with a very Jewish nose and lips, suggest a Semitic origin and strongly mark off their features from the bullet head, flat nose and thick lips of their neighbours . . . Captain Speke, who was the first European to travel among them, reasonably assumes from their own traditions and his own wider observations, that the whole race are closely allied to the pastoral Gallas, who came from Abyssinia. Centuries perhaps before the Christian era, some roving Asiatic race with long-horned cattle came streaming in from Arabia on the east and Palestine on the north and settled themselves in the mountain fastnesses of Abyssinia. Mixing with the agricultural Hamitic Negroes dwelling there, they still retained their Semitic features, their pastoral habits, and their fine breed of cattle . . . the race by their greater forcefulness and pride, subjugated people in their path and though aliens and few in number became . . . the ruling caste.[48]

Among the neighbouring Tutsis we find one of the most dramatic and topical examples of the phenomenon of an imagined Semitic and Israelite identity. The first explorers to reach the area of Rwanda and Burundi were immediately struck by the differences between what they saw as three groups: the Hutus, the Tutsis and the Twa. These groups shared the same territory, spoke the same language and sometimes intermarried. However they appeared to look different. The Twa – a tiny minority – were pygmies who were hunter-gatherers in the forests or else acted as menial servants at court and elsewhere. The Hutu – the vast majority – were peasants who tilled the soil. The Tutsis were perceived as being quite different: they were 'tall and thin and often displayed sharp, angular facial features' and were cattle-herders. As we have seen, the explorer John Hanning Speke (1827–64), who had gone with Burton to search for the equatorial lakes of Africa, had laid some of the groundwork for an explanation of these differences with his theory that ruling groups in the interlacustrine kingdoms had come from a 'superior' civilisation in the north. In *Journal of the Discovery of the Source of the Nile* (London, 1863) Speke connected them with the Galla of southern Ethiopia. The idea that the Tutsis and similar groups in the area were quite superior to others stuck. In a Belgian colonial report of 1925 the Twa were described, in terms reminiscent of Herodotus, as having 'a monkey-like flat face and a huge nose, he is quite similar to the apes whom he chases in the forest'.[49] In another colonial report of the same year the Hutu were similarly disparaged, 'They are generally short and thick-set with a big head, a jovial expression, a wide nose and enormous lips. They are extroverts who like to laugh and lead a simple life.' But according to the same report the Tutsi was something else again, 'he has nothing of the Negro, apart from his colour . . . his features are very fine . . . gifted with a vivacious intelligence, the Tutsi displays a refinement of feeling which is rare among primitive peoples'.[50] In 1926 Mary Hastings Bradley spoke of the 'sophisticated' Tutsis, who had 'a precise theology' and a number of biblical-sounding stories. These, she explains, 'came down from the north with these tribes of pronounced Hamitic and Semitic origins'.[51] A Belgian missionary supposed that the Tutsis' qualities must come from elsewhere, 'We can see Caucasian skulls and beautiful Greek profiles side by side with Semitic and even Jewish features, elegant golden-red beauties in the heart of Ruanda and Urundi.'[52] And in 1902 a French Catholic missionary enthused that their 'intelligent and delicate appearance, their love of money, their capacity to adapt to any situation seem to indicate a Semitic origin'.[53] The anti-Semitism embedded in this last remark – the Jews' love of money and their rootlessness – was a feature of the ministry of more than one Catholic priest in Rwanda and no doubt played a role in the horrors that were to engulf the region in the 1990s. After the Second World War the ferocity of the missions' anti-Semitism was appalling and there was, according to one account I have been given, widespread endorsement of the massacre of European Jewry.

Well before the war 'scientific' theories started to circulate suggesting that the Tutsi and also the Masai came 'from a primordial red race'. Some thought they came from India, a certain Dominican, Father Etienne Brosse, suggested they came from the garden of Eden, while others suggested that the Tutsis were survivors of the lost civilisation of Atlantis. In 1970 Paul del Perugia, a one-time French ambassador to Rwanda, suggested that the Tutsi were 'Magi' who had come from Tibet, some of them finishing up in Iceland. He believed the Tutsis were capable of seeing flying saucers, unlike the more primitive Hutu, and also found reason to include Nineveh, Noah and Babylon in his disquisition on Tutsi origins.[54]

Gérard Prunier points out that while this general discourse was 'semi-delirious', it was taken as serious science by the German and later Belgian colonial authorities, and subsequently came to have an impact upon the native population 'by inflating the Tutsi cultural ego inordinately and crushing Hutu feelings until they coalesced into an aggressively resentful inferiority complex'. The idea of a distant Tutsi origin was used by the Hutu against them. As one journalist has put it, 'Just like the Nazis, the Hutus were told it was their patriotic duty. The same intention existed – the complete elimination of the targeted group. The same words were used: "the final solution". The mistake that was made in earlier massacres – allowing thousands of Tutsis to escape to live in exile, plotting ways to come back – was not to be repeated.' Leon Mugesera, an influential member of the Habyarimana government said in 1992, 'The fatal mistake we made in 1959 was to let them [the Tutsis] get out. They belong in Ethiopia and we are going to find them a shortcut to get there by throwing them into the Nyabarongo River. I must insist on this point.'[55]

As I write many Tutsis, having absorbed such theories over the last century, are moving closer and closer to some sort of Israelite identity. In the wake of their terrible suffering during the genocide of 1994 the eyes of many of them fastened upon a distant hope: the idea that they were indeed Jews and as such could expect eventual redemption. In part this was because of the frequent comparisons that were made in the international media of their holocaust with that of the Jews.[56] On the website of Kulanu there is a piece that fits perfectly into the discourse described above by a certain Mel Laney, himself a blazing eccentric who has been trying to persuade the Egyptian authorities to 'rebuild' the Jewish Temple on the island of Elephantine in the Nile as a kind of centre of African Judaism. Laney writes of the Tutsis, 'These tall, muscular, highly intelligent, and arrogant warriors claim to be remnants of Israel ... The Banyamulenge of South Kivu Province, Congo, have told me the following: They came from Ethiopia in ancient times to protect the high holy places on Mt. Kilimanjaro, and secret gold and diamond mines, for the House of Israel. They came long before their Watutsi brothers who also migrated to the Great Lakes region from Ethiopia. They claim their ancient sacred calling was the basis for the first legends of King Solomon's lost mines ... Watutsi/Tutsi of Rwanda and Burundi have told me the following: Their ancestors were disaffected royal family members from the remnants of the House of Israel living in Ethiopia who migrated to "The Land of the Everlasting Hills" in the Great Lakes Region of Central Africa.'[57]

One source describes attempts to put this Israelite identity into an institutional framework through the creation of a body called Havilah. According to this source there is a growing movement among Tutsi intellectuals in Rwanda, Burundi and Uganda towards a 'Hebrew-Tutsi' identity, which no doubt has much in common with the movement among the Luba[58] and further afield among the Shinlung in the eastern states of India. The 'Israelite' Tutsis have appealed to Israel and to the international community in general and have asked them to condemn and take action against all 'anti-Israelite' violence throughout Africa – including the 500,000 Tutsi-Hebrew-Israelites of Rwanda.[59] In a hostile French-language report from Brussels the accusation is made that the 'process of Judaisation of the Tutsis' is no more than a means of taking over the whole area. According to this report, on 10 October 1999 the Havilah organisation met discreetly in Brussels. The article indicates that the term Havilah is used by the Judaising Tutsis to describe the whole region of the Great Lakes. The meeting was adorned with recognisable Jewish symbols such as the Star of David and also with depictions of the 'drum of Solomon', over which the 'lords of Havilah' are guardians.[60] It appears that the Havilah movement has a number of 'research centres' dedicated to the idea of recovering the 'lost memory' of the Hebraic culture of the Cushitic peoples – the guardians of King Solomon's Mines. One of these, the Sacega Centre, is devoted to the preservation for the peoples of Havilah of the 'memories of ancient Israel, of which they nonetheless guard the Solomonic and Mosaic codes, which are preserved in ancient traditions that thus far have resisted all attempts to decode them.' The Israelite Tutsis, inspired by the teachings of a 'prophet', Jean Bwejeri, who believes that the Tutsis are literally one of the Lost Tribes of Israel, are drawn by the notion of the salvation of Israel and they celebrated the millennium with the thought that the physical reunification of the Lost Tribes of Havilah and Gihon was underway.[61] A thoughtful item on the list-serve of Kulanu in August 2001 from Rabson Wurega, a well-educated member of the Zimbabwean Lemba[62] community, observed, 'I think my brothers and sisters in the West have lost one important understanding of a thought that prevails in Africa and Asia. When I talk of myself, I mean my ancestry, religion of my forefathers, traditions of the family, etc. All these are one thing. There is no room for compartmentalization . . . Basically Christian thinking is western philosophy . . . What I am trying to say is, in understanding groups with Jewish backgrounds in Africa, there is a tendency of pulling out the strand of religion from the whole life-set of a people and seeing them through the lens of Western thinking. If the Tutsi present themselves as descendants of Israel or Abraham they should be understood within their domain of thinking. I am saying simplicity should be allowed to speak for itself.'

The idea of a Tutsi-Israelite identity unquestionably springs from the colonial fantasies mentioned above. Insofar as it stresses the extraneous and superior origins of the Tutsi as against their neighbours, it is unlikely to contribute to the long-term harmony of the region. Jews, it should be pointed out, have had nothing to do with the generation of these myths in the case of the Tutsis. But now there is a perception, which is probably grounded in fact, that the Tutsis are at the receiving end of a kind of anti-Semitic prejudice. Jack Zeller, the kindly president of Kulanu, has observed, 'Some day when we Western Jews can put on a more humble suit of clothing and when the Tutsi have been able to recover from their recent holocaust, maybe we Western Jews can find out more about the Tutsi. Meanwhile, treat them with a well deserved respect as one of our own.'[63]

A little to the east of the Tutsi heartlands we find the Masai – a pastoral people of Kenya and northern Tanzania. It is interesting to note that in the case of the Masai the chief work exploring these ideas was written by a German, indeed by a German officer, one M. Merker. In his detailed and carefully researched work Merker believed that he had found significant parallels between the Masais' myths and customs and those of the biblical Hebrews, including similarities in the names of God; in circumcision; in a belief in the figure of Moses (whom Merker identified with the Masai Marumi or Musana); and in a variety of legends which included the stories of the creation of the world, Adam and Eve and the Fall, the story of the Flood, the theft of the birthright, the bronze serpent, the Ten Commandments. He concluded that both 'the Masai and the "oldest" Hebrews originated from the same people.'[64]

By the end of the nineteenth century the idea that specific African tribes were of Israelite or Semitic extraction had become astonishingly widespread. To deal with every tribe that had been so identified in Africa would require an entire book – particularly if the northern parts of the continent (where quite different factors were in play) were to be taken into account. I shall be obliged therefore to be highly selective and present just a few more examples from throughout the sub-Saharan part of the continent. We might start with the Songhai of the Timbuktu region whose upper classes were viewed as special and therefore extraneous. P. A. Talbot observed, 'the mass of the Songhai are certainly Negroes, though there is little doubt that their ruling families had a strain of Hamitic or even Semitic blood'.[65] And in D. Campbell's more recent book, *In the Heart of Bantuland* (New York, 1969), we hear 'Northward [of Katanga] lives one of the greatest tribes of Central Africa, the Baluba, who are of undoubted Semitic origin. The name Baluba means "the lost tribe", and their language and customs have many Hebrew affinities. Their name for, and idea of, God, with their word for water, and people, and many other words and ideas, show their Semitic strain.'[66] I have received a number of communications from the Luba, who are fully aware of this discourse. One of them suggested an etymology for the name Luba that would convey the sense of a lost tribe.[67] The idea of a Jewish identity for the Luba has recently been described in a publication of the United States Institute of Peace. Since the early 1960s, the report observes, 'Luba administrative, social, and commercial elites have spread all over the Congo country to form an ethnic diaspora that has been viewed with suspicion by the rest of the political class.' According to the report:

> As early as the 1960s, the Baluba regarded themselves as the 'Jews of the Congo,' and some of their most notorious leaders (for example, J. Ngalula) were called 'Moise.' They felt persecuted by most of the other ethnic constituencies, who disliked the privileges the Baluba allegedly garnered under the white administration. During the Second Republic they remained highly visible in politics: President Mobutu's strategy was to consistently absorb the Luba elite into the

> highest levels of the political hierarchy in order to better control it. Since 1978 one of the harshest opponents of the regime among the Luba elite has been Etienne Tshisekedi, later named the 'Zairian Moise,' who, together with ten fellow Kasaians, led a protracted struggle against Mobutu . . . In almost all the regions and provinces, the Luba diaspora is implicitly accused of wanting power only for its own people. Like the Shabans, the Luba are threatened with expulsion by the 'native sons.' The grievances of the 'Jews of Zaire' once again resonate.[68]

This use of a mythology about Jews in which they are perceived as deracinated, wealthy and potent is deeply rooted in the past imagined into existence for the Luba by one of the processes of colonialism.

In the Cape the attempt to place the indigenous population into the frame of an imagined biblical community started at the outset of colonial intervention. From the beginning the issue was highly politicised. The Dutch, who had settled the Cape at a time of great religious faith, believed in the sharp line to be drawn between the saved and the damned. This attitude was transferred to dealings with the African population. The difference between freeman and slave was as evident as the distinction between saved and damned. The Afrikaners were sure that when the Bible spoke of the children of Ham it had the black peoples of Africa in mind and according to them there was scriptural authority for blacks being maintained in slavery. The Bible became the source book for the maintenance of prejudice. Thus the Hottentots, while generally being regarded in a negative spirit, as being devoid of any of the characteristics that might have rendered them human, nonetheless had their very negativity expressed in terms that were culled from the Bible. As Thomas Herbert put it in 1627, 'The natives being propagated from Ham both in their Visages and Natures seem to inherit his malediction.' Features specific to them, such as scarification, similarly were put in a biblical context and in 1612 Patrick Copland observed that, 'they cut their skinnes like Baal's priests'.[69]

Two of the main concerns in the classification of the unknown other were religious and racial. Sometimes the two concerns merged. This may be seen in the work of another German, Peter Kolb, or Kolben. In 1705 Kolb was sent to the Cape to make astronomical observations, although he did not last long in this job. Eventually he turned blind and was dismissed. According to his detractors he spent his time smoking and drinking, although he claimed – as scholars often do when slandered in this way – to be doing research. Regaining his vision the hapless Kolb published a book. The German edition was published in 1719 and was subsequently translated into Dutch, English and French. *The Present State of the Cape of Good Hope* reached a very wide audience and for the next fifty years was the definitive account of the religion of the Hottentots. (In addition he provided painstaking drawings – almost architectural plans – of Hottentot houses.)[70] It should be remembered that the Hottentots or Khoi, in Jan van Riebeeck's notorious phrase, were perceived as 'black stinking dogs' by the majority of Dutch settlers at the Cape.[71] Kolb took an altogether more benign view of the Hottentots and argued that they were 'not so stupid, irrational and inhuman as they have been represented among us', praising their 'most beautiful Simplicity of Manner'.[72] Kolb agreed that in certain specific respects the religion and culture of the Hottentots were no doubt somewhat alien to European Protestant norms. To illustrate this he described the 'ceremony of pissing', in which old men allegedly urinated on people during initiation ceremonies, weddings or funerals as a way of honouring them. Nonetheless Kolb claimed that the general customs and traditions of the Hottentots were similar to those of the Jews. The Hottentot legend that they had entered the country through some sort of a window was seen by Kolb as a distorted folk-memory of the Ark and the Flood. He enumerated what he saw as the similarities between their sacrificial customs, their moon festivals, circumcision rites and so on. But he also asserted that the Hottentots could be counted among the children of Abraham, that they were of Jewish descent. Specifically he maintained that they were descended from Abraham via the troglodytes, issue of his wife Keturah (Genesis 25:1–4), although he conceded that they had no knowledge of this distant ancestor. Further proof of this he adduced from the fact that, like the Jews, they were so resistant to Christianity: after all, the governor of the Cape, Simon van der Stel, who had become the legal guardian of a Hottentot and had raised the child as a Christian, had been warned by his ward that he would live and die 'in the Religion Manners and Customs of My Ancestors'. Recalling this, Kolb concluded that as well as everything else the Hottentots were as 'stiff as the Jews'.[73] Whereas this reading of the history and religious provenance of the Hottentots had its detractors, it also had its adherents. In 1881, the missionary and ethnographer Theophilus Hahn published *Tsuni-Goam, The Supreme Being of the Khoi-Khoi*,[74] which argued that the religion of the Hottentots was a fossilised remnant of ancient Judaism. It followed also therefore that the language of the Hottentots must come from elsewhere. Wilhelm Bleek,[75] a German theologian, Orientalist and philologist came to Natal in 1851 to assist the Anglican Bishop John Colenso. In his doctoral thesis – a comparative study of Hottentot grammar – he maintained that the Hottentots could be traced back ultimately to North Africa because of the similarities he had observed in the structures of Khoi-Khoi, Galla, Coptic and Berber.[76]

The Xhosa, one of the most important of the southern African tribes, were viewed in a similar way. It was generally assumed that their religious structure had developed from some ancient Near Eastern religious system. In 1831 the Glasgow Missionary Society had asked its agents to conduct research on the Xhosa with a view to comparing their traditions and customs with those of the ancient Israelites. Subsequently one missionary wrote an essay along the required lines entitled 'The Antiquity of Circumcision'. Analysis of their customs, language and religion suggested to other Europeans that the Xhosa were in fact the Bedouin of southern Africa[77] and this view was common – that in fact this nomadic and unsettled people were Semitic Bedouin-Arabs. However such a designation was also frequently viewed through a biblical prism: in the 1840s, for instance, John Appleyard maintained that the Xhosa were of 'Ishmaelish descent'. The Ishmaelites were the issue of the elder son of the Jewish patriarch Abraham by his handservant Hagar. Ishmael is viewed as the ancestor of the Ishmaelites and by extension of all the Arabs. The Ishmaelites occur throughout the Old Testament and are often described in a negative way. But there were other explanations as well.[78] In 1827 an English settler in the eastern Cape noted that the Xhosa had religious traditions that included 'some Mahometan and Jewish rites'.[79] At the conclusion of the 1835 war against the Xhosa Harry Smith set himself the task of endeavouring to understand the defeated enemy and spent hours discussing Xhosa traditions and customs with a senior advisor of Chief Maqoma. Smith maintained he had found many things that 'resembled the Law of Moses'.[80] A similar definition was provided by Robert Godlonton (1794–1884), editor of the *Graham's Town Journal* who argued in *A Narrative of the Irruption of the Kafir Hordes into the Eastern Province of the Cape of Good Hope, 1834–35* (Cape Town, 1965) that it was possible to prove the origin of the Xhosa by reference to their language, which he said clearly showed 'traces of its eastern origin in the frequent occurrence of words which are plainly of Hebrew or Arabic extraction'. Godlonton then traced back the Xhosa to some Middle Eastern home. For him the colonial fantasy of inserting the Xhosa into the narrative of Christian sacred history served a gauntly secular aim. As their ancestors had been intruders into the area, the Xhosa did not belong in South Africa.[81]

With the conclusion of the last Frontier War in 1852, the Xhosa more or less gave up armed resistance. Their spirit was broken in 1857 when a fifteen-year-old visionary and prophetess, Nongqawuse, persuaded them that if they killed all their cattle and destroyed their grain, a host of ancestors would rise from the sea, the Europeans would be driven out of southern Africa and a golden period of prosperity and well-being would be inaugurated. When the ancestral horde failed to materialise the starving Xhosa were forced to turn to their enemy for work and food. This story of visions, sacrifice and redemption has such a Hebraic flavour to it that it no doubt added to the conviction that the Xhosa were in some way descended from the peoples described in the Old Testament.

In 1818 a ruthlessly efficient military organisation had been introduced by Shaka, the great Zulu warrior-king, which led to violent readjustments in much of south-eastern Africa. Following the assassination of Shaka in 1828, Dingane seized the throne and by the 1850s a new king, Panda, and his heir Cetewayo, had established a more or less settled form of government. In 1844, the British annexed Natal: the mainly British settlers were acutely aware that to the north there was a powerful Zulu state with a notable military capacity and as a result considerable interest in Zulu customs and traditions was generated. A similar interest no doubt existed among the Zulus with respect to Western traditions and customs, and perhaps particularly in the way it was appropriate to react to imperial, colonial, missionary and broadly Western sources of power. From a Zulu standpoint the fixing of their own identity faced with such an array of foreigners, from the English to white and black Americans, from central European to Dutch Jews, from Indians to Malays, from traders to imperial agents, presented an overwhelming challenge. There were a number of strategems. One invoked the obvious historical analogy of Sparta in the struggle to understand the Zulus.[82] The imposition and indeed acceptance of an

Israelite identity formed part of this attempt at mutual understanding and somewhat complicated the classical opposition of 'blacks' and 'whites', which was to dominate the future of inter-ethnic relationships.

Serious British interest in the Zulus dates back to the 1830s. Not long after Shaka's murder Captain Allen Gardiner had started off from the Cape on a diplomatic mission to forge relations with the new Zulu king. Using the opportunity to preach the Gospel Gardiner made every attempt to inform himself about this new mission field and particularly to find out about local religions. As he explained in his book, *Narrative of a Journey to the Zoolu Country in South Africa*, what struck him most about the religion of the Zulus was the immanent albeit almost forgotten presence of the memory of a supreme deity. But immediately he took the customs of the Zulus to be 'apparently of Jewish origin'. Some of the customs he enumerated included circumcision, the tradition of a younger brother marrying the widow of his deceased brother (levirate marriage), the daubing of the lintels of homes in times of sickness, the festival of the first-fruits and so on. He also mentioned that Ham was a common name among Zulus, as a way of connecting them with Israelite sacred history, while at the same time explaining their colour and in some cases the distance of their traditions from those set out in the Bible.[83]

As British power was extended further east the same discourse continued. Throughout the 1850s Zulus were identified as Jews. Their settled, pastoral life and their religious and social customs were evidence enough of this. G. R. Peppercorne, the magistrate of Pafana Location, observed to the Native Affairs Commission that in fact the Zulus practised a sort of ancient Judaism: 'A general type of the customs and laws of the Ama-Zulu may be found in the early history of the Hebrews.'[84] Peppercorne suggested that any European who wanted to understand Zulu customs had only to read the Old Testament. Zulu polygamy, marriage customs, even attitudes towards work were all described in the appropriate biblical passage. Henry Francis Fynn, who had established a small Zulu chieftaincy in the 1820s and who had spent decades living among them noted, 'I was surprised to find a considerable resemblance between many of the [Zulu] customs and those of the Jews.' These included, 'War offerings; sin offerings; propitiatory offerings; festival of first fruits . . . periods of uncleanness, on the decease of relatives and touching the dead; circumcision; rules regarding chastity; rejection of swine's flesh.' Fynn concluded that in view of 'the nature of semblance of many of their customs to those of the ancient Jews, as prescribed under the Levitical priesthood I am led to form the opinion that the [Zulu] tribes have been very superior to what they are at the present time'.[85]

A similar analysis was madc by John Colenso (1814–83), the famous Cambridge-educated biblical scholar, mathematician and Christian-Socialist who was ordained Bishop of Natal in 1853. He arrived in Natal the following year and quickly became fluent in Zulu (he went on to publish a grammar and dictionary of the language). Colenso was convinced that the two Zulu names for God embraced perfectly the notions of the divine 'contained in the Hebrew words Elohim and Jehovah'.[86] So close indeed were the resemblances, according to Bishop Colenso, that frequently he suggested that anyone who wanted to really understand the Bible had best study Zulu customs. Zulu 'habits and even the nature of their country so nearly correspond to those of the ancient Israelites, that the very scenes are brought continually, as it were, before their eyes, and vividly realised in a practical point of view'. Almost everything about the Zulus, from their lunar calendar to the order of religious feasts, seemed to reflect an Israelite past. 'The Zulu keeps his annual feasts, and observes the New Moons as the old Hebrew did. The very Zulus have their festivals at the beginning of the Southern Spring and at the end of our Autumn, corresponding to the "feast of the first fruits" and the "feast of the ingathering" of the ancient Hebrews.' Bishop Colenso was so convinced of the authenticity of the Zulu traditions, and so convinced that they were purer traditions than those preserved elsewhere, that he went on to write important theological works based in part on Zulu oral tradition. Colenso was called 'father of the people' by the Zulus and became their advocate: in most matters he took the side of the Zulus. His theological work provoked the most violent protests and vilification (some one hundred and forty books were written in opposition to his views) and led to his being deposed from his bishopric. (He refused to budge and for a while there were two parallel Anglican bishops of Natal!) Colenso was not merely a theologian. He threw himself into contemporary anthropological debates in which he stressed the dignity and humanity of the Zulus while rejecting the social Darwinisn which sought to categorise them, like other Africans, as an inferior group lagging behind in the evolutionary race. Colenso's espousal of an Israelite origin for the tribe may thus be seen within a liberal tradition, and his reading of their customs a mechanism in his fight against the forces of racism and conservatism.[87]

In 1901 the linguist and magistrate, James Stuart, spent a day at the Royal Hotel in Ladysmith interviewing three Zulu elders in an attempt to recreate something of the Zulu past. In these conversations one of them, Lazarus Mxaba, traced Zulu history back to ancient Israel and Greece. Many customs of the Zulus, maintained Mxaba, were common to Jews as well: he specifically mentioned the butchering of sacrificial meat and the burning of incense for sacrificial and other ritual purposes. He also maintained that the Jews like the Zulus slit their earlobes. These common features proved to Mxaba that there had been contact between the Jews and the Zulus in the past. Stuart accepted that such common features existed but could not understand how the Zulus could be descended from the Lost Tribes of Israel since they had lost any knowledge of the Godhead. Mxaba pointed out that even the Israelites had forgotten their god and started worshipping the Golden Calf; if the Israelites could forget in such a short time, clearly it was not surprising that in the course of the centuries the Zulus had forgotten too. Stuart mentioned that in fact there were those in Britain who believed that the British too were descended from the Lost Tribes: Mxaba wanted to know what points in common existed between the British and the Jews. Stuart had no ready reply. Mxaba was unimpressed: he was convinced that it was the Zulus who in fact were the lost children of Israel and that they would be redeemed when they remembered and starting worshipping their lost and unknown god. As David Chidester put it, 'By 1900 the comparison between the Zulu and the Jews had been thoroughly internalised in Zulu reflections upon their own religious heritage.'[88]

By the end of the nineteenth century the white conquest of South Africa was practically complete and the Ndebele and Shona peoples in what was by then called Rhodesia had also succumbed. As we have seen many of the South African tribes had been awarded an Israelite pedigree. Others such as the western Sotho or Tswana, who inhabited the northern and eastern grazing areas of the Kalahari, were likened to the ancient Israelites and some observers noted similarities between their customs and those mentioned in the Bible.[89] As white settlers moved into the fertile lands north of the Limpopo they were astonished to discover stone-built buildings, old mine workings and most of all the remarkable ruins known as the Great Zimbabwe complex. These ruins had first been discovered by a German explorer called Karl Mauch who spent from 1865–72 in almost continuous travel through little-known parts of Africa. In 1868 Mauch reported that he had found gold to the north-west of the Transvaal on the Tati river, which gave rise to a short-lived gold rush.[90] In 1871 he came across the Great Zimbabwe ruins. It seemed to him inconceivable that local people, living in their simple adobe huts, could ever have been capable of building these majestic stone constructions. As we have seen elsewhere, anything fine or sophisticated had to be put in a non-African context.

During his examination of the site Mauch came across an undamaged wooden lintel (subsequently shown to have been made from an African hardwood called *Spirostachys Africana*). That evening he wrote in his diary, 'It can be taken as a fact that the wood which we obtained is in fact cedar-wood and from this that it cannot come from anywhere else but from the Lebanon. Furthermore only the Phoenecians could have brought it here; further Solomon used a lot of cedar-wood for the building of the Temple and of his palaces: further – including here the visit of the Queen of Sheba and considering Zimbabe or Zimbaoe or Simbaoe written in Arabic (of Hebrew I understand nothing) – one gets as a result that the Great Woman who built the *rondeau* could have been none other than the Queen of Sheba.' Immediately, with no scrap of evidence, Mauch declared his deepest conviction that these ruins had been erected by the Queen of Sheba and were in fact a copy of Solomon's temple and palace in Jerusalem and that this entire area was the Ophir of the Bible – Solomon's gold lands. In addition the Queen of Sheba was in fact the Queen of Zimbabwe and one of the three wise men mentioned in the New Testament was also from this very place.

Mauch's enthusiasm may seem near-hysterical but it was entirely in the spirit of the time. Indeed, perhaps unwittingly, he simply followed the assumptions about the place that had previously been made by the Arabs and the Portuguese: the ruins had something to do with King Solomon. For the Arabs, Solomon legends – and particularly his association with the djinn – were as much conscripted in the explanation of strange places as were such legends in Christendom and were used in a variety of places in Africa as well as the Middle East and India.

Not long after Mauch had made his momentous discovery, efforts were made to show that Jews had once lived at Great Zimbabwe. In no time at all the Karanga-speaking Shona people, and specifically the Lemba tribe, were being enlisted as Jews and defined in precisely the same way as so many other African tribes and groups had been before and since. The Lemba living in South Africa had been observed in 1867 by the German missionary Alexander Merensky in the vicinity of Potgietersrus. They were amazed to discover that the Lemba had a monotheistic religion and that according to them, 'God had made the man from the same material as the stones, and then his wife. Then He told them to multiply themselves. All people were killed once by water, the sun was dark and there was a great flood; the sea flowed over the land.'[90] Somewhat later a settler-writer in Rhodesia, Richard Nicklin Hall, wrote a book about Great Zimbabwe in which he devoted considerable space to the 'Jewishness' of the surrounding populations. He made a list of twenty-four supposed similarities of custom and belief and concluded, 'Additional parallelisms with Jewish customs could be stated and all these peculiar practices, together with the lighter skin and the Jewish appearance of the Makalanga, distinctly point to the ancient impress of the Idumean Jews, which can also be traced on the present peoples of Madagascar and of the coasts of Mozambique and Sofala . . . the Lemba tribe of Makalanga is noted for the preservation and observance of these Jewish practices, which are distinctly pre-Koranic in origin.'[92]

The belief by the great majority of white settlers that the Great Zimbabwe ruins had been built by the ancient Phoenicians and had some kind of a connection with King Solomon and the Queen of Sheba has persisted until today: white Zimbabweans are often quite incapable of accepting that the ruins were built by Africans. As one woman said to me, 'They are baboons, they do not build anything – they destroy.'[93] The wildest theories are customarily put forward to explain the ruins: that they were built by visitors from outer space, by the Egyptians and so on.[94] But still the preferred option is King Solomon and the Phoenicians. In the early days of the colonisation of Rhodesia a great deal hung on these historical issues. It was firmly in the colonial interest to be able to prove that white supremacy was a fact and that subjugation of native peoples was legitimate. In some sense this theory helped to legitimise the British presence: if the country had once been controlled by a small maritime nation (the Phoenicians) why should it not now be controlled by another small maritime nation (the British)? Clearly if traces could be found of these ancient colonisers it would serve this particular historical vision. The Lemba, with their Semitic-looking customs and apparently Judaic habits, fitted the bill admirably and their identification as Jews thus suited imperial needs.

The Lemba tribe live in the Mberengwe–Mposi area of Zimbabwe and are also to be found in small groups throughout north-east South Africa and in central and eastern Zimbabwe. Another similar group known as Mwenye, which has no knowledge of the Lemba of Zimbabwe and South Africa but which also claims Jewish origins, is to be found in southern Malawi (Mwenye is the preferred name of the Lemba both in South Africa and Zimbabwe).[95] Notwithstanding that this tribe is in many respects indistinguishable from neighbouring tribes, for much of the twentieth century a number of Lemba, and particularly those of South Africa, have claimed to be of Jewish or Semitic ancestry, and a number of outside European observers have made similar claims for them for an even longer period.[96] In 1893 a German missionary called C. Beuster thought that they were probably Baal worshippers and Carl Peters initially perceived 'remnants of the Punic-Baal-Ashera worship'. The Lemba genuinely seemed to have some Semitic-looking features. They did not intermarry, they did not interdine. They had strict laws of purity and severe food taboos. The eating of pork was punished by death. They would only eat meat that had been ritually slaughtered by a fellow Lemba.[97] It is against this background that the suggestion of Jewishness was made to the tribe from the very beginning of colonial intervention. The Lemba themselves claim variously to come from the north or from outside Africa. However a recent and detailed study by the senior curator of Ethnography at the Museum of Human Sciences in Harare, has categorically rejected any suggestion that the Lemba came from elsewhere. According to this paper they are purely African and the idea that they came from abroad has been 'invented' by outsiders who have created 'a false Lemba identity'.[98] As this is what happened everywhere else in Africa it seems tempting to believe that it is precisely what occurred here. However in this particular case there are the strongest grounds for believing that at least some of the Lembas' ancestors did indeed come from outside Africa. It appears that in the relatively remote past they indeed came from South Arabia. They may subsequently have been connected with a coastal civilisation based on a city called Sayuna by mediaeval Arab geographers, in which religious syncretism ran riot – as we can tell from the various references in the literature. There is some genetic evidence to suggest that the

Lemba in fact had some Jewish antecedents. At the very least this evidence shows that a substantial proportion of Lemba males originated from outside Africa. In this the genetic evidence supports Lemba oral traditions very precisely. However their identification as Jews by the earliest explorers and settlers of the region undoubtedly and paradoxically forms part of the discourse that has been described throughout this book.[99]

It is worth noting that in recent times white racists found the Lemba-Israelite tradition appealing: the Scottish laird Gayre of Gayre and Nigg was the editor of a racist journal called *Mankind Quarterly*. In 1967 he wrote a short article in which he posited the connection of the Lemba with the monolithic stone-building culture of Great Zimbabwe and in 1972 he published a book, *The Origin of the Zimbabwean Civilisation*, widely believed to have been commissioned by the Rhodesian Government, which claimed that the Lemba had been involved in the Great Zimbabwe construction.[100] He further argued that the Lemba had Jewish cultural and genetic traits and that their 'Armenoid' genes must have been acquired from Judaised Sabeans who, he maintained, had settled in the area thousands of years ago. The book's clear objective was to show that Africans had never been capable of building in stone or of governing themselves. There is not the slightest evidence that 'Sabeans' or any other Middle Eastern people had settled in this area thousands of years ago, and there is every evidence that Great Zimbabwe was built something less than a thousand years ago, over a considerable number of centuries, by local people.[101]

In similar but less ambiguous vein Carl Peters, the founder of German East Africa, who retired to British South Africa when he was forced to resign from the German Imperial Service accused of cruelty to the local population, wrote some years earlier of the Shona of eastern Zimbabwe, 'How absolutely Jewish is the type of this people! They have faces cut exactly like those of ancient Jews who live around Aden. Also the way they wear their hair, the curls behind the ears, and the beard drawn out in single curls, gives them the appearance of Aden – or of Polish – Jews of the good old type.' This piece of visual invention is of some interest. There is simply no possibility that Peters came across Shona wearing the sidelocks (*peot*) worn by Orthodox Jews. Why did he make it up? Did he make it up? Did he imagine it? It fitted his vision for the Shona to be more or less identical to the Jews from eastern Europe who were frequently to be seen in German towns.

They were powerless, transient, dependent on favours. These were the Jews 'of the good old type'. The other Jews, the assimilated, successful, powerful Jews of Germany were quite another matter.

What we have seen elsewhere in Africa we find in great abundance in the great island of Madagascar. A considerable literature was produced in the nineteenth century on the supposed Israelite origin of some of the island's population. This literature entered the popular discourse but largely originated from scholars. One such was the French Madagascar expert Alfred Grandidier, another Augustus Keane, a one-time professor of Hindustani at University College London. They both claimed that there were great links between Madagascar and the ancient Jews. In the *Gold of Ophir, Whence Brought and by Whom* (London, 1901) Keane argued that Madagascar had been the off-shore base for the colony of Havilah, with Tarshish its port of entry and that Madagascar had links with ancient Israel 'certainly as early as the time of Solomon and possibly even during the reign of his father David'. Grandidier's monumental work, *Histoire Physique, Naturelle et Politique de Madagascar,* also published in 1901, made similar claims. In 1870 James Sibree, a missionary who served from 1863–1916 in Madagascar with the London Missionary Society claimed to have met *Zafin Ibrahim* – descendants of Abraham – at various places on the island of St Marie in east Madagascar. These people claimed to be Jews and Sibree noted a number of customs that he perceived as being Judaic, including a good deal of beef-eating, fasts before and after beef, the purification rituals and the sprinkling of blood on lintels. One of the *Zafin Ibrahim* spoke of his father who had been a 'sorcerer among the Jews'.[102] Similar views continued to be expressed throughout the twentieth century: a suggestion that substantial traces of Hebrew were to be found in Malagasy was made in *L'hébreu à Madagascar* by Jospeh Briant, published in 1946.[103]

Perhaps the most dramatic and tragic of the consequences of the invention of an Israelite identity in the southern African context may be perceived in the life and work of the so-called Prophet of God, Enoch Josiah Mgijima (1858–1929), whose Hlubi family originally came from Natal. In this case the Israelite theory can partly be traced back to an American context[104] but no doubt the widespread use of the Israelite myth in colonial discourse in Natal and elsewhere played a significant role too.

Enoch Mgijima was born in Bulhoek in South Africa's Queenstown district and began to have visions in 1907 while hunting in the mountains. Convinced that he was a sinner and a drunkard he hesitated before accepting his calling as a prophet. However in 1910 he saw Haley's Comet and took this as the longed-for confirmation of his prophetic vocation. His most specific and strongly held belief was that he had to reintroduce the religion of the ancient Israelites to African soil. His ideas swiftly attracted a following. Mgijima associated himself with the like-minded Church of God and Saints of Christ – an American church founded in 1896 by a black American, William Crowdy, who was a firm believer in the idea that Africans were the true and original Israelites and descendants of the Ten Lost Tribes.[105] Because of the starkly political visions that he continued to have and reveal to his followers, Mgijima was eventually asked to leave the church and he founded his own organisation which he called simply the Israelites. In 1920, while sitting on top of Ntabelanga Mountain, he received a message directly from God. Many Israelites flocked to the area and built temporary housing for themselves, thus coming into conflict with local people. The following year the Israelites compounded the crime of squatting by refusing to divulge their names for the census. They explained, reasonably, that this was unnecessary as God knew who they were. After the murder of two Israelites the group started preventing officials from coming to their settlement.

Five years after the destruction at gunpoint of the Maori Israelites' Jerusalem in Maungapohatu in New Zealand, described in chapter nine, a similar drama started unfolding in South Africa.[106] On 24 May 1921 a massive force of policemen arrived at Ntabelanga and the two sides prepared for battle. They drew up in formal military formations: the Israelites were armed with knobkerries, assegais and one or two antiquated guns and knives; the police had modern rifles as well as machine guns. Throughout the lengthy negotiations the Israelites were given the opportunity to surrender but they refused, proclaiming, 'We will fight and Jehova will fight with us.'[107] Mgijima assured them that the police bullets would turn to water and that they would not, could not be harmed. The Israelites fought courageously but the outcome was never in doubt. One policeman was speared while 163 Israelites were left dead on the field of battle with a further 129 wounded. The massacre horrified both black and a good deal of white public opinion.

At the Conference of the Pan-African Freedom Movement in Adis

Ababa in January 1962 where Nelson Mandela was representing the ANC, he picked out the Bulhoek Massacre as perhaps the single worst atrocity in the history of South Africa. It is still remembered. Robert Edgar has noted, 'Almost every African household in South Africa knows about the massacre of the people at Bulhoek'.[108] A Bulhoek Massacre Heritage Memorial was unveiled with due ceremony on 27 May 2001.[109]

We have seen how the myth of the Lost Tribes has penetrated every corner of the African continent. The use and reuse of this myth, and myths about Jews that serve an immense array of ideological and spiritual needs, have had a striking impact on Africa. The spread of the myth connecting Africa with the Jews has been spectacular. It arose in the European and Middle Eastern imagination in the early Middle Ages and may be attributed in part to the ignorance of much of the world brought about by the breakdown of communications between the Islamic Middle East and Christian Europe. It became an axiomatic feature of mediaeval thinking about the world. It was exploited and reinvented by colonialism in many distinct loci in Africa, where it served both missionary and colonial interests. It is now a largely ignored but potent and immanent aspect of the imagined past of a surprising number of Africans.

Chapter Twelve

CROSSING THE RED SEA

These . . . giants . . . the Arabian sons of God . . . can carry a whole camel on one shoulder . . . it is well known that their religion is the Jewish religion.

Obadiah ben Abraham of Bertinoro (*c.* 1450–*c.* 1510)

The most cherished locus for the Lost Tribes, and the one that met with almost universal approval in the Jewish world, was the area around the Red Sea: the land of Cush redolent of the tales of Eldad the Danite to the west, the Arabian desert to the east.[1] For centuries the Jewish world believed if the Lost Tribes were really to be found it was in the lands that bordered the Red Sea that it would be most likely to happen. For well over a thousand years this area of desert and mountain, of great heat and cold, has been the crucible of Lost Tribes identification. As we saw in the introductory chapter Jewish travellers and *shelihim* (emissaries) frequently brought or sent back tales averring that the Lost Tribes had been located in Arabia or in Ethiopia. The great twelfth-century Jewish traveller Benjamin of Tudelah located Reuben, Gad and half the tribe of Manasseh squarely in Arabia where, 'they built strong cities and are in warfare with many kingdoms, and they cannot easily be reached because of their situation, which requires a march of eighteen days through uninhabited deserts, and this renders them difficult of access. Khaibar is also a large city with 50,000 Jews in it, of whom many are learned. They are valiant and engaged in wars with the inhabitants of Shinear, with those of the northern country, and with those of the Yemen who live near them – the latter province borders India.'[2] Benjamin's account of his travels was first published in Constantinople in 1543 but was already widely known about in Europe. Its English translation – which appeared in *Purchas his Pilgrimes* – appeared in 1625.[3]

A number of Jewish *shelihim* brought or sent back tales from the East in the following centuries that corroborated and embroidered these accounts. The regularity and insistence of these reports on the Ten Tribes were frequently related to the general level of persecution of Jews, which in turn gave rise to Messianic hopes and expectations. One such report was included in a letter sent by the Jewish community of Jerusalem in 1456 with an emissary – Abraham ha-Levi – dispatched to raise funds for the Jews in the Holy City. Rumours had been heard of a Jewish kingdom battling it out in Cush with Prester John and these were taken to be signs of imminent redemption.[4] There were many such reports from emissaries from Jerusalem and the other Holy Cities of the land of Israel throughout the fifteenth and sixteenth centuries. The reports were not necessarily well known in their time – although they certainly did spread through many of the Jewish communities – but they serve as an indication of what was commonly believed with respect to the Lost Tribes.[5]

Obadiah ben Abraham of Bertinoro was one of the most distinguished Italian rabbis of his day and his commentary on the Mishnah remains a standard work of Jewish scholarship. He emigrated from Italy to Palestine in 1485. From Jerusalem he wrote colourful letters back to his elderly father and his brother in which he described the things he saw and heard on his journey and in the land of Israel. Obadiah fell into conversation with Jews from Aden, 'which is the Land with the famous Garden of Eden and it lies in a south-easterly direction next to the Land of Cush. Except that they are divided by the Red Sea. And these Jews told me that in their land there were many great communities of Jews . . . and some fifty days distance in the desert is that well-known river the Sambatyon and it encircles the whole land inhabited by Jews like a thread and it throws up stones and sand and only rests on the Sabbath . . . and they have the tradition that these people are all the sons of Moses, pure and innocent like the administering angels . . . there are no sinners among them. And beyond the Sambatyon the sons of Israel are like the sand of the sea, kings and princes, but they are not pure and innocent like those enclosed by the Sambatyon. And those Jews told me this quite clearly and explicitly and said there was no doubt about it at all and it was as clear as daylight to them . . .' Elsewhere he confirms that the tribe of Dan, with five kings or princes, was to be found in the land of Prester John where it waged constant war against the Priest King.[6]

In 1528 the Jerusalem Kabbalist R. Abraham ben Eliezer ha-Levi reported that the tribes of Dan and Gad were living in Ethiopia.[7]

Fourteen years later in 1542 Rabbi Moses Bassola of Ancona went on a pilgrimage to the Holy Land. When he arrived in Beirut he met four Jews from 'Babylonia'. With one of them, a Hebrew-speaking individual called Moses, he was able to have an interesting conversation. Moses told him that he had heard from Arabs who had seen it with their own eyes that there was indeed such a thing as the Sambatyon River, and that the sons of Moses inhabited it 'without a doubt'. And later he revealed that in Jerusalem he had heard from a Jew from Ethiopia that in the south there were 'many Jews, kings and princes, who sometimes fought with the Indians and he said that some of them [came at the time of] the First Temple and some the Second'. Further on he reveals that he met someone else in Jerusalem who thirty years previously had met a man who claimed to be from the tribe of Simeon. This man had claimed that in his home country there were four tribes, including Issachar, who studied the Torah. In addition he had met an old man in Safed who had three sons. 'The youngest of the sons had spent two years sitting on a roof alone and a white dove flew down in front of him and he took it in his hand and saw on one of its wings written in square Hebrew characters – "behold the Ten Tribes are coming" ... and after reading this he took the dove in his hand and ran to show it to his father and then he felt a mighty blow on his hand so he was forced to open it and the dove flew off and was never seen again'.[8]

Some twenty years before Rabbi Moses Bassola of Ancona went on pilgrimage to the Holy Land, a very short, dark individual of great personal magnetism calling himself David Reubeni appeared in the ghetto in Venice. This was in 1524. Like Eldad ha-Dani he was painfully thin. Their meagre frames were no more meagre than our knowledge of their pasts. In the case of Reubeni we know nothing much about his life prior to his arrival in Venice. We know he was not really called David Reubeni and that he was not a prince of the Israelites. The story this fantastic character had to tell was that he had been charged by his brother, Joseph, king of the tribe of Reuben, one of the Lost Tribes of Israel, which flourished still in Arabia, to obtain military assistance from the Pope and Christian potentates in his people's constant war against the Turks. This accomplished confidence trickster had the rough manner of command and spoke a kind of Hebrew no one could readily understand. It has been suggested, but on excessively flimsy evidence, that he was a Falasha – an Ethiopian Jew.[9]

His brother Joseph, so he said, commanded no less than 300,000 Israelite warriors. In February 1524 he proceeded from Venice to Rome. He was given a warm welcome at the Vatican by Pope Clement VII (1523–34), where he appeared riding a white horse. Reubeni introduced himself as 'the General of the Army of Israel' and claimed that 'My brother, the king of the Jews, has sent me here to you, my lord King, for help. And now help us that we may go fight Suleiman the Turk, so that we might take the Holy Land out of his power.' What he wanted was firearms with which to bring about the union of the Jewish tribes who inhabited both sides of the Red Sea, before embarking on a new crusade. Pope Clement VII was intrigued by this scheme: after all, just three years before, Suleiman had taken Belgrade and then Rhodes, and Christendom seemed at risk as never before. In addition the possibility of an alliance with this powerful Israelite army no doubt seemed potentially useful in the Pope's delicate relationship with his arch-enemy the Emperor Charles V. In their discussions the Pope negotiated special privileges with respect to the Christian sites of *terra sancta* for the Roman Catholic Church.

The Jews of Italy were astonished that a mere Jew could be received with such distinction at the Vatican. Señora Benvenida Abrabanela sent him considerable sums of money from Naples and a precious silk banner embroidered with the Ten Commandments. Reubeni subsequently received a formal invitation from King João III of Portugal and embarked there on a ship flying a Jewish flag. In Portugal, too, he was received with great pomp and ceremony. The excitement and bewilderment caused by a Jew being entertained by the most distinguished men in the land seemed to presage a long-awaited deliverance from persecution and was almost too much for the oppressed Marranos. One of them, a young man called Diogo Pires (*c.* 1501–32), who took the Jewish name of Solomon Molcho, interpreted Reubeni's mission in purely Messianic terms and was impelled to the belief that the end was nigh. After a number of barely credible adventures Reubeni and Molcho tried to convince the Emperor Charles V to send arms to the Lost Tribes. The Emperor was not amused. According to Joseph ha-Kohen, the author of a sixteenth-century Hebrew martyrology, 'The Emperor remained firm and would not listen to him, being impatient, and even issued an order to put him [Molcho] and his friend Prince David and his men into prison.' Molcho was burned to death at the stake and Reubeni died some years later in a prison of the Holy Inquisition in Spain.[10]

Obadiah ben Abraham wrote of the Jewish giants descended from the biblical 'Rechabites' who were called by Arabs the 'Arabs of Shaddai', according to Obadiah. This term signified that they were the 'Arabian sons of God . . . and the Ishmaelites say of them that each can carry a whole camel on one shoulder and can use his other hand to carry a dagger with which to fight his enemy . . . it is well-known that their religion is the Jewish religion and it is said that they are descendants of the Rechabites'.[11] In Jewish Lost Tribe discourse the Rechabite theme was persistent. In the 1830s the ubiquitous Joseph Wolff, who travelled much of the world at the expense of the London Society for the Promoting of Christianity Amongst the Jews, visited the Yemen and recorded, 'I spent six days with the children of Rechab – they drink no wine, plant no vineyards, sow no seed, live in tents and remember the words of Jonadab, the son of Rechab. With them were the children of Israel, of the tribe of Dan, who reside near Terim in Hadramawt, who expect, in common with the children of Rechab, the speedy arrival of the Messiah in the clouds of heaven.'[12] It is not clear to whom Wolff was referring in this incredible passage. There were no Jews in the Yemen who even begin to answer to such a description.

There were certainly internal circumstances within the Yemen that fed into a Lost Tribes discourse. At the time of Wolff's visit there, for instance, there was an almost endemic Messianism. Both Islam and Judaism – not to mention other religions – nurture the idea of a redeemer who will appear at the end of time following a period of anarchy and unrest and who will herald a new era of justice and peace. Muslim Messianic figures are normally called al-Mahdi. In Shia Islam the long-awaited redeemer is usually identified as Muhammad ibn al-Hassan al-Askari, the Twelfth Imam. In Sunni tradition the identity of the Mahdi is less precise: it is believed simply that he will be of the family of the prophet. A key feature of the lives of the Jews of the Yemen was their predisposition towards Messianism. The adventures of periodic false Messiahs, often tinged with the tragic-comic, were some of the most potent forces at work in Yemeni society, and influenced Muslims as well as Jews.

In the early nineteenth century a Yemeni Muslim, Faqih Sarid, declared himself al-Mahdi, conquered a good part of the Yemen and had coins minted with the words 'Expected Deliverer' stamped on one side and 'Ruler of the World' on the other. In the words of a contemporary British historian, 'He declared that he had the divine mission to purify the faith of Mohammed, to abolish taxation throughout the Yemen and to drive the infidel from Aden: and he promised to all who should join him in his task, complete invulnerability against the sword and gunshot.' To the consternation of his followers he was executed by the Imam in 1840. A few years later extraordinary signs and wonders persuaded Muslims and Jews that Messianic events could be expected again. In 1846 a great star fell: its red and white light was brighter than the moon and it stopped in the East long enough for a man to read a sura of the Koran. A little later hailstones the size of ostrich eggs fell over the Yemeni highlands.

A new Muslim Messiah, Sharif Ismail, threw himself into the fray declaring that he would throw the infidel British out of Aden and rid the Yemen of its non-Muslims, in other words, the Jews. Against this background, encouraged no doubt by reports from Europe where similar scenes of Messianic expectation prevailed in the 1840s, the Jews started to nurture hopes that their own Messiah would soon be revealed. A plethora of Jewish Messianic movements emerged. These self-proclaimed redeemers – Shukr Kuhayl I (1861–5), a humble maker of leather components for water pipes from Sanaa who was decapitated by the Imam, Shukr Kuhayl II (1868–75), a plausible swindler who claimed to be the reincarnation of Shukr Kuhayl I and took up with his widow, and the equally dubious Yosef Abdullah (1888–93) – all drew on Jewish traditions but also proved receptive to Muslim eschatological imagery. Thus in the Jewish Messianic movements infidel British forces in Aden and the Ottoman Turkish occupying forces in the Yemen were perceived as being enemies of the Messianic cause. At times the Jews appeared even to have been in favour of the preservation of the traditional rule of Islam. Jewish Messianic writing of the time paints a colourful picture of wild Jewish hopes and aspirations: Jewish armies would be created and at the critical moment a mighty flotilla containing warriors from the Ten Tribes of Israel would come to their aid.[13]

In 1824 Rabbi David Deveit Hillel set off on a journey from Safed in northern Palestine to Syria, Kurdistan, Iraq, Persia and India. Like many before and since his object was to locate the Ten Lost Tribes. Like most Jewish seekers of the Lost Tribes, when he left Safed he supposed them to be in Ethiopia or somewhere in Arabia. His journey was not totally without success for he had every reason to believe that he had found at least traces of them in Syria. Here he had met two Bokharan Jews who convinced him that they were members of the Ten Tribes and the same thing happened in Kurdistan.[14] Seven years later, in 1831, Rabbi Yisrael of Shklov,[15] also living in Safed, sent an emissary – Rabbi Barukh ben Shmuel of Minsk – to the Yemen on behalf of his Safed community to raise funds. Two years earlier another emissary had visited Sanaa, the capital of the Yemen, where he had met a Jew in a synagogue who told him he was a member of the tribe of Dan and had come from an independent Jewish kingdom in the eastern reaches of the Yemen. Moreover he had said his name was Issachar and he had spoken of the wealth, might and greatness of the kingdom of the Jews of which he had the good fortune to be a citizen. He disappeared abruptly after this encounter.[16] This was quite a specific sighting on a good authority and it caused some excitement in Palestine. And of course it fell fast on the heels of the return of David Deveit Hillel who had brought similarly encouraging news.

But there was another reason why these sightings caused the interest they did. In Russia the anti-Jewish decrees of Tsar Nicholas I (1825–55), which used harsh police methods to force the Jews to assimilate into Russian society, had caused despair there and throughout the Jewish communities of Europe. The measure that caused the greatest anguish was promulgated in 1827 and called for the conscription of Jewish adolescents into the Tsarist armies. The young conscripts – the so-called Cantonists – were taken from the age of twelve, sometimes younger, for a period of twenty-five years' regular army service starting from their eighteenth birthday. A good part of the rationale of this scheme was to wean the children away from Judaism. As with the Chmielnicki massacres of 1648 the various decrees of Nicholas had the knock-on effect of reducing the Ashkenazi community of Palestine to an even more abysmal level of poverty than previously and it is against this background that emissaries were now sent forth armed with the news of these recent sightings. It was also the persecutions in Russia that helped to bring about a new period of intense Messianic speculation.

Rabbi Yisrael of Shklov no doubt had a number of things in his mind when he sent off his emissary. The fact that he was caught in the grip of Messianic fervour himself is reflected in his desire to recreate in Palestine the ancient institution of ordination for the Sanhedrin (the ancient Jewish council court) – a necessary precondition, as he pointed out, for the Redemption and the coming of the Messiah.[17] He believed that it was only among the Ten Lost Tribes that this ancient practice was still followed: once the tribes were found instructions could be given which would enable ordination to be reintroduced in the land of Israel. The emissary, R. Barukh ben R. Shmuel of Pinsk, a particularly resourceful and versatile man, with medical skills and a knowledge of the world, was given two tasks by his community: to raise funds in Syria, Kurdistan, Mesopotamia and Persia and to seek out the Lost Tribes in the Yemen. He was provided with a special letter addressed to 'our holy and pure brethren, the sons of Moses . . . who dwell beyond the Shabatyon ... and the Ten Tribes ...' This epistle, written in beautiful Hebrew by Rabbi Yisrael, and signed first by him and then by other Palestinian rabbis, spoke of the hardships and piety of the Jews of the Diaspora, and particularly of the Holy Land. In addition the letter requested the Ten Tribes to send teachers and money and further asked for the reply to be couched in the Hebrew tongue (the letter was dispatched to Europe where it was published and made quite a stir). Shmuel duly arrived in the Yemen in 1833, some two years after leaving Safed. Accompanied by the erudite president of the Jewish Court of Law (*beit din*) in Sanaa, Rabbi Yahya ben Solomon Abyad, Shmuel courageously set off to explore the little-known desert areas of the northern part of the country which had rarely, if ever, been visited by a European. In the desert near Haydan they met a mysterious Jewish shepherd who claimed to belong to the 'sons of Moses'. They gave him a letter to deliver to his people and returned to Haydan to await an answer. The answer did not come and because the high holidays were approaching they returned to Sanaa. The Imam al-Mahdi Abdullah, the king of the Yemen, was impressed by Shmuel's medical skills, which he had used to cure the king of an illness, and appointed him court physician. Shmuel suggested that the Imam put ten thousand troops at his disposal which he would lead against the Turks in the Tihama on condition that he was made governor of Mocha. The Imam suspected treachery and had him murdered.[18] This story, along with others about the Ten Tribes of Israel living in the desert regions and fighting alongside the Arab tribes, was published with no hint of scepticism in the well-known *Even Sapir* of the Jewish scholar, antiques merchant and traveller, Jacob Saphir.[19]

In 1840 the remarkable Karaite scholar Abraham Firkovich (1785–

1874), one of the greatest if not *the* greatest collector of Hebrew manuscripts of all times and thus a monument of reliability, added to Lost Tribes excitement by forging a Hebrew colophon purporting to be a message from the Lost Tribes. Six years later another emissary from Safed, Rabbi Omram, an immigrant from North Africa, was sent to find the Lost Tribes in Arabia. He was robbed by Bedouin and was unable to continue with his mission. The following year, 1847, Rabbi Joseph Schwartz sent an emissary by the name of Moses Yafeh from Hebron. Moses was going to India and China to raise funds for the Holy Land and had promised to inform him about the Ten Tribes on the way. He was as good as his word. From Aden he reported that the British governor had told him about warrior Jews in Habash (Ethiopia) and suggested that Schwartz ask the Chief Rabbi in Jerusalem to send a special mission to them. From India he reported that he had heard that the river Sambatyon was in China.[20] In 1848 a young Jew called Ezekiel Asha from Russia set out to the Yemen in quest of the Lost Tribes and was last heard of entering Ethiopia. Ten years later another young Jew, one David Ashkenazi, set off from Jerusalem to the Yemen and Ethiopia on a similar mission.

Later in the century there were further confirmations of the broad outline of the legend. David Carasso was a Jewish merchant from Salonika, who spent the years 1874–9 in the Yemen on business. He wrote an interesting account in Ladino of the history of the Jews of the Yemen and the events of his journey. Carasso described 'warrior Jews' who lived in the vicinity of Saada in good relations with the Arab nomads of the area and who, he claimed, formed over a third of the total population of Arabia.[21] Reports from Joseph Halévy, who visited the Yemen in 1870,[22] and Yomtob Sémach who went on behalf of the Alliance Israélite Universelle in 1910, of warlike, armed Jews living on the fringes of the Arabian desert cannot but have lent credence to the notion that the Lost Tribes of Israel were indeed alive and well in South Arabia.[23] While in Palestine the arrival in the 1880s of Yemenite Jews dressed in exotic garb and speaking their own form of Hebrew aroused considerable interest and stimulated further speculation about the Lost Tribes.

These ideas were to continue to have some currency for the next few decades. In 1928 Wolfgang von Weisl, an Austrian journalist, visited the Yemen and his account of his travels was carried by a number of newspapers throughout the world including the *London Evening*

Standard, which reported that there were several thousand Jews there subject to the Imam but in addition, 'to the north-east across the great Arabian desert live other Jews, possible descendants of the "Ten Lost Tribes of Israel" who have maintained their freedom through their fighting abilities and who look down upon their brethren in the Yemen ... Then there are the independent Jew, the enemies of the Imam, the Jews of the North: they live in seventy cities and they fight against the Yemen'.[24]

The conviction that the Lost Tribes were to be found in the more remote areas of the Yemen was one that was shared by the Yemenite Jews themselves. Over the centuries they had elaborated numerous legends about the tribes, and particularly about the supposed valour of the tribe of Dan.[25] The Messianic movements that rocked the Yemenite community from time to time frequently drew on these legends: the idea that a mighty army sent by the Lost Tribes would one day sweep in from the desert and bring Jewish tribulations to an end is a frequent motif in Yemenite Jewish apocalyptic literature. When Joseph Halévy visited the Yemen in 1870 the entire Jewish community, from the Chief Rabbi down, was convinced that the real purpose of his journey was to find the warlike Danites.[26]

During the late nineteenth and early twentieth century the motif of the Lost Tribes of Israel and echoes of travellers' reports from the Yemen are to be found in the works of a number of Jewish writers.[27] Naphtali Herz Imber (1856–1909), the central European Hebrew poet who wrote *Hatikvah* (The Hope) – the Israeli national anthem – wrote a Hebrew poem called 'The Sons of Moses', which describes his desire to visit those parts of Arabia where the Lost Tribes lived and to learn from them how to wage war.[28] In 1897 Abraham Luncz,[29] the blind Palestinian Jewish writer, became so tired of the subject of the Ten Tribes that he complained indignantly in a letter to the influential Hebrew journal *Ha-Shiloah* that foreign Jews visiting Palestine were much more eager to seek news of the Lost Tribes of Israel than they were to have up-to-date information about the history and geography of Palestine and the general state of the country.[30]

The interest in the Lost Tribes after the rise of Zionism continued to grow. It peaked in the 1940s and 1950s when two events – the destruction of European Jewry and the establishment of the State of Israel – persuaded many that the End of Days was at hand. This gave rise to a renewed enthusiasm for the 'dispersed of Israel', as they were called. As Emanuela Trevisan Semi has shown, during the 1940s and 1950s various committees and organisations were established to promote the well-being and eventual redemption of the 'dispersed of Israel'. They were led by a number of prominent Zionists, including a future president of the State of Israel, Yitzhak Ben Zvi, old-style Zionists like Nahum Slouschz, the so-called 'father' of the Falashas, Jacques Faitlovitch, Israel Ben-Zeev and others.[31] And as we have seen above, this interest persists and is occasionally transformed into calls for immigration rights into Israel for sundry 'Jewish' groups throughout the world.

We have seen in the first chapter that for hundreds of years Ethiopia was perceived as the home of some of the Lost Tribes.[32] Ethiopia was the locus par excellence of the Israelites-in-Africa myth and until the nineteenth century attempts were still being made to locate the Lost Tribes in this mountainous kingdom. John Pory, the English translator of Leo Africanus' *Description of Africa*, refers to Jews of an independent polity in Ethiopia 'who maintain themselves free and absolute'. And this is confirmed by the seventeenth-century Portuguese Jesuit missionary Balthazar Tellez in *Travels of the Jesuits in Ethiopia* and by Jacques Basnage, the French Protestant historian in 1706, both of whom also claimed that the 'Jews' in Ethiopia used Hebrew in their synagogues (which incidentally they did not).[33] And as we have seen above many Jewish traditions maintained these beliefs.

Gradually claims of an independent Jewish kingdom in Ethiopia peopled by the Lost Tribes coalesced around a small Agau-speaking tribe generally known as Falashas who lived principally in the area around Lake Tana.

Some of the factors that were responsible for the creation of an imagined Israelite identity in so many different parts of Africa and the world were absent in Ethiopia. For one thing Ethiopia was a predominantly Christian country. For another it had a written culture. And thirdly it was not colonised until the 1930s and then only partially and briefly. In any case the invention of an Israelite identity in Ethiopia had already occurred: the national epic of the land – the *Kebra Nagast* – celebrates the Israelite origins of the royal house and this became 'the basic metaphor for legitimacy and authority within Ethiopian culture'.[34] It was even embodied in the 1955 Ethiopian constitution, 'The imperial dignity shall remain perpetually attached to the line ... [which] descends without interruption from the dynasty of Menelik, son of the Queen of Ethiopia, the Queen of Sheba, and King Solomon of Jerusalem.'[35]

The act of comprehending the otherness of Ethiopians was not strictly part of a colonial enterprise. For those Westerners who penetrated the kingdom there was plenty that was strange, but some of the techniques employed elsewhere for the demystification of African societies would not serve here. Nonetheless some of the oddball theories produced in other places did surface in Ethiopia, such as those preserved in *Un peuple antique ou une colonie gauloise au pays de Menelik. Les Gallas: une grande nation africaine* (1901), a book by the French missionary Martial de Salviac, who somehow concluded that the Gallas (who live in lowland south-east Ethiopia and are now known as Oromo) were in fact Gauls. In addition, in independent Ethiopia the missionaries did not have the free rein they had elsewhere in Africa: their activity was restricted because of the suspicions of the established national church and the court. The missions were only permitted to preach to non-Christians and the non-Christians who held out the greatest appeal were the Falashas – the so-called Ethiopian Jews. The London Society for Promoting Christianity among the Jews commenced its activities in Ethiopia in 1860 but between 1860 and 1922 European missionaries were never active in the country for more than a few months at a time. The work was done by 'native agents'. This was in part because when two of the society's missionaries, Henry Stern and Henry Rosenthal, had been imprisoned by the Emperor Tewedros II, a British Expeditionary Force of twelve thousand men under Sir Robert Napier was obliged to storm the imperial fortress at Amba Magdala in order to free them. This intervention saved the missionaries, drove the Emperor to suicide and plunged the country into civil war.[36]

There are, however, important parallels that can be drawn between the invention of a new identity for the Falashas and the situation elsewhere in Africa. Before the contact with Western missionaries and Jews in the nineteenth century the Falashas had an identity that was essentially constructed from the *Kebra Nagast* and the Bible. They participated in the national myth that the first emperor of Ethiopia was the son of King Solomon by the Queen of Sheba. They perceived themselves as Israelites, as did the Christian population to a considerable extent. When James Bruce, the Laird of Kinnaird who travelled in

Ethiopia between 1769 and 1774, came across the Falashas they explained that 'they came with Menelik from Jerusalem', so Bruce could note that 'they perfectly agree with the Abyssinians in the story of the Queen of Saba'.[37] They did not perceive themselves as Jews (*ayhud* in Ge'ez). When Joseph Halévy (the first Western Jew to visit the Falashas to our knowledge) was in Ethiopia in 1867–8 he observed that the term 'Jewish' was practically unknown.[38] In earlier periods it was used as one of many designations of the Falashas by the Christians but the term *ayhud* was equally used to describe pagans or Christian heretics.[39] As a result of European intervention a new identity was imagined for the community and was essentially absorbed by it. This was a categorical identity as Jews – an identity somewhat divorced from the stories of the national epic of King Solomon and the Queen of Sheba (in which 'Jews' are portrayed in a negative way). It appears that from the sixteenth century on, Ethiopian non-Falasha sources began to suggest that the Falashas had come to Ethiopia after the destruction of the Second Temple by the Romans: in other words that they were Jews rather than Israelites, which may reflect a Portuguese understanding of Falasha origins.[40] By the time the Anglican missionary Samuel Gobat (whom we have already encountered as a supporter of British Israelism)[41] visited the Falashas in 1830 there was a mixed tradition: as he put it, 'they do not know of what tribe they are; nor have they any adequate idea as to the period when their ancestors settled in Abyssinia. Some say that it was with Menelic, the son of Solomon; others believe that they settled in Abyssinia after the destruction by the Romans.'[42] Gobat, however, was clear as to who they were. He observed that their 'superstitions are the same as those of the Christians, only that they are modelled after the Jewish fashion'. He never once questioned the Jewishness of the Falashas.[43] Their Jewishness became institutionalised, so to speak, when, perhaps at the suggestion of Joseph Wolff – the Jewish convert to Christianity, missionary and seeker of the Lost Tribes whom we have sighted periodically throughout this book – Gobat urged the London Society for the Promoting of Christianity Amongst the Jews to take over the mission to the Falashas.[44] Increasingly Falashas began to make historical connections between themselves and Jews, perhaps Egyptian Jews, particularly with the idea – a quite novel one for them – of being a Lost Tribe of Israel, and more specifically the Lost Tribe of Dan.[45] In this they were aided by the Jewish 'missionaries' who came to save their 'Jewish' brethren from the snares laid by the Christian missionaries, chief among whom was Jacques Faitlovitch himself, not merely a great supporter of the Falashas but also one of the chief Lost Tribes enthusiasts of the twentieth century. The myth of the Lost Tribes in the African hinterland propagated so effectively by Eldad ha-Dani a thousand years before had come home to roost. It had been helped on its way by the wide acceptance of the broad outlines of the Lost Tribes myth in so many mediaeval and later texts. In particular there are two *responsa* (rabbinic replies to specific legal queries) of the sixteenth-century Egyptian Talmudic scholar David Ben Abi Zimra, known as the *Radbaz*, which are unequivocal, 'Those Jews that come from the land of Cush are without doubt from the Tribe of Dan.'[46] This *responsum* was certainly based on Eldad, and it now has the force of legal halakhic precedent.

In 1973 the Sephardi Chief Rabbi of Israel, Ovadiah Yosef, declared the Falashas to be 'descendants of Jewish tribes who moved South to Cush and there is no doubt that the aforementioned authorities who ruled that they originate from the Tribe of Dan carefully investigated and reached this conclusion on the basis of most reliable testimony and evidence'.[47] The ruling of the Sephardi Chief Rabbi opened the way for the subsequent mass emigration of the entire Falasha population to Israel. It was the ruling of the *Radbaz* that he principally invoked: the Falashas' imagined Israelite identity as the Lost Tribe of Dan gave them the right of entry to the Jewish State. The Israeli Ministry of the Interior, acting on the advice of an inter-ministerial committee, converted the religious ruling of the Sephardi Chief Rabbi into law. Henceforth the Lost Tribe of Dan was entitled to enter Israel and receive automatic Israeli citizenship under the 1950 Law of Return.[48]

Another Ethiopian group – the Qemant – appear to have once shared many of the characteristics of the Falashas. While most of them have now converted to Christianity there are still some who cling to their Judaic-animist religion: indeed there is a movement of renewal among the Qemant led by Qemant intellectuals in Gondar.[49] And over the last few years an Israelite identity has been proclaimed for the four million inhabitants of Gojjam in Western Ethiopia. One of the propagators of this idea, Dr Muse Tegegne, believes that Jews – the Lost Tribes – settled in Ethiopia 3,500 years ago but adopted Christianity 'to camouflage their Jewishness'.[50]

His Geneva-based organisation takes a similar position to that adopted by some Tutsis. 'Felege Guihon International,' he notes, 'stands for the protection of the Nile waters . . . It struggles against social stigma in the Horn of Africa and against the genocide in the Great Lakes. It fights inhuman acts perpetuated against the Semitic pre-Talmudic Hebrews of the Nile region in general and that of the Orits (Gojjamis) of western Ethiopia in particular.' In addition Tegegne believes that the Ark of the Covenant resides in Gojjam and that it is 'the home of the legacy of the Queen of Sheba and is the Semitic capital of the region'.[51]

In neighbouring Somalia a more recent Israelite identification has been made of a group called the Yibro who have made a number of attempts to get Israeli embassies throughout the world to show an interest in them and who have been described in a recent book enticingly titled: *The Yibro Somali Magi: the Forgotten Jews of the Horn of Africa.*[52] *The New York Times* (15 August 2000) carried an article about the Yibro that noted:

> The Sultan of the Jews in Somalia is a handsome, silver-haired man named Ahmed Jama Hersi who does not know the first thing about Judaism. He is a Muslim, as were his ancestors back at least 800 years. But he and his people are treated badly, cursed as descendants of Israelites. The name of the tribe is Yibir, or Hebrew. 'Even our young people,' he said, 'they are ashamed when you ask them what tribe they belong to. They will not say Yibir.' Not much is known about the lineage of the Yibir, one of Somalia's 'sab,' or outcast, clans . . . Mr. Hersi, 68, who has been the elected leader of the Yibir for 22 years, was asked to speak at one of the opening sessions of the peace conference two months ago. He noted that the Yibir had suffered terribly during the years of war but wanted badly to forgive and move on. 'In the civil war I lost my son, my wife, my brother, my dignity and my self-respect,' he told the delegates. 'But still I have come here to work for reconciliation.' Part of the bad treatment, he concedes, is the support of many Yibir for the dictator Muhammad Siad Barre. When he was overthrown in 1991, Mr. Hersi fled the country with surviving members of his family to live in Nairobi, Kenya's capital. But part of it is simply that they are one of the low castes of Somalis, and particularly that they are believed to be ethnic Jews in a strongly Muslim country.

From Somalia to Ethiopia and from Ethiopia to the Yemen the myth of the Lost Tribes in the Red Sea area – the locus in many ways of the most influential aspects of the myth – with a literary pedigree that goes back a thousand years and more, gets stronger as the years go by.

CONCLUSION

Throughout history the various groups in the world designated as Lost Tribes may be termed imagined communities, either imagined into existence by themselves or by others. The appellation 'Israelites' serves a variety of functions, none of which has much bearing on the objective reality of their past. In some cases the mechanism serves the purposes of anti-Semitism: it reflects the mediaeval Christian view of the magic Jew, the poisoner of wells, the killer of Christ – frightening 'others' – for instance the Tartars – portrayed as Israelites. Similarly self-identifying 'Israelites' may well find a life-enhancing meaning in their adopted identity and use it as a means of attacking Jews whom they see as usurpers and frauds on a gigantic scale. In other cases the designation of a group as the people of God serves a quite different function – it associates them with the prestigious, it confirms their good fortune or it may convey some material benefit, including evangelisation, education opportunities and so on.

The worldwide acceptance of Israelite identities often modelled on the Lost Tribes from Japan to New Zealand, from Burma to South America, from the United States to Ireland and from Somalia to South Africa is indeed strange. Why, in the wake of the Holocaust, should anyone want to pretend to be Jewish? In some cases – notably Japan – the Holocaust has been a trigger for such identification, and elsewhere, particularly in Africa, Jewish suffering is perceived as a paradigm of African suffering at the hands of whites or nature. In Israel there has been a good deal of scepticism about many of these groups, who are ridiculed or at best tolerated at a distance. But perhaps this will change.[1]

The topic of this 'Israelite' tradition is not part of the meta-narrative of Western historiography but is an important element in the way people view this world, its inhabitants and their origins. As Lyman has pointed out, one result of this is that the Ten Tribes 'have been lost from – and lost to – conventional modes of secular temporal historiography'.[2] And in a sense necessarily so because traditions of origin, in all their potency, defy the historian. Alexander Piatigorsky has reminded us that 'any "origins" are exempt from history, being mere symbols of that which history preserves or forgets'.[3] In *The Invention of Tradition* Eric Hobsbawm and Terence Ranger have collected articles that show how contemporary anxieties of all sorts have influenced the way we view the past. Societies throughout the world have a marked tendency to construct a genealogically useful past for themselves in which unwanted narratives and elements are purged, dispensed with and forgotten. The same mechanism is used for the explanation of 'others'. Of the mass of available facts we select those that are user-friendly. The myth of the Lost Tribes of Israel was immensely user-friendly: it was a catch-all device for understanding unknown peoples and races and a means of labelling human entities for whom there was no available label – as for some it became a channel for the better perception of self. The way Europe viewed the rest of the world over the last couple of centuries was no doubt hierarchical. From a British perspective the European states were ranged – according to their merits – below a pre-eminent Britain. The colonised world was ranked below European powers. To some extent this was based on the supposed inferiority of other 'racial' groups. But as David Cannadine has shown, it was also based on analogies with home. Thus the factory workers brought into existence by the Industrial Revolution were in some sense equated with the swarming denizens of the 'dark continents', while the criminal classes or 'undeserving poor' of the great cities were likened unto the 'Negroes' of empire.[4] Similarly analogy played a role in the construction of Israelite identities: a superior tribe or people (the British, the Tutsis or the Maoris) could by analogy be identified as the chosen people. A mysterious population about which little was known – the Pathans, Tibetans, Incas or Japanese – could be equated with the Lost Tribes. Peoples throughout the world for no very particular reason could be identified as Jews simply by analogy with one of the best-known and most feared minorities in Britain – let us say the immigrant Jews of the East End – or with Jewish minorities in Europe as a whole. As P. D. Morgan has observed in an influential article, the world of the colonised and the coloniser was one 'entire interactive system, one vast interconnected world'.[5]

Time has been harsh to the beliefs described throughout this book, which often appear quite nonsensical. Yet the recruitment of the myth of the Lost Tribes of Israel in the construction of identities throughout the world has contributed to two important and not at all nonsensical agendas: the construction of the 'other' and the construction of the self.[6] In the world of this new century the myth of the Lost Tribes will have every conceivable assistance in its travels: globalisation and the worldwide web will take the myth to the few remaining corners of the globe that it has not yet visited; the paradigm of Israelite identity will be available and accessible to all in a new order in which individual choice is likely to play a much greater role than ever before in the selection of religious and ethnic identity.

On the whole what this book has shown is that the universal use of the myth of the Lost Tribes in so many different, radically different, contexts is a Western mechanism for understanding the 'other' and particularly the other in the colonial and foreign context. It was readily accepted as a feature of modernisation in many societies and one that could be modelled to satisfy various needs. The development of the myth as a device to populate practically the entire globe with Jews presages nineteenth- and twentieth-century myths of universal Jewish conspiracies and power. It is mirrored in an interesting way by the development of another myth: the intriguing myth of the wandering Jew. Whereas in the famous chronicle of Mathew Paris that appeared in 1228 (based on an account received by Paris from a visiting Armenian bishop) this legendary wanderer was a non-Jew – the porter of Pontius Pilate, who roughly pushed Jesus in the back and told him to put a move on as he made his way to be crucified. According to the bishop Jesus retorted, 'I am walking as it is written I would and I shall rest soon: but you will walk the world until I return.' This archetypal wanderer, never at rest, had taken on various Jewish characteristics by the end of the mediaeval period and is perceived as a Jew who suffers for the crimes of his people. By the beginning of the seventeenth century an anonymous letter containing the account of a German bishop finally replaced Paris's chronicle as the definitive account. The wanderer, now a Jewish shoemaker, is given the name Ahasuerus and wanders through time and space, 'a living witness against the Jews and unbelievers.'[7] In both cases – the myth of the Lost Tribes and the myth of the wandering Jew – immensely powerful symbols of alterity, had reified around a Jewish entity.

For those that imposed a Lost Tribes identity the desire to typify the 'other' in a lucid way is clear. For those that accepted or sought this identity perhaps a psychological explanation would not be out of place. In seeking links of kinship with the ancient Israelites – the people of the Book – the book often described as the anchor of Western civilisation – individuals were in some sense aspiring to oneness with an intellectual, moral and spiritual universe. They were, if you will, aspiring to reach back to that period before individuation – to the stage of 'primitive narcissism' – to the period in the womb before the 'fall' into physical existence. The evocation of such historic models as the Israelites is in some essential way a longing for a lost past and a desperate desire to be reunited with the beginning.

NOTES

One: The Lost Tribes of Israel

1. The continued belief in the Lost Tribes is unabated. The last serious book on the subject was by A. Godbey who taught at Duke University in North Carolina. Godbey's idiosyncratic book set out to disprove the continued existence of the Lost Tribes, although at times the author seemed in two minds. He makes repeated attacks on Lost Tribe hunters but in some instances leaves the door open for further speculation. See A. Godbey, *The Lost Tribes a Myth: Suggestions towards Rewriting Hebrew History*, North Carolina, 1930. A vast number of recent works still attempt to prove the continued existence of the Lost Tribes, e.g. D. A. Law, *From Samaria to Samarkand: the Ten Lost Tribes of Israel*, New York and London, 1992; Y. Benjamin, *Mystery of the Lost Tribes*, New Delhi, 1989; H. Kersten, *Jesus Lived in India*, Dorset, 1994 (especially chapter 3); J. Eidelberg, *The Japanese and the Ten Tribes of Israel*, Givatayim, 1980. This is no more than a mildly representative list: hundreds more books subscribe to Mormon or British-Israelite or other fantasies. See pp. 25ff. The present writer does not believe that the Ten Tribes are still to be found and accepts their disappearance as a historical fact that requires no further proof. The importance of the myth as a continuing narrative is the stuff of the present work.
2. T. Parfitt, *Operation Moses*, London, 1985.
3. A. M. Hyamson, *The Lost Tribes*, London, 1903, p. 1.
4. This uncertainty may best be illustrated by looking at another very old tradition. In ancient India the term 'Aryan' meant someone who performed certain Vedic rituals: this is all it meant. In Judaism the sense of 'Jew' was always ambiguous.

5. There is some genetic support for the historical division of the tribes. See T. Parfitt, M. Thomas, N. Bradman, D. Goldstein, 'Origins of Old Testament Priests', in *Nature*, no. 394, July 1998, pp. 138–40.
6. H. Tadmor, 'The Period of the First Temple, the Babylonian Exile and the Restoration', in *A History of the Jewish People*, ed. H. Ben-Sasson, Massachusetts, 1976, p. 138.
7. Some may have returned with the exiles from Judah when they went back to the land of Israel. Those elements of the Ten Tribes left behind in the land of Israel, while retaining a separate identity for a while (see II Chronicles 30:1–6; II Chronicles 34:21) may be supposed to have been absorbed into the tribes of Judah and Benjamin.
8. This may be simply a slightly corrupted form of Hebrew 'another country'.
9. Giuseppe Veltri, 'The East in the Story of the Lost Tribes of Israel', paper presented at a conference on Orientalism and the Jews at the University of Toronto, May, 2001.
10. N. Cohn, *The Pursuit of the Millennium*, London, 1970, pp. 28–9.
11. Josephus, *Jewish Antiquities*, xi 133.
12. The Babylonian Talmud is a further compilation of Oral Law started around the fifth century that comments on the Mishnah, included in its text.
13. Jerusalem Talmud, Sanhedrin 29:b.
14. A. Neubauer, 'Where are the Ten Tribes?', in *The Jewish Quarterly Review*, vol. i, 1899, p. 20; W. Rosenau, 'What happened to the Ten Tribes?', Hebrew Union College Jubilee Volume, 1925, p. 79.
15. *Pesikta Rabbati*, tr. W. G. Braude, New Haven and London, 1968, p. 599. I am indebted to my student Ingrid Sherlock for bringing this reference to my attention.
16. T. Parfitt, *The Jews in Palestine: 1800–1882*, Royal Historical Society Studies in History, No. 52, Woodbridge, 1987, p. 120; T. Parfitt, 'The Use of Hebrew in Palestine: 1800–1882', in *Journal of Semitic Studies*, Autumn 1972, vol. 17, no. 2, p. 238, n. 5.
17. *Sepher Eldad* has been printed in many different editions. E.g. *Eldad ha-Dani*, ed. A. Epstein, Pressburg, 1891; E. N. Adler, *Jewish Travellers*, London, 1930. See C. E. Nowell, 'The Historical Prester John', *Speculum*, vol. xxviii, no. 3, July 1953, pp. 435–45.
18. E. N. Adler, *Jewish Travellers: a Treasury of Travelogues from Nine Centuries*, New York, 1966, pp. 4–21. Giuseppe Veltri has suggested that the stones in the river may be taken to represent the Tablets of the Law and points out that fire is the symbol of the presence of God in the book of Exodus.

19. D. Wasserstein, 'Eldad Ha-Dani', in *Prester John, the Mongols and the Ten Lost Tribes*, ed. C. F. Beckingham and B. Hamilton, Aldershot, 1996, pp. 214 ff.
20. D. Wasserstein, 'Eldad ha-Dani', p. 217.
21. M. Schloessinger, *The Ritual of Eldad ha-Dani*, Leipzig and London, 1908.
22. S. M. Lyman, 'The Lost Tribes of Israel as a problem in History and Sociology', in *International Journal of Politics, Culture and Society*, vol. 12, no. 1, 1998, p. 13. On Najran see T. Parfitt, *The Road to Redemption: the Jews of the Yemen: 1900–1950*, Leiden, 1996, p. 247 ff.
23. S. Kaplan, *The Beta Israel (Falasha) in Ethiopia*, New York and London, 1992, p. 43.
24. E. Ullendorff and C. Beckingham, *The Hebrew Letters of Prester John*, Oxford, 1982, p. 154; D. Wasserstein, 'Eldad ha-Dani', p. 225, n. 20.
25. H. Graetz, *History of the Jews*, London, 1901, vol. iii, p. 186.
26. A. Neubauer, 'Where are the Ten Tribes?', pp. 14–28, 95–114, 185–201, 408–23.
27. *Encyclopaedia Judaica*, vol. vi, p. 577.
28. E. Ullendorff and C. Beckingham, *The Hebrew Letters of Prester John*, p. 153. But, cf. D. Wasserstein, 'Eldad ha-Dani', *passim*.
29. S. Purchas, *Purchas His Pilgrimes*, Glasgow, 1905; *The Itinerary of Benjamin of Tudela*, ed. M. N. Adler, London, 1907.
30. A. Godbey, *The Lost Tribes*, p. 381.
31. A. Ya'ari, *Sheluhei Eretz Yisrael*, Jerusalem, 1947, p. 144. See A. Gross, 'The Expulsion and the Search for the Ten Tribes' in *Judaism*, vol. 41, no. 2, Spring 1992, pp. 130 ff.
32. Ibid. S. Weil, *Beyond the Sambatyon: the Myth of the Ten Lost Tribes*, Tel Aviv, 1991, p. 89.
33. *Massot Eretz Yisrael lerabbi Moshe Bassola*, ed. I. Ben Tzvi, Jerusalem, 1938, pp. 88–90 (the translation is mine).
34. Obadiah travelled from Italy to Palestine in 1485. See A. Ya'ari, *Sheluhei Eretz Yisrael*, p. 144; S. Weil, *Beyond the Sambatyon*, 1991, p. 89.
35. I. Ben Zvi, *The Exiled and the Redeemed*, Philadelphia, 1958, p. 180.
36. Marco Polo, *The Travels*, tr. R. Latham, Harmondsworth, 1958, pp. 303–4.
37. M. T. Hodgen, *Early Anthropology in the Sixteenth and Seventeenth Century*, Philadelphia, 1964, p. 71.
38. G. Boas, *Essays on Primitivism and Related Ideas in the Middle Ages*, Baltimore, 1948, p. 137.

39. J. Mandeville, *The Travels of Sir John Mandeville*, London, 1900, pp. 174 ff.
40. A. H. Hyamson, 'The Lost Tribes and the influence of the search for them on the return of the Jews to England', in *Jewish Quarterly Review*, vol. xv, 1903, pp. 640–76.
41. B. Hamilton, 'Prester John and the Three Kings of Cologne', in *Prester John, the Mongols and the Ten Lost Tribes*, pp. 177 ff.
42. E. Ullendorff and C. E. Beckingham, *The Hebrew Letters of Prester John*, p. 60.
43. J. Mandeville, *Travels*, London, 1953.
44. M. Hodgen, *Early Anthropology*, pp. 207–53.
45. See p. 199.
46. Rabanus Maurus' *De rerum naturis*, also known as *De universo*, is an encyclopedic compilation that he assembled between 842 and 846. The earliest edition was edited and printed by Adolf Rusch in about 1466. This edition was reprinted by George Colvener in his collected edition of Rabanus' works in 1627, and again by J. P. Migne in the series *Patrologia Latina* in 1851.
47. I am indebted to Dr Ian Christie-Miller for this information.
48. P. D. A. Harvey, *Mediaeval Maps*, London, 1991, p. 7.
49. H. Baudet, *Paradise on Earth*, New Haven and London, 1965, *passim*.
50. M. L. Margolis and A. Marx, *History of the Jewish People*, Philadelphia, 1927, p. 379; N. Cohn, *The Pursuit of the Millennium*, pp. 78–9; J. Trachtenberg, *The Devil and the Jews*, Philadelphia, 1961, ch. 2.
51. *The Book of Ser Marco Polo*, tr. and ed. H. Yule, London, 1903, vol. i, p. 56.
52. H. W. Weinbrot, *Britannia's Issue: the Rise of British Literature from Dryden to Ossian*, Cambridge, 1993, p. 409.
53. Christie-Miller's PhD thesis, 'A Critical Analysis Of Jean Thenaud's Kabbalistic Manuscript Arsenal 5061', London, 1997 which deals with the sixteenth-century French Christian Hebraist Jean Thenaud. The thesis describes the latter's work 'La Marguerite', which argues that Phrygian was the first language.
54. M. Olender, *The Languages of Paradise: Race, Religion and Philology in the Nineteenth Century*, Massachusetts and London, 1992; M. Olender, 'Sur un "oubli" linguistique', in *La conscience de soi de la poésie: Poésie et Rhétorique*, Paris, 1997, pp. 267 ff.
55. J. F. Lafitau, *Customs of the American Indians Compared with the Customs of Primitive Times*, tr. and ed. W. N. Fenton and E. L. Moore, Toronto, 1974, vol. ii, p. 253.

56. K. N. Chaudhuri, 'From the Barbarian and Civilised to the Dialectics of Colour: an Archaeology of Self-Identities', in *Society and Ideology: Essays in South Asian History*, ed. P. Robb, Oxford, 1993, p. 31.
57. E.g. http://web.tiscalinet.it/imninalu/english.htm
58. S. Greenblatt, *Marvellous Possessions: The Wonder of the New World*, Chicago, 1991, p. 92.
59. I am indebted to Emanuela Trevisan Semi who makes this point in a forthcoming paper.
60. L. Glaser, *Indians or Jews? An Introduton to a Reprint of Manasseh ben Israel's The Hope of Israel*, California, 1973, pp. 21–2.
61. François du Creux, *The History of Canada or New France*, ed. J. B. Conacher, vol. i, Toronto, 1951, p. xxiv.
62. S. Zantop, *Colonial Fantasies: Conquest, Family and Nation in Precolonial Germany: 1770–1870*, Durham and London, 1997, introduction.
63. R. Elphick, 'Africans and the Christian Campaign in Southern Africa', in *The Frontier in History: North America and Southern Africa Compared*, ed. H. Lamar and L. Thompson, New Haven and London, 1981, pp. 270 ff.
64. S. Zantop, *Colonial Fantasies*, p. 17. Discussion of these elements is absent in Edward Said's much cited works.
65. A. McClintock, *Imperial Leather: Race, Gender and Sexuality in the Colonial Contest*, New York, 1995; R. Young, *Colonial Desire: Hybridity in Theory, Culture and Race*, London, 1995; N. Armstrong, 'The Occidental Alice', in *Differences: A Journal of Feminist Cultural Studies*, no. 2, 1990. See also E. Said, 'Orientalism Reconsidered', in *Europe and Its Others*, ed. F. Barker, Colchester, 1985; S. Zantop, *Coloncal Fantasies*.
66. H. Bhabha, 'The Other Question: the stereotype and Colonial Discourse', in *Screen*, vol. 24, no. 6, 1983.
67. D. Cannadine, *Ornamentalism: How the British Saw Their Empire*, London, 2002, pp. xix ff.

Two: As the Sand of the Sea: Israelites, the Spanish and the New World

1. *The Journal of Christopher Columbus*, tr. C. Jane, ed. L. A. Vigneras, New York, 1960.
2. Rodrigo de Jerez may have been the sailor who Columbus had planned to send to the Great Khan a few days before, on 30 October.
3. *The Journal of Christopher Columbus*, p. 51.
4. *The Journal of Christopher Columbus*, pp. 51 and 206.
5. D. Katz, *Philo-Semitism and the Readmission of the Jews to England, 1603–*

1655, Oxford, 1985, p. 130; Yosef ha-Cohen, *Divrei-ha-yamim lemalkhei Zarfat umalkhei beit Otman ha Togar*, Sabbionetta, 1554; English translation, C. H. F. Bialloblotzky, *The Chronicles of Rabbi Joseph ben Joshua ben Meir, the Sphardi*, London, vol. ii, 1836, pp. 4–12, quoted in M. Pollack, 'The Revelation of a Jewish Presence in Seventeenth-Century China: its impact on Western Messianic Thought', in *The Jews of China*, New York, London, 1999, vol. i, ed. J. Goldstein, pp. 50–70.

6. Pedro Martir de Angleria, *Décadas del Nuevo Mundo*, tr. J. T. Asensio, Buenos Aires, 1944; F. A. MacNott, *De Orbe Novo, The Eight Decades of Peter Martyr d'Anghera*, New York, 1912; L. E. Huddleston, *Origins of the American Indians: European Concepts, 1492–1729*, Austin, 1967, p. 4; *The Gold of Ophir: Travels, Myths, and Legends in the New World*, ed. E. Dahlberg, New York, 1972, pp. 31 ff.
7. S. M. Lyman, 'Postmodernism and the construction of Ethnocultural identity: the Jewish-Indian theory and the Lost Tribes of Israel', in *Sociological Spectrum*, 1997, no. 17, pp. 259 ff. See also *Magna Bibliotheca Anglo-Judaica: A Bibliographical Guide to Anglo-Jewish History*, ed. C. Roth, London, 1937.
8. *The Journal of Christopher Columbus*, pp. 3–4; T. Todorov, *The Conquest of America: the Question of the Other*, New York, 1992, p. 50.
9. *The Journal of Christopher Columbus*, p. 24.
10. S. Greenblatt, *Marvellous Possessions*, p. 92.
11. Luis de Granada, *Quarta parte de la Introduccion de la Fe*, Madrid, 1730, vol. vi, p. 266, quoted in *Manasseh ben Israel: the Hope of Israel*, ed. with introduction and notes by H. Méchoulan and G. Nahon, Oxford, 1987, p. 45.
12. K. N. Chaudhuri, 'From the Barbarian and Civilised to the Dialectics of Colour', p. 23.
13. Ibid.
14. Pedro Martir de Angleria, *Décadas del Nuevo Mundo*, p. 29.
15. R. H. Popkin, 'The rise and fall of the Jewish Indian Theory', in *Manasseh Ben Israel and His World*, ed. Y. Kaplan, H. Méchoulan and R. H. Popkin, Leiden, 1989, p. 64.
16. L. E. Huddleston, *Origins of the American Indians*.
17. L. Glaser, *Indians or Jews?*, pp. 13–14, 21–2. See also D. Duran, *Historia de las Indias de Nueva Espana e Islas de la Tierra Firme*, Mexico, 1967, 2 vols; English translation, *Book of the Gods and Rites and the Ancient Calendar*, tr. and ed. F. Horcasitas and D. Heyden, Norman, Oklahoma, 1971. See T. Todorov, *The Conquest of America*, p. 210.

18. R. H. Popkin, 'The rise and fall of the Jewish Indian Theory,' p. 63.
19. See below, pp. 90 ff.
20. E. K. Kingsborough, *Antiquities of Mexico*, London, 1829–30, vol. vi, p. 283.
21. Juan de Torquemada, *Primera Parte de los veinte i un libros rituales i monarchia indiana, con el origen y guerras de los Indios Occidentales, i–iii*, Madrid, 1723.
22. E. K. Kingsborough, *Antiquities of Mexico*; L. Glaser, *Indians or Jews?*, pp. 21–2.
23. R. H. Popkin, 'The rise and fall of the Jewish Indian Theory', p. 64.
24. L. E. Huddleston, *Origins of the American Indians*, pp. 5–6; L. Glaser, *Indians or Jews?*, p. 21.
25. E. K. Kingsborough, *Antiquities of Mexico*, vol. vi, p. 271.
26. Diego de Landa, *Relacion de las Cosas de Yucatan*, ed. and tr. A. M. Tozzer, Massachusetts, 1941, pp. 16–17, quoted in D. Katz, *Philo-Semitism and the Readmission of the Jews to England*, p. 132.
27. E. K. Kingsborough, *Antiquities of Mexico*, vol. vi, p. 235. As it happens hundreds of Peruvians, descendants of the Incas, started to convert to Judaism in the 1980s. By the early 1990s several groups had already gone to Israel as converts and as immigrants. In November 2001 a group of 83 were given an orthodox conversion in Peru. The community had come to the conclusion as Christians that if they were to follow the laws of the Bible properly, as they wished, they would in fact have to become Jews. For other examples of group conversions see T. Parfitt and E. Semi, *Judaising Movement*, London, 2002, *Passim*.
28. E. K. Kingsborough, *Antiquities of Mexico*, vol. vi, p. 272.
29. E. K. Kingsborough, *Antiquities of Mexico*, vol. vi, p. 275.
30. *Book of the Gods and Rites and the Ancient Calendar*, p. 25.
31. *Book of the Gods and Rites and the Ancient Calendar*, pp. 26 ff.
32. D. Duran, *Historia de las Indias de Nueva Espana e Islas de la Tierra Firme*; T. Todorov, *The Conquest of America*, p. 210.

Three: The Invisible Hebrews – A Myth of Albion

1. C. Roth, *A History of the Jews in England*, Oxford, 1949, p. 150; C. Garrett, *Respectable Folly: Millenarians and the French Revolution in France and England*, Baltimore, 1975, p. 184.
2. H. W. Weinbrot, *Britannia's Issue*, pp. 418 ff.
3. D. S. Katz, *Philo-Semitism and the Readmission of the Jews to England*; D. S. Katz, *The Jews in the History of England, 1485–1850*, Oxford, 1996, p. 112.
4. D. S. Katz, *The Jews in the History of England*, p. 112.

5. L. Hyman, *The Jews of Ireland from Earliest Times to the Year 1910*, Ireland, 1972, pp. 8–10.
6. P. Ackroyd, *Blake*, London, 1995, p. 74.
7. D. S. Katz, *The Jews in the History of England*, pp. 303 ff. On Gordon see P. Colson, *The Strange History of Lord George Gordon*, London, 1937; C. Hibbert, *King Mob*, Harmondsworth, 1982. One of the ways in which many of the eighteenth-century Hebraisers of British culture attempted to make a connection between the Jews of the Bible and the contemporary British was by finding signs of Hebrew in the history of English. In 1869 R. Govett published *English Derived from Hebrew: with Glances at Greek and Latin*, London, 1869. H. D. Weinbrot, *Britannia's Issue*, pp. 403–31, 482–91.
8. C. Hill, *The World Turned Upside Down*, London, 1972.
9. E. P. Thompson, *Witness Against the Beast: William Blake and the Moral Law*, London, 1993, pp. xiii ff.
10. *The Dictionary of National Biography from the Earliest Times to 1900*, Oxford, 1917, p. 1350 ff; R. Mathews, *English Messiahs*, London, 1936, pp. 85–126.
11. R. Brothers, *A Revealed Knowledge of the Prophecies and Times*, London, 1795, p. 34.
12. D. S. Katz, *The Jews in the History of England*, pp. 312–13; J. F. C. Harrison, *The Second Coming: Popular Millenarianism, 1780–1850*, London, 1979.
13. P. Ackroyd, *Blake*, p. 174.
14. J. Wilson, 'British Israelism', in *Patterns of Sectarianism: Organisation and Ideology in Social and Religious Movements*, ed. B. R. Wilson, London, 1967, p. 351.
15. *The Dictionary of National Biography*, p. 685 ff; D. S. Katz, *The Jews in the History of England*, p. 313; J. K. Hopkins, *A Woman to Deliver Her People: Joanna Southcott and English Millenarianism in an era of Revolution*, Texas, 1982.
16. In New Zealand Christadelphian schismatics refer to themselves as Christian Israelites.
17. *The Dictionary of National Biography*, pp. 1073 ff; D. S. Katz, *The Jews in the History of England, The Jews in the History of England*, p. 313.
18. H. W. Weinbrot, *Britannia's Issue*, pp. 477–9.
19. See pp. 91 ff and n. 22 below.
20. G. Keating, *History of Ireland*, tr. P. S. Dinneen and published in 1908 for the Irish Texts Society.
21. H. Howarth, *The Irish Writers (1880–1940)*, London, 1958, p. 260.

22. F. Budgen, *James Joyce and the Making of Ulysses*, Bloomington, 1960, p. 170; *Letters of James Joyce*, ed. S. Gilbert, London, 1957, vol. i, p. 146; L. Hyman, *The Jews of Ireland*, pp. 167 ff. This kind of thing persists. A recent theory has it that the ancient Egyptians established a colony in Ireland 3,500 years ago, after landing in County Kerry. Lorraine Evans, *Kingdom of the Ark*, London, 2000. Simon & Schuster, the publishers, describe the book as the 'startling story of how the ancient British race is descended from the pharaohs'.
23. A. Hertzberg, 'The New England Puritans and the Jews', in *Hebrew and the Bible in America: the First Two Centuries*, ed. S. Goldman, Dartmouth, 1993, p. 115.
24. Ibid.
25. Ibid., p. 114; G. A. Kohut, *Ezra Stiles and the Jews*, New York, 1902; E. S. Morgan, *The Gentle Puritan – a Life of Ezra Stiles, 1727–1795*, New Haven, 1962; W. Wilner, 'Ezra Stiles and the Jews' in *Publications of the American Jewish Historical Society*, no. 8, 1900, pp. 119–26.
26. A. A. Chiel, 'Ezra Stiles and the Jews: a Study in Ambivalence', in *Hebrew and the Bible in America: the First Two Centuries*, ed. S. Goldman, Dartmouth, 1993, pp. 156 ff; L. E. Huddleston, *Origins of the American Indians*, pp. 113–4; R. Wauchope, *Lost Tribes and Sunken Continents: Myth and Method in the Study of American Indians*, Chicago, 1962, p. 57.
27. *Ethnicity*, eds J. Hutchinson and A. D. Smith, Oxford, 1996, p. 260.
28. A. M. Hyamson, 'Anglo-Israelism', in *Encyclopaedia of Religion and Ethics*, ed. J. Hastings, no. 1, New York, 1913, p. 482; O. M. Friedman, *Origins of the British Israelites*, San Francisco, 1993; R. Sanders, *Lost Tribes and Promised Lands*, New York, 1992.
29. O. M. Friedman, *Origins of the British Israelites*, p. 14; R. R. Chambers, *The Plain Truth about Armstrongism*, Grand Rapids, 1972, p. 32.
30. It is of interest that in the sixteenth century in France François I was widely believed to be the literal heir of the kings of Israel, to have a special relationship with the archangel Michael and to be an angel himself. I am indebted to Dr Ian Christie-Miller for this information.
31. A. M. Hyamson, 'Anglo-Israelism', p. 482.
32. *Banner of Israel*, 5 April, 1899.
33. J. Wilson, 'British Israelism', p. 350.
34. P. France, *The Rape of Egypt: How the Europeans Stripped Egypt of its Heritage*, London, 1991, p. 185.
35. The bishopric had started out as a joint Anglo-Prussian venture.
36. E. Hine, *Oxford Wrong in Objecting to the Anglo-Saxons being Identical with Israel*, New York, 1880, p. 137.

37. T. Rolsing, *Anglo-Israel and the Jewish Problem: the Ten Lost Tribes of Israel Found and Identified in the Anglo-Saxon Race*, Philadelphia, 1892.
38. O. M. Friedman, *Origins of the British Israelites*, p. 16.
39. H. W. J. Senooir, *The British Israelites*, London, 1885, p. 1.
40. M. H. Gayer, *The Heritage of the Anglo-Saxon Race*, London, 1941, p. 11.
41. J. Wilkinson, *The Ten Tribes: Where are they not And Where are they?*, London, no date; also J. Wilkinson, *Englishmen not Israelites*, London.
42. J. Wilkinson, *The Ten Tribes*, p. 20.
43. J. C. Stevens, *Genealogical Chart Showing the Connection Between the House of David and the Royal Family of Britain*, Liverpool, 1877.
44. A. K. Robinson, *Predestination as Taught in the Bible and Verified in History*, Leeds, 1895, pp. 132 ff.
45. O. M. Friedman, *Origins of the British Israelites*, p. 25.
46. C. Daines, *When Jesus Lived in Britain*, California, no date, pp. 4–5.
47. A. M. Hyamson, 'Anglo-Israelism', p. 482; O. M. Friedman, *Origins of the British Israelites*, pp. 33 ff., pp. 59 ff.
48. E. J. Hobsbawm, *The Age of Empire: 1875–1914*, London, 1996, p. 252.
49. J. Wilson, 'British Israelism'; *Israel's Messenger*, 22 April 1921; M. H. Gayer, *The Heritage of the Anglo-Saxon Race*, London, 1941, pp. 112.
50. J. Wilson, 'British Israelism', p. 376.
51. J. O. Sanders, *Heresies Ancient and Modern*, London, 1948, p. 121.
52. Mathews has noted, 'When the Jews were carried off into Babylon captivity the Ark of the Covenant, according to the biblical book of Jeremiah was hidden. The Ark of the Covenant allegedly, again according to the Bible, contained the writings of Moses. To this day the Ark has never been found, ergo neither have Moses' writings been found. After seventy years of captivity, Cyrus, king of the Persian Empire, allowed the Jews to return to Jerusalem. They were led by Ezra, who during the Babylon captivity, worked as a scribe in the Babylon library. According to the Bible, Ezra had a dream in which he wrote the first five books of the Bible attributed to Moses. Much of what Ezra wrote came from the Persian (Aryan) library in Babylon. Ezra created a history for his people by plagiarizing Aryan stories from the library. One example is Moses being placed in the water as an infant. This was a copy of the earlier Sumerian story. The book *Bible Myths and Their Parallels in Pagan Religions* covers many such gleanings of our pagan beliefs that "found" their way into the Bible. So in answer to your question, yes, I view parts of the Bible as being of Aryan origin. It is those parts that spoke to me when I was a

follower of Christian Identity. As far as any part of the Bible being useful, I would have to say yes. It helps, as I previously said, to bring some of our Kinsmen to think racially through Christian Identity beliefs and it helps the rest of us understand the mind of our enemy and what makes him tick.'

53. M. Barkun, *Religion and the Racist Right: the Origins of the Christian Identity Movement*, North Carolina, 1994, pp. 122, 228, 230; R. E. Exekiel, *The Racist Mind: Portraits of American Neo-Nazis and Klansmen*, New York, 1995.
54. *London Review of Books*, no. 14, 19 July 2001, p. 23.
55. B. Sayyid, 'Sign o'times: Kaffirs and Infidels fighting the Ninth Crusade', in *The Making of Political Identities*, ed. E. Laclau, London, 1994, p. 270.

Four: The Puritans, American Indians and the End of Days

1. Anon., *Of the Newe Landes*, Antwerp, 1511(?), in *The First Three English Books on America*, ed. E. Arber, pp. xxvii, xxxiii–iv, quoted in D. Katz, *Philo-Semitism*, p. 134.
2. Included in *The First Three English Books on America*, Edinburgh, 1885.
3. F. A. MacNott, *De Orbe Novo, the Eight Decades of Peter Martyr d'Angera*, New York, 1912.
4. L. E. Huddleston, *Origins of the American Indians*, p. 33; D. Katz, *Philo-Semitism*, p. 134. It is worth noting that Huddleston throughout his extremely useful book on Indian origins (followed by others) constantly plays down the importance of the Israelite theory. Indeed his book seems to approve of 'right' theories and frown on 'wrong' ones. In any event he shies away from the Israelite theory when he can. In the case of Peter Martyr, for instance, he notes categorically, 'he did not postulate a Judaic origin'. But by referring to Hebrew, circumcision and Solomon in the context of Indian origins it is clear that in some sense he took Israelite origins somewhat for granted – or at the very least it was in the background of his thinking as a widespread discourse towards which he nods.
5. L. E. Huddleston, *Origins of the American Indians*, p. 35.
6. G. Fletcher, 'The Tartars or, Ten Tribes', in *Israel Redux*, ed. S. Lee, London, 1677, pp. 1–28; Anon., *Relations, of the Most Famous Kingdoms*, London, 1611, p. 336, quoted in D. Katz, *Philo-Semitism*, p. 135.
7. E. Brerewood, *Enquiries Touching the Diversity of Languages and Religions through the Chief Parts of the World*, London, 1614, p. 95–6.
8. G. Postel, *Des Histoires Orientales*, Paris, 1575, pp. 34–7. A. Thevet,

La Cosmographie Universelle, Paris, 1575, p. 1022; D. Katz, *Philo-Semitism*, p. 135.

9. L. E. Huddleston, *Origins*, pp. 113–4; R. Wauchope, *Lost Tribes and Sunken Continents: Myth and Method in the Study of American Indians*, Chicago, 1962, p. 57.
10. A. Ya'ari, *Sheluhei Eretz Yisrael*, p. 145.
11. M. F. Modder, *The Jew in the Literature of England*, Philadelphia, 1960, p. 19.
12. I. Archer, *The Personal Reigne of Christ*, London, 1642, pp. 25–6, quoted in D. Katz, *Philo-Semitism*, p. 128.
13. It is worth noting that not all Puritans held this view: some understood Israel in Romans 1:25 ff to refer to the New Testament Church of Gentile and Jew. See P. Toon, 'The Question of Jewish Immigration', in *Puritans, the Millennium and the Future of Israel: Puritan Eschatology, 1600–1660*, ed. P. Toon, Cambridge and London, 1970, pp. 115 ff, 126 ff.
14. A. H. Silver, *A History of Messianic Speculation in Israel from the First through the Seventeenth Century*, New York, 1927, p. 173.
15. R. Popkin, 'The Marrano theology of Isaac la Peyrère', in *Studi internazionali di filosofia*, vol. v, 1973, pp. 97–126.
16. R. Mason, *The God of Spinoza: a Philosophical Study*, Cambridge, 1997; S. Smith, *Spinoza, Liberalism and the Question of Jewish Identity*, Yale, 1997; R. Popkin, 'The Excommunicant', *London Review of Books*, 15 October 1998.
17. D. S. Katz, *Philo-Semitism*, passim; *The Jews in the History of England*, pp. 109, 123; G. Leti, *La Vie d'Olivier Cromwel*, Amsterdam, 1746.
18. B. S. Capp, *The Fifth Monarchy Men*, London, 1972, p. 38.
19. H. W. Weinbrot, *Britannia's Issue*, p. 414.
20. M. F. Modder, *The Jew in the Literature of England*, p. 32.
21. D. S. Katz, *Philo-Semitism*, p. 110.
22. C. Hill, *Intellectual Origins of the English Revolution*, Oxford, 1965, p. 102.
23. *Menasseh ben Israel: the Hope of Israel*, eds H. Méchoulan and G. Nahon, Oxford, p. 48.
24. L. Wolf, *Manasseh ben Israel's Mission to Oliver Cromwell*, Jewish Historical Society, London, 1901; H. Graetz, *History of the Jews*, vol. v, 1901, p. 48.
25. *Menasseh ben Israel: the Hope of Israel*, eds H. Méchouland and G. Nahon; C. Roth, *A Life of Menasseh ben Israel, Rabbi, Printer and Diplomat*, Philadelphia, 1935.
26. L. Hyman, *The Jews of Ireland*, p. 350.

27. R. H. Popkin, 'The Lost Tribes, the Caraites and the English Millenarians', in *Journal of Jewish Studies*, vol. xxxvii, 1986, pp. 213–23.
28. *Menasseh ben Israel: the Hope of Israel*, ed. H. Méchoulan and G. Nahon, p. 1 ff.
29. Ibid., p. 25.
30. H. Graetz, *History of the Jews*, vol. v, pp. 34–5.
31. *Menasseh ben Israel: the Hope of Israel*, eds H. Méchoulan and G. Nahon, p. 23.
32. C. Roth, *A Life of Manasseh ben Israel*, p. 65.
33. M. Pollack, 'The Revelation of a Jewish Presence in Seventeenth-Century China', p. 55.
34. E. Levi de Montezinos, 'The Narrative of Aharon Levi, alias Antonio de Montezinos', in *The American Sephardi*, nos 7–8, 1975, pp. 62–83.
35. 'The Relation of Master Antonie Montesinos', in *Iewes in America*, ed. T. Thorowgood, London, 1605, quoted in D. Katz, *Philo-Semitism*, p. 143; *Menasseh ben Israel: the Hope of Israel*, eds H. Méchoulan and G. Nahon, passim.
36. The reference is to the Hephtalites who defeated Peroza, King of Persia in AD 481.
37. H. Graetz, *History of the Jews*, vol. v, p. 37.
38. A. Ya'ari, *Sheluhei Eretz Yisrael*, p. 146.
39. D. S. Katz, *Philo-Semitism*, passim; D. S. Katz, *The Jews in the History of England*, pp. 109, 123.
40. G. Leti, *La Vie d'Olivier Cromwel*; H. Graetz, *History of the Jews*, vol. v, p. 48; D. S. Katz, *The Jews in the History of England*, p. 121.
41. H. Graetz, *History of the Jews*, vol. v, p. 48.
42. C. Hill, *Intellectual Origins of the English Revolution*, p. 102; L. Wolf, *Menasseh ben Israel's Mission to Oliver Cromwell*; C. Roth, 'The resettlement of the Jews in England in 1656', in *Three Centuries of Anglo-Jewish History*, ed. V. D. Lipman, Cambridge, 1961.
43. C. Hill, *Change and Continuity in Seventeenth-Century England*, London, 1974; C. Hill, *Antichrist in Seventeenth-Century England*, London, 1971, p. 95.
44. L. E. Huddleston, *Origins of the American Indians*, p. 123; H. F. Wright, 'The Controversy of Hugo Grotius with Johannes de Laet on the Origin of the American Aborigines', in *Catholic Historical Review*, 1917, no. iii, pp. 257–75; J. F. Lafitau, *Customs of the American Indians*, vol. i, p. 259.
45. T. Thorowgood, *Jews in America or Probabilities that Those Indians are Judaical, made more probable by Some Additions on the Further Conjectures*,

London, 1660, p. 17; A. Hertzberg, 'The New England Puritans and the Jews', pp. 110 ff.

46. G. Scholem, *Sabbatai Sevi: The Mystical Messiah 1626–1676*, Princeton, 1973, p. 332. Joseph Mede (1586–1638) of Cambridge and his student, the Cambridge Platonist Henry More, were among those who thought that the end of the world was nigh and that it would occur sometime between 1650 and 1680. They argued that the American Indians were the children of Satan, who had been expelled from the Old World during Christ's ministry on earth and had made their way to the Americas. Mede thought America would be spared the mighty conflagration that would accompany Christ's return but that it would also miss the benefits of the blessed millennium. The Indians would make up Gog and Magog whom the Devil would persuade to march on the new Jerusalem. The bloodiest stories about the Indians peddled by some of the Spanish were retold by More with the intention of demonstrating how thoroughly demonic they were. Given the picture of Jews in standard Christian theology, the commonplace identification of Jews as agents of the Devil in mediaeval Europe and their frequent identification as Gog and Magog, it is clear that Mede and More's theory is not all that far removed from the Israelite theory.
47. R. W. Cogley, *John Eliot's Mission to the Indians before King Philip's War*, Massachusetts, 1999.
48. D. S. Katz, *Philo-Semitism*, pp. 156–7.
49. A. Hertzberg, 'the New England Puritans and the Jews', pp. 118 ff.
50. L. Glaser, *Indians or Jews?*, p. 46; D. Katz, *Philo-Semitism*, p. 157.
51. D. S. Katz, *Philo-Semitism*, p. 157.
52. A. Hertzberg, 'The New England Puritans and the Jews', p. 111.
53. D. Gookin, *Historical Collections of the Indians of New England*, Boston, 1792, reprinted in the series, Research Library of Colonial America, New York, 1972.
54. D. Gookin, *Historical Collections*, pp. 4 ff.
55. C. Crawford, *An Essay upon the Propagation of the Gospel*, Philadelphia, 1799, pp. 16–17; W. Penn, *His Own Account of the Lenni Lenape by Albert Cook Myers*, Philadelphia, 1737.
56. *Menasseh ben Israel: the Hope of Israel*, ed. H. Méchoulan and G. Nahon, p. 69 and n. 29.

Five: A Star in the West: Israelites and the Americas

1. J. F. Lafitau, *Customs of the American Indcans* vol. i, pp. xxxix ff, 260 ff.

2. J. F. Lafitau, *Customs of the American Indians*, ii, p. 255.
3. J. Eyre, *Observations upon the Prophecies Relating to the Restoration of the Jews*, London, 1771, quoted in D. S. Katz, *The Jews in the History of England*, p. 311.
4. R. H. Popkin, 'The rise and fall of the Jewish Indian Theory', pp. 70–1.
5. L. E. Huddleston, *Origins of the American Indians*, p. 57; D. S. Katz, *Philo-Semitism*, p. 139.
6. C. Beatty, *Journal of a Two Months Tour with a View to Promoting Religion among the Frontier Inhabitants of Pennsylvania and of Introducing Christianity among the Indians to the Westward of the Alegh-geny Mountains*, London, 1768, pp. 25, 83 ff.
7. R. Wauchope, *Lost Tribes and Sunken Continents: Myth and Method in the Study of American Indians*, Chicago, 1962, p. 57.
8. C. Crawford, *An Essay upon the Propagation of the Gospel*, Philadelphia, 1799, pp. 16–17.
9. The volume of Crawford I consulted in the University of Oklahoma Library contains a handwritten note: 'a late account, however, mentions that their man proved to be an impostor and is now in an elevated station . . .'; C. Crawford, *An Essay upon the Propagation of the Gospel*, p. 33; L. Glaser, *Indians or Jews?* p. 53; R. H. Popkin, 'The rise and fall of the Jewish Indian Theory', p. 72.
10. C. Crawford, *An Essay upon the Propagation of the Gospel*, pp. 20–1, 34.
11. Cf. C. Crawford, *An Essay upon the Propagation of the Gospel*, p. 25.
12. C. E. Leonoff, *Pioneers, Pedlars and Prayer Shawls*, British Columbia, 1978, p. 11; D. Rome, *The First Two Years: a record of the Jewish Pioneers on Canada's Pacific Coast, 1858–1860*, Montreal, 1942; D. Rome, 'Jewish Pioneers of British Columbia', in *Jewish Western Bulletin*, 16 August 1957, p. 3.
13. *The American Museum*, December 1791, vol. ii, p. 262.
14. E. Boudinot, *A Star in the West or a Humble attempt to discover the long Lost Tribes of Israel preparatory to their return to their beloved city, Jerusalem*, New Jersey, 1816, pp. 101–3.
15. Ibid., p. 297.
16. See J. Evarts, *Cherokee Removal*, ed. F. P. Pruchia, Knoxville, 1981, p. 3.
17. R. H. Popkin, 'The Rise and Fall of the Jewish Indian Theory', p. 74.
18. S. J. Gould, 'Morton's Ranking of Races by Cranial Capacity. Unconscious manipulation of data may be a scientific norm', in *Science*, no. 200, 1978, pp. 503–9.

19. The son of George, the third Earl of Kingston.
20. See *The Gentleman's Magazine*, London (New Series), no. 7, 1837, p. 537; R. Wauchope, *Lost Tribes and Sunken Continents*, pp. 50 ff.
21. E. K. Kingsborough, *Antiquities of Mexico*, vol. vi, p. 283.
22. See B. Simon, *The Ten Tribes of Israel Historically Identified with the Aborigenes of the Western Hemisphere*, London, 1836, p. viii.
23. M. J. Koehler, 'Some Early American Zionist Projects', in *Publications of the American Jewish Historical Society*, 1900, vol. viii, pp. 106–113; *The Selected Writings of Mordecai Noah*, eds M. Schuldiner and D. J. Kleinfeld, Connecticut, 1999; I. Goldberg, *Major Noah: American-Jewish Pioneer*, New York, 1937.
24. J. Schwartz, *A Descriptive Geography and Brief Historical Sketch of Palestine*, Philadelphia, 1850, pp. 493–517.
25. J. J. Benjamin II, *Eight Years in Asia and Africa from 1846 to 1855*, Hanover, 1863, p. 175.
26. *Publications of the Ohio Archeological and Historical Society*, 1904, vol. 13, pp. 452–3.
27. S. D. Peet, 'The migrations of the Mound-Builders', in *The American Antiquarian and Oriental Journal*, 1891, no. 13, pp. 131–50.
28. F. M. Cross, 'The Phoenecian Inscription from Brazil: a Nineteenth century forgery', in *Orientalia*, 1968, no. 37, pp. 437–60.
29. R. C. Mainfort and M. L. Kwas, 'The Bat Creek Stone: Judeans in Tennessee', in *Tennessee Anthropologist*, 1991, no. 16, pp. 1–19.
30. See C. H. Gordon, 'The Ten Lost Tribes', in S. Goldman, *Hebrew and the Bible in America: the First Two Centuries*, Dartmouth, 1993, p. 66; C. H. Gordon, *Before Columbus: Links between the Old World and Ancient America*, New York, 1971, pp. 1175 ff; J. H. McCulloch, 'The Bat Creek Inscription: Cherokee or Hebrew?', in *Tennessee Anthropologist*, no. 13, Fall, 1988, pp. 79–123; B. Ford, 'Semites in America', in *Science Digest*, no. 71, January 1972, pp. 43–53; C. Covey, *Calalus: A Roman Jewish Colony in America from the Time of Charlemagne through Alfred the Great*, New York, 1975; see particularly the chapter entitled, 'The Next Fourteen, Notably the Pair with Hebrew Words', pp. 83 ff; M. McKusick, 'Canaanites in America: a New Scripture in stone', in *Biblical Archeologist*, no. 42, 1979, pp. 137–40. See S. Williams, 'Fantastic Archeology: Fakes and Rogue Professors', in *Symbols*, Harvard, December, 1988, pp. 17–23.
31. J. D. Baldwin, *Ancient America*, New York, 1872, pp. 166–7.
32. R. H. Popkin, 'The rise and fall of the Jewish Indian Theory', pp. 81–2.

33. J. O. Sanders, *Heresies Ancient and Modern*, London, 1948, p. 107.
34. D. Chidester, *Christianity: a Global History*, New York, 2000, p. 409.
35. *The Messenger*, Auckland, 31 October 1907, vol. 1, no. 19.
36. *Journal of Discourses*, 11 April 1875, vol. 18:26. I am indebted to Ingrid Sherlock for this reference.
37. R. Wauchope, *Lost Tribes and Sunken Continents*, p. 66. On these Mormon historical efforts see P. R. Cheesman, *The World of the Book of Mormon*, Bountiful, 1984; D. Farnsworth, *The Americas Before Columbus*, Salt Lake City, 1956; T. S. Ferguson, *One Fold and One Shepherd*, Salt Lake City, 1962; B. W. Warren and T. S. Ferguson, *The Messiah in Ancient America*, Provo: Books of Mormon Research Foundation, 1987; D. Brinton, *Myths of the New World*, New York, 1868.
38. See C. H. Gordon, *Riddles in History*, New York, 1974, pp. 49, 151–2.
39. *The Prophet Joseph Smith: Essays on the Life and Mission of Joseph Smith*, eds L. Porter and S. Black, Salt Lake City, 1989; T. G. Madsen, *Joseph Smith the Prophet*, Salt Lake City, 1989.
40. L. D. Friedman, *Hollywood's Image of the Jew*, New York, 1982, p. 228, quoted in S. M. Lyman, 'Postmodernism and the Construction of Ethnocultural identity: the Jewish-Indian theory and the lost tribes of Israel', in *Sociological Spectrum*, 1997, 17:259 ff.
41. R. Landes, 'Negro Jews in Harlem', in *Jewish Journal of Sociology*, 1967, 9:2, p. 176, quoted in T. Parfitt and E. Trevisan-Semi, *Judaising Movements*, London, 2001, p. 16.
42. S. Howe, *Afrocentrism: mythical pasts and imagined homes*, London, New York, 1998, p. 36; M. Bernal, *Black Athena: the Afroasiatic Roots of Classical Civilization*, New York, 1989.
43. On the Falashas see pp. 216 ff.
44. J. Malciom, *The African Origins of Modern Judaism*, Trenton-Asmara, 1996.
45. T. Parfitt and E. Trevisan-Semi, *Judaising Movements*, p. 98.
46. See pp. 46 ff.
47. H. Brotz, *The Black Jews of Harlem*, New York, 1964, p. 49, quoted in T. Parfitt and E. Trevisan-Semi, *Judaising Movements*, p. 93.
48. C. Crawford, *An Essay upon the Propagation of the Gospel*, p. 33.
49. See p. 214.
50. A. Ya'ari, *Sheluhei Eretz Yisrael*, p. 149.
51. J. Wolff, *Narrative of a Mission to Bokhara in the Years 1843–1845 to Ascertain the Fate of Colonel Stoddart and Captain Conolly*, London, 1845, vol. i, pp. 64–5. Perhaps, or perhaps not, a reference to B.

Simon, who wrote *The Ten Tribes of Israel Historically Identified with the Aborigenes of the Western Hemisphere.*

Six: From the Chi'ang to the Karen: Israel in the East

1. T. Thorowgood, *Jewes in America*, p.17.
2. A copy of Isaiah from the Dead Sea Scrolls has a variant reading of 'Sinim' which suggests that what is meant is the people of southern Egypt and this is the sense understood by a number of Jewish commentaries including Rashi, David Kimchi and the Targum Jonathan. See M. Pollak, 'The Revelation of a Jewish Presence in Seventeenth-Century China', pp. 67–8.
3. J. Wolff, *Narrative of a Mission to Bokhara in the Years 1843–1845 to Ascertain the Fate of Colonel Stoddart and Captain Conolly*, London, 1845, vol. i, p. 15.
4. J. Finn, *Stirring Times*, London, 1878, vol. i, p. 130.
5. In the case of China and the Far East generally the confusion that underlay these identifications was compounded by the ignorance of Eastern society that prevailed at the time: as late as the eighteenth century it is doubtful if any Englishman could read a Chinese text. Any way of explicating this vast, complex and alien society – by comparison with more readily understandable peoples, for instance – was readily seized upon. It should be mentioned that there was an ancient Jewish community in China that has been exhaustively studied. See *The Jews of China*, ed. J. Goldstein, New York and London, 1999, vol. i. For a recent bibliography on the Jews of China see F. D. Shulman, 'The Chinese Jews and the Jewish, Diasporas in China from the Tang Period (AD 618–906) through the mid-1990s: a Selected Bibliography', in *The Jews of China*, ed. J. Goldstein, New York and London, 2000, vol. ii, pp. 157–83. See also M. Pollack, *Mandarins, Jews and Missionaries: the Jewish Experience in the Chinese Empire*, Philadelphia, 1980. On Chinese attitudes towards Jews see Zhou Xun, *Chinese Perceptions of the 'Jews' and Judaism: a History of the Youtai*, Surrey, 2001.
6. T. Parfitt, *The Thirteenth Gate*, London, 1987, pp. 68 ff.
7. *Israel's Messenger*, Shanghai, 22 April, 1921.
8. S. Y. R. Cammann, 'The Chi'ang people of western Szechuan: the miscalled West China Jews', in *Faces of the Jewish Experience in China*, ed. D. A. Leventhal, Hong Kong, 1990, vol. ii, pp. 75–6.
9. Ibid., pp. 64–87.
10. I am much indebted to Dr Zhou Xun of the School of Oriental and

African Studies, University of London, who first brought the work on the Chi'ang to my attention and who kindly sent me some articles and read this part of the chapter.

11. See Rev. T. Torrance, 'The religion of the Ch'iang', in *Journal of the North-China Branch of the Royal Asiatic Society*, Shanghai, 1923, vol. 54, pp. 150 ff.
12. S. Y. R. Cammann, 'The Chi'ang people of western Szechuan', p. 69.
13. T. Torrance, 'The basic spiritual conceptions of the religion of the Chiang', in *Journal of the West China Border Research Society*, 1933–34, pp. 31–48; T. Torrance, 'Notes of the West China aboriginal tribes', *Journal of the West China Border Research Society*, 1932, pp. 17–19; T. Torrance, *China's First Missionaries: Ancient Israelites*, London, 1937, and T. Torrance, 'The emigration of the Jews: Israel in China', in *Scottish Geographical Magazine*, no. 56, 1940, pp. 59–64.
14. J. F. Lafitau, *Customs of the American Indians*, tr. and ed. W. N. Fenton and E. L. Moore, vol. i, p. 179; G. Candidus in H. Brouwer, *A Voyage to the Kingdom of Chile in America performed by Mr Elias Herckeman in the year 1642 and 1643. With a description of the isle of Formosa and Japan [by George Candidius]*, Frankfurt am Main, 1649.
15. *Israel's Messenger*, vol. 1, no. 15, 4 November 1904.
16. D. C. Graham, *The Customs and Religion of the Chi'ang*, Washington, 1958.
17. S. Y. R. Cammann, 'The Chi'ang people of western China', p. 65.
18. See K. Primack, *Jews in Places you Never Thought Of*, Hoboken, New Jersey, 1998, p. 33.
19. There are three main divisions of Indian Jewry: the Bene Israel, traditionally of the Konkan coast near Bombay (Mumbai); the Jews of Cochin; and the immigrant community of Iraqi Jews called Baghdadis. These communities have attracted a good deal of scholarly attention. See J. B. Segal, *A History of the Jews of Cochin*, London, 1993; B. J. Israel, *The Bene Israel of India*, Bombay, 1984; T. Timberg, *The Jews of India*, Delhi, 1986; S. Weil, 'Double Conversion among "the Children of Manasseh"', in *Contemporary Society: Tribal Studies* (Professor Satya Narayana Ratha Felicitation Volumes) vol. 1, Structure and Progress (eds G. Pfeffer and D. Behera), New Delhi, no date. Today one would add the Judaising communities of the Shinlung and the Telugu-speaking communities of Andhra Pradesh. There are, in addition, a number of discrete communities known as Banu Yisrail who, while living as Muslims, did not traditionally inter-marry with others and

who treasure a tradition that they descended from the Jews of Medina in the Hijaz.

20. J. Carel, *With the Scattered in the East*, Jerusalem, 1960, vol. i, p. 35.
21. Today the Karens number several million people; traditionally they were farmers who farmed the relatively rich soil of southern Burma. The contemporary religions of the Karen people are mainly Animism and Buddhism, although about a third are now Christians. According to their website, 'The Karens descend from the same ancestors as the Mongolian people. The earliest Karens . . . settled in Htee-Hset Met Ywa (Land of Flowing Sands), a land bordering the source of the Yangtse Kiang river in the Gobi Desert. From here we migrated southwards and gradually entered the land now known as Burma in about 739 BC. We were, according to most historians, the first settlers in this new land . . .' According to this account the Karens suffered untold hardships at the hands of their Burman overlords until the arrival of the British, when their lot began to improve. Today many Karens seek a state of their own.
22. J. E. Joshua, 'The lost Jews of Burma', in *The Jewish Tribune*, July, 1934.
23. F. Mason, *The Karen Apostle: or, Memoir of Ko Thah-Byu*, London, no date, p. 7.
24. D. M. Smeaton, *The Loyal Karens of Burma*, London, 1887, p. 76.
25. D. M. Smeaton, *The Loyal Karens of Burma*, pp. 66 ff.
26. F. Mason, *The Karen Apostle*, p. 2.
27. F. Mason, 'Traditions of the Karens', in *Baptist Missionary Magazine*, no. xiv, 1834, pp. 382–93.
28. Ibid.
29. F. Mason, *The Karen Apostle*, p. 2.
30. D. M. Smeaton, *The Loyal Karens of Burma*, p. 75.
31. H. I. Marshall, *The Karen People of Burma*, New York, p. 12.
32. F. Mason, 'Traditions of the Karens', pp. 382–93.
33. M. Lacrampe and M. Plaisant, 'Les Karians du Pégou', in *Nouvelles annales des voyages*, no. cxxii, Paris, 1849, pp. 181 ff.
34. T. Stern, '*Ariya* and the Golden Book: a Millenarian Buddhist Sect among the Karen', in *Journal of Asian Studies*, no. 27, 1968, p. 303.
35. A. R. McMahon, *The Karens of the Golden Chersonese*, London, 1876, pp. 57, 120; F. Mason, *The Karen Apostle*, p. 93; F. Mason, *Burmah, its People and Productions*, Rangoon, 1882–3.
36. T. Stern, '*Ariya* and the Golden Book', p. 303.
37. J. E. Joshua, 'The Lost Jews of Burma', in *The Jewish Tribune*, April,

1934. I am indebted to Yulia Egorova for bringing this and a number of other references to my attention.

38. J. E. Joshua, 'The Lost Jews of Burma', in *The Jewish Tribune*, May, 1934. In a private communication Hillel Halkin, who is writing a book on the Sons of Manasseh, noted that in 1998 he and Rabbi Avichail of Jerusalem met an old Karen man in Thailand who told the following tale: 'once all the peoples of the earth were one family and spoke the same language. One day a beautiful girl evinced the desire to go to the sky. She built a tower that reached the sun: she continued up until she reached the moon. However the moon fell in love with her and they married. But when she wanted to go back to earth the moon destroyed the tower. All the tribes ran in different directions: the Chinese in one direction, the Indians in another. This was the time that the different languages were created.'
39. Ibid.
40. J. E. Joshua, 'The Lost Jews of Burma', in *The Jewish Tribune*, August, 1934.
41. T. Stern, '*Ariya and the Golden Book*', p. 303.
42. K. Primack, *Jews in Places you Never Thought Of*, p. 33.

Seven: The Land of Hard Bondage: the Lost Tribes in India

1. According to census data there were 22,480 Jews in India in 1941. See A. A. Bhende and R. E. Jhirad, *Demographic and Socio-Economic Characteristics of Jews in India*, Mumbai, 1997, p. 3.
2. Ananda, *Hindu View of Judaism*, New Delhi, 1996.
3. Yulia Egorova is currently writing a doctoral thesis at the School of Oriental and African Studies, University of London, devoted to the subject of Indian perceptions of Jews.
4. F. Bernier, *Travels in the Mogul Empire: AD 1656–1668*, London, 1891.
5. English translation by J. Toland, *The Agreement of the Customs of the East Indians with those of the Jews and other Ancient Peoples*, London, 1705.
6. M. T. Hodgen, *Early Anthropology in the Sixteenth and Seventeenth Centuries*, Philadelphia, 1964, p. 346.
7. One idea was that all the circumcision in the world had started with the Jews. A counter-argument then current had it that the Jews could not have passed the habit of circumcision to Africans on the grounds that it was absolutely *necessary* for the latter to circumcise in order to have childrerk. But de la Créquinière observed that he himself had seen Africans in Guinea, America and Asia and 'they are not otherwise

made as to these Parts than we are'. Others had argued that the Jews too needed to circumcise to have children. But if so, how did they manage for forty years in the wilderness when they did not circumcise and how about those converts from Judaism who did not circumcise and who had children?

8. J. Toland, *The Agreement of the Customs of the East Indians*, pp. 132, 136–40.
9. Ibid., p. 19.
10. Abbé J. A. Dubois, *Hindu Manners, Customs and Ceremonies*, ed. Henry Beauchamp, Oxford, 1906, pp. 198–9. (This is an edition of a later improved version carried out by the Abbé.)
11. J. Rhenius, *Memoir of the Rev. C. T. E. Rhenius*, London, 1841, p. 71.
12. R. Lovett, *The History of the London Missionary Society 1795–1895*, London, 1902, vol. ii, p. 24; J. Adam, *Memoir of John Adam, Late Missionary of Calcutta*, London, 1833, p. 225.
13. G. Moore, *Lost Tribes*, London, 1861, pp. 143–60.
14. C. Buchanan, *Memoir of the Expediency of an Ecclesiastical Establishment for British India*, London, 1812, pp. 150–1.
15. C. Buchanan, *Christian Researches in Asia: with notices of the translation of the Scriptures into the Oriental Languages*, London, 1811.
16. G. Higgins, *Anacalypsis*, London, 1833–6, was first published in an edition of 200 copies, it was partially reprinted in 1878, and in full in an edition of 350 copies in 1927. In 1965 it was reprinted in full in an edition of 1,000 copies by University Books, New York.
17. G. Higgins, *Anacalypsis*, vol. 1, p. 50.
18. Ibid., p. 438.
19. Ibid., p. 432.
20. Ibid.
21. Ibid, p. 740.
22. Ibid., p. 771. On Higgins and his influence on theosophy see L. Shepard, 'The "Anacalypsis" of Godfrey Higgins, precursor of H.P.B.', in *Theosophical History*, July 1985, vol. 1, no. 3, pp. 46 ff.
23. See pp. 81 ff.
24. A. H. Godbey, *The Lost Tribes, a Myth – Suggestions towards Rewriting Hebrew History*, Durham, 1930, p. 372; J. Wolff, *Narrative of a Mission to Bokhara*, vol. i., p. 283.
25. G. Moore, *Lost Tribes*, pp. 143–60.
26. J. Wolff, *Narrative of a Mission to Bokhara*, vol. i, p. 14; J. Wolff, *Travels and Adventures*, London, 1860, vol. ii, p. 15.
27. J. Wolff, *Narrative of a Mission to Bokhara*, p. 16.

28. Ibid., p. 19.
29. Ibid., p. 17.
30. C. Crawford, *An Essay upon the Propagation of the Gospel*, pp. 18–19.
31. William Yates, *Memoirs of Mr John Chamberlain, Late Missionary in India*, Calcutta, 1824, p. 395.
32. W. T. Gidney, *The History of the London Society for Promoting Christianity amongst the Jews, 1809–1908*, London, 1908, p. 198.
33. E. Boudinot, *A Star in the West or a Humble attempt to discover the long Lost Tribes of Israel*, pp. 30–1.
34. J. Samuel, *An Appeal on behalf of the Jews Scattered in India, Persia and Arabia*, London, 1840, p. 8.
35. See J. Reit and M. Weis to the Afghan Minister Fhuja-ud-Daula 2.ii.1928, in the Faitlovitch Collection in the Sourasky Central Library of the University of Tel Aviv, file 117.
36. I. Ben Zvi, *The Exiled and the Redeemed*, Philadelphia, 1958, p. 216.
37. This suggestion that the Taliban, conscious of their 'Israelite' origins, do not engage in anti-Israeli rhetoric to the same extent as other Islamist groups is discussed on the website: www.tbwt.com/content/article.asp?articleid=1824.
38. Ibid.
39. M. Hamid, *The Unholy Alliance, Indo-Israel Collaboration against the Muslim World*, Lahore, 1978.
40. M. Tayab, *Indo-Israel Relations: A study of Indo-Israel Collusion against the Arab World*, Lahore, 1974, p. 35.
41. See p. 92.
42. Daniel Defoe, *Essay upon Literature, or an Enquiry into the Antiquity and Original of Letters Proving that the Two Tables written by the Finger of God in Mount Sinai was the first Writing in the World and that all other Alphabets derive from the Hebrew*, London, 1726, p. 77.
43. A. Ya'ari, *Sheluhei Eretz Yisrael*, p. 150.
44. *Israel's Messenger*, 18 November 1904, vol. 1, no. 16.
45. *The Bene Israelite*, Bombay, 31 January 1898, vol. 5.
46. J. Reit and M. Weis to the Afghan Minister Fhuja-ud-Daula 2.ii.1928 Fait. Coll. file 117.
47. J. J. Benjamin II, *Eight Years in Asia and Africa from 1846–1855*, Hanover, 1863, pp. 176 ff.
48. *The Bene Israelite*, 7 June 1899, vol. 6.

Eight: The Burmese Frontier: The Land of Strangers

1. S. Weil, 'Double Conversion among the "Children of Manasseh"',

vol. 1; *Structure and Progress*, ed. G. Pfeffer and D. Behera, New Delhi, no date, pp. 84 ff; A. A. Bhende and R. E. Jhirad, *Demographic and Socio-Economic Characteristics of Jews in India*, Mumbai, 1997.

2. See J. Francisco, '"Discovering" the Telugu Jews of India', in K. Primack, *Jews in Places you Never Thought Of*, pp. 253 ff. There is no 'historic' element to the Benei Ephraim. They have come to Judaism for reasons that will always be somewhat obscure, but the ambitions of the two Sadoc brothers – or their disappointment with the Baptist church – may figure among them. Having said that the community as it is presently constituted has a genuine sense of Jewish identity: for the children and young people it is their main identity in the village where they live. They are sincere in their desire to be recognised as Jews, both by their neighbours and by foreign Jews, they practise Judaism as best they can and learn Hebrew again as best they can. They feel embittered that they have been ignored by Jews elsewhere and point to their Christian neighbours who receive sustenance from overseas Christian churches in the US and elsewhere. The community seemed to me to be marked by piety, a desire to better their lot and a determination to raise the flag of Judaism in Andhra Pradesh. Because of their vague idea of descent from Israelites they feel ethnically as well as religiously Jewish.
3. The Organisation for Rehabilitation through Training, an international Jewish charitable institution for technical education.
4. See N. Natrajan, *The Missionary among the Khasis*, New Delhi, 1977.
5. See N. W. Williams, The Welsh Calvinistic Methodist Mission in Assam 1930–1950 with special reference to Missionary Attitudes to Local Society, Customs and Religion, University of London PhD, 1990, p. 70.
6. S. Weil, 'Double Conversion among the "Children of Manasseh"', p. 88.
7. Ibid.
8. M. Samra, 'Buallawn Israel: the Emergence of a Judaising Movement in Mizoram, north-east India' in *Religious Change, Conversion and Culture*, ed. Lynette Olson, Sydney, 1996, p. 105.
9. S. Weil, 'Double Conversion among the "Children of Manasseh"', p. 89. Messianic activity was engendered by the missions some of which, as in the case of the Kachar Nagas, was directed against the British as well as the Kukis. The best known of the revivalist missions, which adopted a syncretistic blend of traditional and Christian belief and praxis, was that of Pau Chin Hau in the Chin Hills, started at the beginning of the twentieth century.

10. F. Downs, 'Christian Conversion Movements among the Hill Tribes of north-east India in the Nineteenth and Twentieth Centuries', in *Religion in South Asia: Religious Conversion and Revival Movements in Mediaeval and Modern Times*, ed. G. A. Oddie, Columbia, London, 1977, pp. 155 ff. M. Samra, 'Buallawn Israel: the Emergence of a Judaising Movement in Mizoram', p. 106.
11. M. Samra, 'Judaism in Manipur and Mizoram: a By-Product of Christian Mission', in *The Australian Journal of Jewish Studies*, vol. vi, no. 1, 1992, pp. 7–22; M. Samra, 'The Tribe of Manasseh: "Judaism" in the Hills of Manipur and Mizoram', in *Man in India*, no. 71 (1), 1991 and M. Samra, 'Buallawn Israel: the Emergence of a Judaising Movement in Mizoram'.
12. M. Samra, 'Judaism in Manipur and Mizoram', pp. 7–22.
13. S. Weil, 'Double Conversion among the "Children of Manasseh" ', p. 90.
14. *The Jewish Tribune*, November 1936, vol. 7, no. 9, p. 12.
15. K. Primack, *Jews in Places you Never Thought of*, p. 21.
16. M. Samra, 'Judaism in Manipur and Mizoram,' p. 11.
17. M. Samra, 'Buallawn Israel: the Emergence of a Judaising Movement in Mizoram', p. 112.
18. Samra refers to him as Mela Chala in 'Buallawn Israel' but in a private communication he notes, 'I have been questioned by some of the Mizos about the name Mela which they don't recognise. I cannot recall where I got the name so it appears that I got it wrong. For completeness Chala's full name was Challianthanga.' I am indebted to Dr Samra for this, a number of other points and for having supplied with me copies of his articles.
19. As one informant put it, 'Chala was the first among Mizo people who came to know, to see, that Mizos are sons of Israel, of Manasia. God revealed to Chala through his spirit, saying that the Mizos are all descendants of Ten Lost Tribes of Israel. That is God's revelation to Chala, who was first to realise that Mizos are Israel. Therefore his followers all realised from about 1953 that they were Israelites of the tribe of Manasseh. All the villagers of Buallawn embraced Chala's vision and asserted they were Israelites. All people of Mizoram heard and knew that they were all Israel but unfortunately they were all uneducated people.' M. Samra, 'Buallawn Israel: the Emergence of Judaising Movement in Mizoram', p. 112.
20. Ibid; S. Weil, 'Double Conversion among the "Children of Manasseh" ', p. 93.

21. M. Samra, 'Buallawn Israel: the Emergence of a Judaising Movement in Mizoram', p. 116.
22. B. B. Goswami, 'By-product of Christianity on the Hill Tribesmen of north-east India', in *Review of Ethnology*, vol. 7:1–9, pp. 42–6.
23. C. L. Hminga, 'Christianity and the Lushai people', MA thesis, School of World Mission, Fuller Theological Seminary, 1963 quoted by S. Weil, 'Double Conversion among the "Children of Manasseh" ', p. 94.
24. I am grateful to Dr Samra for having corrected my spelling of Thangruma in *The Thirteenth Gate*, London, 1987, and for a number of other points about him; J. R. Ross, *Fragile Branches: Travels Through the Jewish Diaspora*, New York, 2000, p. 101.
25. M. Samra, 'The Tribe of Manasseh: "Judaism" in the Hills of Manipur and Mizoram', unpublished paper, p. 8.
26. Ibid.
27. M. Samra, 'Judaism in Manipur and Mizoram', pp. 7–22.
28. S. Weil, 'Double Conversion among the "Children of Manasseh" ', p. 95. Professor Nathan Katz told me in a private communication that the term Benei Menashe was already being used to describe Jews in Rangoon in the 1940s. The term was also used of the Cochinis and it may be that in this case it referred to them.
29. T. Parfitt, *The Thirteenth Gate*, p. 53.
30. A. H. Godbey, *The Lost Tribes, a Myth*, p. 372; J. Wolff, *Narrative of a mission to Bokhara*, vol. i, p. 283.
31. S. Weil, 'Double Conversion among the "Children of Manasseh" ', p. 92. Weil also spells it Chapchar Kut on p. 93.
32. J. R. Ross, *Fragile Branches*, p. 116.
33. Zaithanchhungi, *Israel-Mizo Identity*, Mizoram, 1994.
34. M. Samra, 'The Tribe of Manasseh', p. 4.
35. M. Samra, 'Buallawn Israel: the Emergence of a Judaising Movement in Mizoram', pp. 122–3.
36. S. Weil, 'Double Conversion among the "Children of Manasseh" ', p. 94.
37. C. S. Liebman, *Religion, Democracy and Israeli Society*, Amsterdam, 1997.
38. From a letter dated 3 February 1984, from Levy Benjamin, General Secretary of Manasseh People, Shinlung-Israel, north-east India, to the Chief Rabbinet [sic] Council Israel, quoted in M. Samra, 'Buallawn Israel: the Emergence of a Judaising Movement in Mizoram', p. 117.

39. Appendix A of the 1991 census report on religion: see A. A. Bhende and R. E. Jhirad, *Demographic and Socio-Economic Characteristics of Jews in India*, p. 4.
40. K. Primack, *Jews in Places you Never Thought of*, p. 28.
41. K. Primack, *Jews in Places you Never Thought of*, pp. 31 ff.
42. W. Elliman, 'Menashe's children come home', in *Hadassa Magazine*, October 1999. Avichail noted in 1998 that the Shinlung 'Jewish religious community' numbers 5,000. See K. Primack, *Jews in Places you Never Thought of*, p. 34.
43. T. Parfitt, *The Thirteenth Gate*, p. 54.

Nine: Doomed to Wander: Lost Tribes in the Pacific and New Zealand

1. J. C. Beaglehole, *The Life of Captain James Cook*, Stanford, 1974.
2. J. C. Beaglehole, 'The place of Tasman's voyage in history', in *Abel Tasman and the Discovery of New Zealand*, Wellington, 1942; A. Sharp, *The Voyages of Abel Janszoon Tasman*, Oxford, 1968.
3. In 1841 a Jew called Alexander Salmon landed in Tahiti and married a princess of the Teva clan. See I. Cohen, *Jews in Remote Corners of the World*, New Jersey, 1971, p. 4.
4. G. Robertson, *The Discovery of Tahiti: a Journal of the Second Voyage of H.M.S.* Dolphin, ed. H. Carrington, London, 1948, p. 228.
5. J. Dunmore, *French Explorers in the Pacific*, Oxford, 1965, vol. i, p. 117.
6. J. Diamond, *Guns, Germs and Steel*, London, 1997, pp. 54–5.
7. D. Chidester, *Savage Systems*, Charlottesville and London, 1996, pp. 9–10; H. G. Grey, *Ko Na Mahinga a nga tupuna Maori: the Mythology and Traditions of the New Zealanders*, London, 1854; G. Grey, *Journal of an Expedition Overland from Auckland to Taraniki by way of Rotoru, Taupo, and the West Coast: Undertaken in the Summer of 1849–50, by his Excellency the Governor-in-Chief of New Zealand*, London, 1851.
8. C. Crawford, *An Essay upon the Propagation of the Gospel*, pp. 19–20.
9. J. R. Elder, *Letters and Journals of Samuel Marsden*, London, 1932.
10. A. S. Thomson, *The Story of New Zealand*, London, 1859.
11. D. Cohen, 'New Zealand's Zion', in *The Jerusalem Report*, 18 September 1997, pp. 28–9. I am indebted to Dr Norman Simms of the English Department of Waikato University, Hamilton, New Zealand for drawing this article to my attention.
12. R. Taylor, *Te Ika a Maui or New Zealand and its Inhabitants*, London, 1855, pp. 190–1.
13. Ibid., p. 8.
14. Ibid., p. 179.

15. J. S. Polack, *New Zealand: Being a Narrative of Travels and Adventures during Residence in the Country between the Years 1831 and 1837*, London, 1838; J. S. Polack, *Manners and Customs of the New Zealanders*, London, 1840.
16. Cf. Maurice Shadbolt's novel, *Season Of The Jew*, about Te Kooti's uprising. Also see Heretaunga Pat Baker's unfinished work, Part I, 'Behind the Tattooed Face' and Part II, 'The Superior God'.
17. See S. Binney, G. Chaplain and G. Wallace, *Mihaia The Story of Rua Kenana*, Oxford University Press, Wellington, 1980.
18. *New Zealand Herald*, 28 October 1998. I am indebted to Dr Norman Simms for drawing this article to my attention. Maori identification with Jews was fairly widespread in the first half of the twentieth century. See I. Cohen, *Jews in Remote Corners of the World*, p. 30.
19. R. I. Levy, *Tahitians: Minds and Experience in the Society Islands*, Chicago and London, 1975, p. 219.
20. *The Messenger*, 31 October 1907, no. 19, pp. 145–8.
21. I am greatly indebted to Mrs Ann Gluckman of Auckland, New Zealand for her help, particularly for sending me an unpublished paper which I have used in this chapter and for drawing the article in *The Messenger* to my attention.
22. I. Cohen, *The Journey of a Jewish Traveller*, London, 1925, p. 67.
23. *The Journals of Captain James Cook*, London, 1955, ed. J. C. Beaglehole, vol. i, p. xxvii, n. 1.
24. *Israel's Messenger*, 20 October 1905, vol. 2, no. 14.
25. *Israel's Messenger*, 30 December 1904.

Ten: Our Own People of Joseph's Seed: Japan

1. Ben-Ami Shillony, 'The Japanese and the Jews: Two Societies that Surprised the World', in *International House of Japan Bulletin*, Summer 1985, vol. 5, no. 3, p. 1.
2. D. G. Goodman and M. Miyazawa, *Jews in the Japanese Mind: the History and Uses of a Cultural Stereotype*, New York and London, 1995, pp. 7ff.
3. T. Thorowgood, *Jews in America*, p. 17.
4. D. G. Goodman and M. Miyazawa, *Jews in the Japanese Mind*, pp. 59 ff. A synopsis of McLeod's findings was reported in *Israel's Messenger* at the height of the Russo-Japanese War. *Israel's Messenger*, vol. 1, no. 14; 21 October 1904; I. Cohen, *Jews in Remote Corners of the World*, p. 155. An 'appended edition' was published in 1879 and printed for the author at the *Rising Sun* Office, Nagasaki.

5. N. McLeod, *Epitome of the Ancient History of Japan*, London, 1879, pp. 20 ff.
6. *Israel's Messenger*, 7 October 1904, vol. 1, no. 13.
7. D. G. Goodman and M. Miyazawa, *Jews in the Japanese Mind*, pp. 64–5.
8. *Israel's Messenger*, vol. 5, no. 17, 27 November 1908, pp. 14–15.
9. D. G. Goodman and M. Miyazawa, *Jews in the Japanese Mind*, pp. 59 ff.
10. J. Wilson, 'British Israelism', in *Patterns of Sectarianism: Organisation and Ideology in Social and Religious Movements*, ed. B. R. Wilson, London, 1967; *Israel's Messenger*, 22 April 1929, p. 33; M. H. Gayer, *The Heritage of the Anglo-Saxon Race*, London, 1941, pp. 112 ff.
11. *Israel's Messenger*, 22 April 1921.
12. M. H. Gayer, *The Heritage of the Anglo-Saxon Race*, pp. 112 ff.
13. *Israel's Messenger*, 7 October 1904, vol. 1, no 13, pp. 147 ff.
14. *Israel's Messenger*, p. 5, 6 October 1922.
15. Another audacious theory has it that Japanese has Middle Eastern roots: R. Yoshiwara and R. Ahlberg, *Sumerian and Japanese: a Comparative Language Study*, Chiba, Japan, 1991.
16. D. G. Goodman and M. Miyazawa, *Jews in the Japanese Mind*, p. 6ff.
17. Ibid., p. 2.
18. T. Parfitt, *The Jews of Africa and Asia*, Minority Rights Report no. 76, London, 1987, p. 11; T. Parfitt, *The Thirteenth Gate*, pp. 88 ff.
19. One of these volunteers went on to write the 1965 bestseller, *Shalom Israel*, describing the pleasures of kibbutz life. D. A. Kapner and S. Levine, 'The Jews of Japan', *Jerusalem Letter*, 1 March 2000; Ben-Ami Shillony, 'The Japanese and the Jews: Two Societies that Surprised the World' p. 1.
20. At the more sober end of the spectrum of interest in Jews in Japan is the Japanese Association of Jewish Studies, which encourages research in Jewish studies and produces a scholarly journal entitled *Studies in Jewish Life and Culture*, naturally written in Japanese.
21. See below pp. 216 ff.
22. See E. Trevisan Semi, 'Conversion and Judaisation: the "Lost Tribes" Committees at the Birth of the Jewish State', in T. Parfitt and E. Trevisan Semi, *Judaising Movements: Studies in the Margins of Judaism*, London, 2002, p. 54.
23. Beit Shalom used to be known as the Holy Jesus Society, or the Christian Friends of Israel.
24. The Makuya held a rally in front of the United Nations headquarters

in New York in 1971. Similarly 3,000 members led a pro-Israel demonstration in Tokyo after the 1973 Yom Kippur War.

25. *Sisu Yerushalayim*, a pamphlet of the Makuya Bible Seminary, Tokyo, no date, p. 16.
26. *Makuya and Israel: In Memory of Abraham I. Teshima*, Tokyo, 1976.
27. In 1985 I was granted an audience with His Imperial Highness Prince Mikasa No Miya Takahito at the Institute of Middle Eastern Studies of which he is the founder and director. He denied believing the Israelites-in-Japan theory in any way. As he put it, 'As far as the imperial insignia and the mirror are concerned – nothing can be proven one way or the other because they have never been seen by me or anyone else. They form the core of the great shrine of Ise. The rest is a mixture of conjecture and fantasy. There have been dozens of people over the last forty or so years who have been convinced of the connection between the two peoples.'

Eleven: Africa: Abraham's Seed

1. I am indebted to Professor Andrew George of SOAS for this observation.
2. D. Chidester, *Savage Systems*, p. 37.
3. See K. N. Chaudhuri, 'From the Barbarian and Civilised', p. 23.
4. Ibid.
5. E. Brerewood, *Enquiries Tracing the Diversity of Languages and Religions through the Chief Parts of the World*, London, 1613, quoted in D. Chidester, *Savage Systems*, p. 17.
6. D. Chidester, *Savage Systems*, pp. 35–7.
7. See above pp. 25 ff.
8. *The Cambridge History of Africa c. 1790–c. 1870*, ed. A. D. Roberts, Cambridge, 1986, vol. 5, p. 474.
9. E. Long, *The History of Jamaica*, London, 1774, vol. ii, pp. 353–6.
10. M. Van Wyck Smith, 'Waters flowing from darkness: the two Ethiopias in the early European image of Africa', in *Theoria*, 1986, no. 68, pp. 67–77.
11. J. S. Prichard, *Researches into the Natural History of Mankind*, London, 1836, vol. ii, p. 97, quoted in *The Cambridge History of Africa*, vol. 5, p. 477.
12. C. Seligman, *Races of Africa*, p. 61, quoted in S. Howe, *Afrocentrism: Mythical Pasts and Imagined Homes*, p. 115.
13. See above.

14. T. Lewicki, *Arabic External Sources for the History of Africa to the South of Sahara*, London, no date.
15. Ibn Khaldun, *The Muqaddimah*, vol. i, p. 119, quoted in K. N. Chaudhuri, 'From the Barbarian and Civilised', p. 29.
16. The original manuscript of his work in the National Library at Rome is written in sixteenth-century dialectal Italian with traces of Arabic and other Mediterranean languages. Ramusio's first edition transformed this manuscript into an elegant Venetian text. *The Description of Africa* was published in the 1540 edition and subsequent editions of Giovanni Battista Ramusio's *Delle navigationi et viaggi.*
17. According to the 1588 edition of the *Description*, Leo died in Rome shortly before 1550, but there is some evidence to suggest that he may have returned to North Africa and to Islam.
18. E. Jones, *Othello's Countrymen: the African in English Renaissance Drama*, London, 1965, p. 21.
19. J. J. Williams, *Hebrewisms of West Africa: from Nile to Niger with the Jews*, New York, 1930, pp. 208, 224, 232, 281, 292.
20. J. Pory, *A Geographical Historie of Africa written in Arabicke and Italian by John Leo a More, borne in Granada, and brought up in Barbarie*, London, 1600, p. 379.
21. J. Ogilby, *Africa: being an accurate description of the regions of Aegypt, Barbary, Lybia, and Billedulgerid*, London, 1670, p. 34.
22. R. Whately, 'On the Origin of Civilisation', in *Lectures delivered before the Young Men's Christian Association from November 1854 to February 1855*, London, 1879, p. 22, quoted in M. le Roux, *In Search of the Understanding of the Old Testament in Africa: the Case of the Lemba*, University of South Africa PhD thesis, 1999.
23. S. Dulucq, 'Zulu/Spartiates et autres analogies antiquisantes: des usages de l'Antiquité dans l'Afrique des XIXème et XXème siècles', in *Retrouver, imaginer, utiliser l'Antiquité*, eds Sylvie Caucanas, R. Cazals and P. Payen, Toulouse, 2001, pp. 135–40.
24. Ibid.
25. D. Chidester, *Christianity: a Global History*, New York, 2000, p. 414.
26. E. L. Woodward, *The Age of Reform 1815–1870*, Oxford, 1938, p. 486.
27. See pp. 36 ff.
28. H. W. Nevinson, *Fire of Life*, London, 1935, p. 432.
29. Captain H. Clapperton, *Narrative of Travels and Discoveries in Northern and Central Africa in the Years 1822, 1823 and 1824*, London, 1926.
30. Reverend S. Johnson, *The History of the Yorubas from the Earliest Times to the Beginning of the British Protectyorate*, London, 1921, pp. 3–5.

31. S. Howe, *Afrocentrism*, p. 120.
32. S. Dulucq, 'Zulu/Spartiates et autres analogies antiquisantes: des usages de l'Antiquité dans l'Afrique des XIXème et XXème siècles', pp. 138 ff.
33. A. Holl, 'West African Archaeology: Colonialism and Nationalism', in *A History of African Archaeology*, ed. P. Robertshaw, London, 1990, pp. 296 ff; D. P. de Pedrals, *Archéologie de l'Afrique noire*, Paris, 1950; M. Robin, 'Notes sur les premieres populations de la région de Dosso', in *Bulletin du comité d'études historiques et scientifiques de l'A.O.F.*
34. J. J. Williams, *Hebrewisms of West Africa: from Nile to Niger with the Jews*, p. 24.
35. F. Ratzel, *History of Mankind*, London, 1896, vol. iii, p. 142.
36. J. J. Williams, *Hebrewisms of West Africa*, p. 26.
37. T. E. Bowdich, *Essay on the Superstitions, Customs and Acts Common to the Ancient Egyptians, Abyssinians and Ashantees*, Paris, 1821, p. 40, quoted in J. J. Williams, *Hebrewisms of West Africa*, p. 26.
38. H. M. Stanley, *Coomassie and Magdala*, New York, 1874, p. 167.
39. F. Willett, *African Art: an Introduction*, London, 1986, pp. 109 ff.
40. J. J. Williams, *Hebrewisms of West Africa*, pp. 60, 66–92. It would be tedious to keep reiterating that my own view is that there are no Hebrew influences on Ashanti, Hottentot, Zulu, Xhose or on the languages of the Masai, Luba, Tutsi or any of the other languages viewed as descended from or influenced by Hebrew.
41. R. Patai, 'The Ritual Approach to Hebrew-African Culture Contact', in *Jewish Social Studies*, no. 24, 1962, pp. 86–96; J. J. Williams, *Hebrewisms of West Africa*.
42. H. Norden, *White and Black in East Africa*, Boston, 1924, p. 248.
43. H. Johnston, *History and Description of the British Empire in Africa*, London, p. 31.
44. M. Twaddle, *Kakungulu and the Creation of Uganda*, London, 1993, p. 9.
45. The same arguments in favour of Judaism were used a hundred years later by descendants of Incas in Peru who converted from Christianity to Judaism.
46. M. Twaddle, *Kakungulu and the Creation of Uganda*, pp. 284 ff; A. Oded, 'The Bayudaya of Uganda: a Portrait of an African Jewish Community', in *Journal of Religion in Africa*, 1974, no. 6, pp. 173, 167–86; K. Primack, *Jews in Places You Never Thought of*, pp. 168–244.

47. T. Parfitt, 'Savage-Pictures', in *Le fait de l'analyse, (Sauvagerie)*, March 1999, p. 160.
48. T. Broadway Johnson, *Tramps round the Mountains of the Moon*, Boston, 1909, pp. 184 ff.
49. 'Rapport annuel du Territoire de Nayanza', 1925, quoted in G. Prunier, *The Rwanda Crisis: History of a Genocide*, London, 1995, p. 6.
50. 'Rapport sur l'administration belge de Ruanda-Urundi', 1925, quoted in G. Prunier, *The Rwanda Crisis*, p. 6.
51. M. H. Bradley, *Caravans and Cannibals*, New York, 1926, p. 65.
52. Father van den Burgt, *Dictionnaire Français-Kurundi*, p. lxxv, quoted in G. Prunier, *The Rwanda Crisis*, p. 7.
53. J. B. Piollet, *Les missions catholiques français au XIXeme siècle*, Paris, 1902, pp. 376–7, quoted in G. Prunier, *The Rwanda Crisis*, p. 8.
54. P. del Perugia, *Les derniers Rois-Mages*, Paris, 1970, quoted in G. Prunier, *The Rwanda Crisis*, p. 8. The ravings of del Perugia are somewhat reminiscent of the theories white Zimbabweans are fond of advancing with respect to the Zimbabwe Ruins.
55. P. Bones, 'Rwanda – The Children's Return', at www.walkleyindex.com.
56. www.africa2000.com/indx/rwanda2c.htm. Similar developments took place during the Nigerian Civil War with respect to the Ibos. One discourse that I have often heard is formulated by a contributor to the Kulanu list-serve (29 January 2002) who observed, 'Some Ibos feel that the word Ibo and Ivri are related ... Many European newspapers called the Ibo, "the Jews of Africa" because they are energetic and educated. I thought that this was done to justify their genocide. After all it's OK to kill Jews or people who are like them ... They are resented for some of the reasons that Jews are disliked. They value education and have a "can do" attitude. They suffered the way Jews have suffered because there was a "silent conspiracy" to destroy them.'
57. www.ubalt.edu/kulanu.
58. See below, p. 191.
59. *Jerusalem Post*, 23 November 1998.
60. A report from Agence France Presse on 18 September 1998, indicated the famous gold mines of Solomon were to be found in the region of Kivu.
61. www.africa2000.com/indx/rwanda2c.htm;
www.geocities.com/burundi-bwacu/Doc0052.html;
www.grandslacs.net/bbsgen/messages/98.html.

62. See below, p. 200.
63. Cf. p. 127.
64. From R. Patai, 'The ritual approach to Hebrew-African Culture Contact' in *Jewish Social Studies*, 24, 1962, pp. 86–96; M. Merker, *Die Masai*, Berlin, 1904, pp. 290–332.
65. P. A. Talbot, *Peoples of Southern Nigeria*, Oxford, 1926, vol. i, p. 27.
66. D. Campbell, *In the Heart of Bantuland*, New York, 1969, p. 266.
67. A part of the letter reads, 'Here is what could be a possible explanation of this statement from linguistics. The source is potentially correct if we take the verb kulubakana – very common in Tshiluba – luluwa. Mwana mulubakana means a confused child, or a lost child. Muluba, the shorter form of mulubakana, means a "lost person". The plural is mulubakana, balubakana thus, /muluba/ baluba/. Baluba would thus be "lost people".'
68. www.usip.org/pubs/pworks/zaire11/chap1–11.html.
69. T. O. Lloyd, *The British Empire 1558–1995*, Oxford, 1996, p. 141; D. Chidester, *Savage Systems: Colonialism and Comparative Religion in Southern Africa*, Charlottesville and London, 1996, p. 38.
70. Cf. F. Willett, *African Art: an Introduction*, London, 1986, p. 99.
71. *The Cambridge History of Africa c. 1790–c. 1870*, ed. A. D. Roberts, vol. 5, p. 473.
72. Ibid.
73. D. Chidester, *Savage Systems*, pp. 50 ff.
74. T. Hahn, *Tsuni-Goam, The Supreme Being of the Khoi-Khoi*, London, 1881.
75. Wilhelm Bleek was a Prussian student of African languages, the son of a famous German biblical scholar, one of those whom Matthew Arnold later called the 'Higher Critics'. In the next two decades, Bleek worked on the grammars of several South African languages, including the Bantu languages (Bleek selected the name of this language family). *The Natal Diaries of W. H. I. Bleek*, ed. O. Spohr, Cape Town, 1965.
76. D. Chidester, *Savage Systems*, p. 88.
77. Ibid., p. 88.
78. Ibid., p. 124.
79. Ibid., p. 95.
80. Ibid., p. 98.
81. Ibid., pp. 122 ff; R. Godlinton, *A Narrative of the Irruption of the Kafir Hordes into the Eastern Province of the Cape of Good Hope, 1834–5*, Cape Town, 1965.

82. S. Dulucq, 'Zulu/Spartiates et autres analogies antiquisantes', pp. 135 ff.
83. A. Gardiner, *Narrative of a Journey to the Zoolu Country in South Africa*, Cape Town, 1966, first edition, London, 1836, pp. 95 ff. Chidester's theory has it that at the outset colonists in southern Africa were persuaded that the natives had no religion. It was only at a second stage that they were thought to be practising Judaism. In other words at the first stage of colonial intervention local peoples were negated. With further information an Israelite identity might be established. This as a general rule is not what I have found. Gardiner might be a test case. He was one of the first to encounter the Zulus. Like so many others, from Columbus onwards, the Israelite model was the first thing to occur to him. Regrettably, Chidester, to whom I am so much in debt for this section of this chapter, did not quote Gardiner. It is clear that an Israelite identity or influence was the first thing to strike him and generally in the wider discourse an Israelite identity is imposed as a first stage of comprehension.
84. D. Chidester, *Savage Systems*, p. 125.
85. J. Stuart and D. M. Malcolm, *The Diary of Henry Francis Fynn*, Pietermaritzburg, 1950, pp. 86 ff.
86. G. Parsons, 'Rethinking the Missionary Position: Bishop Colenso of Natal', in *Religion in Victorian Britain*, ed. J. Wolffe, vol. 5: *Culture and Empire*, Manchester, 1997, pp. 135–75; J. W. Colenso, 'The Diocese of Natal', in *The Monthly Record of the Society of the Propagation of the Gospel in Foreign Parts*, 4 November 1853, no. 4, pp. 241–64, quoted in D. Chidester, *Savage Systems*, p. 133.
87. G. Parsons, 'Rethinking the Missionary Position', pp. 135–75.
88. D. Chidester, *Savage Systems*, p. 168; M. le Roux, In Search of the Understanding of the Old Testament, pp. 22–5. Over the last century the internalisation of an imposed Israelite identity has proceeded apace in southern Africa and has helped to spawn such movements as the African Hebrew Community, the Church of God, the Saints of Christ, the Zionist Church and the International Pentecostal Holiness Church, all of which have strong Israelite elements.
89. H. A. Bryden, *A History of South Africa*, London, 1904, p. 127; E. Casalis, *The Basutos or Twenty-Three Years in South Africa*, London, 1861, p. 180.
90. *The Cambridge History of Africa c. 1870–c. 1905*, ed. A. D. Roberts, vol. 6, p. 362.
91. M. le Roux, 'African Jews for Jesus' (paper read at UNISA Con-

ference, Pretoria, 1999, kindly loaned to me by the author).

92. R. N. Hall, *Great Zimbabwe*, London, 1905, p. 101; T. Parfitt, *Journey to the Vanished City*, p. 266.
93. Recorded and broadcast in 'Solomon's Tribe': a series of two forty-minute documentaries about the Lemba tribe for BBC Radio Four and the BBC World Service, September 1992 (producer Julian Hale).
94. Ibid.
95. T. Price, 'The Arabs of the Zambezi', in *The Muslim World*, 1954, vol. xliv, no. 1, pp. 31 ff.
96. T. Parfitt, *Journey to the Vanished City*, p. 264; N. J. Van Warmelo, 'The classification of cultural groups', in W. D. Hammond-Tooke, *The Bantu-speaking Peoples of Southern Africa*, Johannesburg, 1937, pp. 80–2; H. von Sicard, *Ngoma Lungundu*, Upsala, 1952.
97. T. Parfitt, *Journey to the Vanished City*, passim.
98. A. Ruwitah, 'Lost Tribe, Lost Language? The Invention of a False Remba Identity', in *Zimbabwea*, October 1997, no. 5, pp. 53 ff. 'Remba' is the Shona form of 'Lemba'.
99. T. Parfitt, *Journey to the Vanished City*, passim; J. M. Cuoq, *Recueil des sources Arabes concernant l'Afrique Occidentale du VIII au XVI siècle*, Paris, 1975; T. Lewicki, *Arabic External Sources for the History of Africa to the South of Sahara*, London, no date; A. Malecka, 'La côte orientale de l'Afrique au moyen age de la Himyary', in *Folia Orientalia*, 1962, vol. iv, pp. 331 ff; Abu al-Fidah wrote of 'Seruna' – certainly an error for Sayuna which looks similar in Arabic script; R. E. Gregson, 'Trade and Politics in South-East Africa: The Moors, the Portuguese and the Kingdom of Mwenemutapa', in *African Social Research*, 1973, no. 116, p. 417; H. T. Norris, *The Adventures of Antar*, London, 1980; D. C. Chiciga, 'A Preliminary Study of the Lemba in Rhodesia', unpublished history seminar paper, University of Rhodesia, 1972, p. 15; on the genetic evidence see Mark Thomas, Tudor Parfitt, Deborah A. Weiss, Karl Skorecki, James F. Wilson, Magdel le Roux, Neil Bradman and David B. Goldstein; 'T Chromosomes Travelling South: the Cohen Modal Haplotype and the Origins of the Lemba – the "Black Jews of Southern Africa"' in *American Journal of Human Genetics*, February 2000, no. 66.
100. Gayre of Gayre, *The Origin of the Zimbabwean Civilisation*, Salisbury, 1972.
101. P. S. Garlake, *Great Zimbabwe*, London, 1973; R. N. Hall, *Great Zimbabwe*, London, 1905; C. Peters, *The Eldorado of the Ancients*, New York, 1902.

102. J. Sibree, *Madagascar and Its People*, London, 1870.
103. J. Briant, *L'hébreu à Madagascar*, Madagascar, 1946.
104. See pp. 99 ff.
105. In general terms, both in Africa and elsewhere, we see that often Christianity was soon appropriated by indigenous peoples for their own purposes. In South Africa the first 'Ethiopian' churches seceded from established churches as early as 1892.
106. See pp. 153 ff.
107. *The Bulhoek Tragedy: the Full Story of the Israelite Settlement at Ntabelanga*, East London (South Africa), 1921, p. 23.
108. R. Edgar, *Because They Chose the Plan of God: the Story of the Bulhoek Massacre*, Johannesburg, 1988, p. 38.
109. Ibid.; J. Cochrane, *Servants of Power: the Role of the English Speaking Churches 1903–1930*, Johannesburg, 1987.

Twelve: Crossing the Red Sea

1. A Lost Tribes identity was not always imposed from outside. Throughout history, as we have seen, there were always eager claimants for this ancient lineage. A tradition of origin from the Lost Tribes was particularly common among North African and Middle Eastern Jewish communities. In the area of present-day Iraq, for instance, a number of quite different groups have claimed descent from the Lost Tribes of Israel. Among these may be counted the Jews of Kurdistan who took their cue from Isaiah 27:13, which has it that the tribes were 'lost in the land of Assyria'. Indeed both Christian and Jewish groups in Kurdistan subscribe to this belief. The ubiquitous Joseph Wolff certainly knew of these local traditions. He was ready to believe that 'the Chaldeans in the mountains of Kurdistan are of Jewish origin though I cannot go so far as to affirm that they are of the Lost Tribes.' Yitzhak Ben Zvi, a future president of the State of Israel, on the other hand, had little doubt that the Kurdish Jews had something to do with the Lost Tribes. And such claims were made frequently elsewhere from Morocco to Tunisia and from Syria to the Caucasus. Kurdish Muslims have a tradition which explains their origin thus: one day King Solomon ordered five hundred jinn to go forth and find the five hundred most exquisite virgins in Europe. This they did – taking their time over this important task. Sadly when they got back Solomon was dead so the jinn 'took them unto themselves as their wives. And they begot many beautiful children . . . and that is the way the Kurds came into being.' Y. Sabar, *The Folk Literature of the Kurdistani Jews:*

an Anthology, New Haven and London, 1982; I. Ben Zvi, *The Exiled and the Redeemed*, Philadelphia, 1957, p. 40. However an American missionary in the 1830s had presented a detailed case for the Mesopotamian Nestorians. In 1835 Asahel Grant was appointed by the American Board of Foreign Missions to work as a physician among the Nestorians: he very soon came to the conclusion that they were descendants of the Lost Tribes, as indeed were the Yezidis, and he devoted a book to the subject – *The Nestorians or the Lost Tribes*, New York, 1845. Here he maintained that the Nestorians were 'indeed the representatives and lineal descendants of the Ten Tribes' and argued that the places to which the Tribes were banished – Assyria, Halah, Habor, Gozan, Hara and Media – were now inhabited not by Jews but by Nestorians. The Ten Tribes had not moved on from the first place of their exile – they simply became Nestorians. His evidence he found in their language – Aramaic – their own traditions and their names, their sacrifices, first-fruits and tithes, their ceremonies, the separation of women and so on. As he puts it, 'The observance by the Nestorian Christians of the peculiar rites and customs of the Jews furnishes very strong evidence of their Hebrew origin.' Grant also found ample evidence in their physiognomy, 'the physiognomy of the Nestorian Christians bears a close resemblance to that of the Jews of the country in which they dwell. Even the natives who are accustomed to discriminate by the features between the various classes of people are often unable to distinguish a Nestorian from a Jew and I have taxed my own powers of discrimination with no better success ... Other members of this mission and one English gentleman who visited us have noticed this striking resemblance saying of this or that Nestorian: "He has the most marked Jewish physiognomy I ever saw."' Grant concluded that the conversion of the Lost Tribes was prophesied and should occasion therefore no surprise, 'We have found it "a light shining in a dark place" while amid the obscurity of the long night of ages we have sought and found the erring daughter of Zion, purified from her idolatry, waiting in her espousal covenant to be received into perfect fellowship with her Beloved.' A. Grant, *The Nestorians or the Lost Tribes*, pp. 205, 222 ff.

2. A. Neubauer, 'Where are the Ten Tribes?', in *The Jewish Quarterly Review*, 1899, vol. i, p. 192.
3. S. Purchas, *Purchas His Pilgrimes*, Glasgow, 1905.
4. A. Ya'ari, *Sheluhei Eretz Yisrael*, Jerusalem, 1951, p. 144.
5. Ibid., p. 145.

6. A. Ya'ari, *Iggerot Eretz Yisrael*, Tel Aviv, 1943, pp. 98–144. The translation is mine.
7. A. Ya'ari, *Sheluhei Eretz Yisrael*, p. 144; S. Weil, *Beyond the Sambatyon: the Myth of the Ten Lost Tribes*, p. 89.
8. *Massot Eretz Yisrael lerabbi Moshe Bassola*, ed. I. Ben Tzvi, Jerusalem, 1938, pp. 88–90 (the translation is mine).
9. This suggestion was made by Umberto Cassuto, *Tarbitz*, Jerusalem, 1963, vol. xxxii, pp. 339–58, 346–7, and referred to in E. Ullendorff and C. Beckingham, *The Hebrew Letters of Prester John*, p. 158.
10. C. Roth, *The Jews in the Renaissance*, pp. 23 ff; H. Graetz, *History of the Jews*, vol. iv, p. 523; *The Jew in the Mediaeval World*, ed. J. R. Marcus, Philadelphia, 1938, pp. 251 ff.
11. I. Ben Zvi, *The Exiled and the Redeemed*, p. 180; A. Ya'ari, *Letters from the Land of Israel*, pp. 98–144. The translation is mine.
12. J. Wolff, *Narrative of a Mission to Bokhara*, pp. 58 ff.
13. In some of the Arabic Jewish Messianic texts (the majority are written not in Arabic but in Hebrew) the Messiah is referred to by the Arabic phrase *al-Mahdi al-muntazar* – 'the expected Mahdi' – while the Mahdis already referred to are perceived by the Jewish writers as essential precursors of the Jewish Messianic contenders. See B.-Z. Eraqi Klorman, *The Jews of the Yemen in the Nineteenth Century: a Portrait of a Messianic Community*, Leiden, New York and Cologne, 1993.
14. A. Ya'ari, *Sheluhei Eretz Yisrael*, pp. 146–7.
15. R. Yisrael ben Shmuel of Shklov was a disciple of the Gaen of Vilna. In 1809 with his family he joined the third group of the Gaon's disciples to emigrate to Palestine. In time he became the head of the Safed *kolel* of the Perushim. He died in Jerusalem in 1839. A. Ya'ari, *Iggerot Eretz Yisrael*, pp. 324–5; A. Luncz, *Yerushalayim*, Jerusalem, 1901, vol. v, p. 289.
16. A. Ya'ari, *Iggerot Eretz Yisrael*, pp. 347–8.
17. Ibid., p. 353.
18. A. Ya'ari, *Sheluhei Eretz Yisrael*, pp. 146–8; Y. Nini, *The Jews of the Yemen 1800–1914*, Chur, Reading etc., 1991, pp. 119, 120, 219; A. Ya'ari, 'Shelihim me-Eretz Yisrael la-Aseret ha-Shevatim', *Sinai*, vol. 6, no. 3, pp. 348–52.
19. Yaakov Saphir (1822–85), Hebrew author and traveller, was born in Lithuania and taken to Palestine when he was ten. He later travelled widely in the East. Y. Saphir, *Even Sapir*, Jerusalem, 1866, p.52; Y. Ratzaby, *Yemen Paths*, Tel Aviv, 1988, pp. 47–66; Y. Ratzaby, 'Shelihim

to the Yemen in the years 1883, 1889', in *Shalem*, 1974, no. 1, pp. 427–53. For a discussion of the internal implications of these tales see B.-Z. Eraqi Klorman, *The Jews of the Yemen in the Nineteenth Century: a Portrait of a Messianic Community*, Leiden, 1993, pp. 100 ff.

20. A. Ya'ari, *Sheluhei Eretz Yisrael*, p. 149.
21. D. S. Carasso, *Zikhron Teiman O El Viage de Yemen*, Constantinople, 1875, p. 130; M. Franco, *Essai sur l'histoire des Israélites de l'Empire Ottoman depuis les origines jusqu'à nos jours*, Paris, 1897, pp. 214 ff. In 1910 Sémach noted that in the area of Saada Jews were to be found 'strong and tall, they belong to a bellicose race, and are always armed in the Arab way with a curved *djambie* and the rifle'. Y. Sémach, *Une Mission de l'Alliance au Yémen*, Paris, p. 109.
22. Joseph Halévy (1827–1917) was a French Semitic scholar and traveller. He was sent by the Alliance to Ethiopia to study the Falashas in 1868 and in 1869–70 by the Académie des Inscriptions et Belles-Letters to the Yemen where, disguised as a native rabbi, he collected 686 Sabean inscriptions. In 1879 he was appointed Professor of Ethiopic at the Ecole des Hautes Etudes. Halévy's journey to Najran is without question one of the great journeys of exploration of the nineteenth century. It is noteworthy that in the first half century after the British occupation of Aden in 1837, with the exception of Halévy, only one other European penetrated more than fifty miles inland from the coast.
23. See H. Habshush, *Travels in Yemen*, p. 63; Y. Sémach, *op. cit.* p. 21.
24. *London Evening Standard*, 1928; see also *Ha-Aretz*, 5 October 1928. Weisl's report emphasised the persecution of the Jews in the Yemen and was taken seriously by the Jewish organisations. See, for example, the American Jewish Committee's report to the Board of Deputies, New York, 30 November, 1928. British Middle East experts took him less seriously particularly with respect to the question of whether the Jews were persecuted or not. Thus Lieutenant Colonel H. F. Jacob to L. Wolf, London, 25 December 1928, contended that they were not maltreated and indeed 'in Najran and parts of the Jauf the Jews enjoy special privileges', Archive of the Board of Deputies of British Jews Acc 3168/318–22.
25. Y. Ratzaby, *Yemen Paths: Selected Studies in Yemenite Culture*, Tel Aviv, 1987, pp. 244 ff.
26. E. Brauer, *Ethnologie der jemenitischen Juden*, Heidelberg, 1934, p. 8.
27. Perhaps the best known of these is Mendele Mokher Sefarim's Hebrew novel *The Journey of Benjamin III*, which satirised the popular obsession with the subject.

28. In the early days of modern Jewish settlement in Palestine there was a belief that emphasised what was seen as the racial kinship of Jew and Arab. A number of writers took this further and wrote about Hebrew-speaking Jewish Bedouin groups sighted in the hinterland of Palestine. Hemdah ben Yehuda (1873–1951), for instance, in one of her stories wrote of a tribe descended from the original Hebrews: in her description, which appears to owe something to the travellers' reports cited above, these nomads are of singular intelligence, tall, noble of bearing and handsome. They were the very antithesis of the way in which European Jews at the time viewed themselves. In addition they legitimised the whole Zionist idea of settling Palestine, 'these wild brethren of ours who have preserved our land for two thousand years . . . their feet have not trodden alien soil, and our language lives on in their mouth from those times until this very day . . . faithful children!' See H. Ben Yehuda, 'Havvat Bnei Reikab', in *Sippurei Nashim*, Israel, 1984, p. 69.
29. A. M. Luncz (1854–1918) emigrated from Kovno to Palestine in 1869 and became a key figure in 'enlightened' circles in Jerusalem where he was active as writer, editor and publisher.
30. Luncz makes this point in a letter to *Ha-Shiloah* in reply to a criticism by Ahad ha-Am of one of his books. See *Ha-Shiloah*, 1892, vol. vii, p. 282; S. Werses, 'Stories about the Ten Tribes and the Sambatyon and their absorption into Modern Hebrew Literature', in *From Mendele to Hazaz*, Jerusalem, 1987, p. 307. I am indebted to Dr Herman Zeffert for bringing the letter of Luncz to my attention.
31. See E. Trevisan Semi, 'Conversion and Judaisation: the "Lost Tribes" Committees at the Birth of the Jewish State', in T. Parfitt and E. Trevisan Semi, *Judaising Movements: Studies in the Margins of Judaism*, London, 2002, pp. 53 ff.
32. See Chapter One.
33. D. Kessler, *The Falashas*, London, 1996, p. 84.
34. S. Kaplan, *The Beta Israel (Falasha) in Ethiopia*, New York and London, 1992, p. 23.
35. E. Ullendorff, *Ethiopia and the Bible*, London, 1968, p. 139.
36. H. A. Stern, *Wanderings among the Falashas in Abyssinia*, second edition with introduction by R. L. Hess, London, 1968, p. xxiv; S. Kaplan, 'The Beta Israel (Falasha) Encounter with Protestant Missionaries: 1860–1905', in *Jewish Social Studies*, winter 1987, vol. xlix, no. 1, p. 29.
37. J. Bruce, *Travels to Discover the Source of the Nile*, Edinburgh, 1805, vol. ii, p. 406.

38. J. Halévy, 'Excursion chez les Falacha en Abyssine', *Bulletin de la société de géographie*, 1869, vol. 5, no. 17, p. 287.
39. J. Quirin, *The Evolution of the Ethiopian Jews: a History of the Beta Israel (Falasha) to 1920*, Philadelphia, 1992, p. 14.
40. S. Kaplan, *The Beta Israel (Falasha) in Ethiopia*, p. 172, n. 48.
41. See p. 48.
42. S. Gobat, *Journal of a Three Years Residence in Abyssinia*, London, 1847, p. 467.
43. Ibid., p. 309.
44. H. A. Stern, *Wanderings among the Falashas*, p. xix.
45. S. Kaplan, *The Beta Israel (Falasha) in Ethiopia*, p. 165.
46. M. Corinaldi, *Jewish Identity: the Case of Ethiopian Jewry*, Jerusalem, 1998, p. 13; S. Kaplan, *The Beta Israel*, p. 25.
47. M. Corinaldi, *Jewish Identity*, pp. 111 ff.
48. M. Corinaldi, *Jewish Identity*, p. 112; T. Parfitt, *Operation Moses*, p. 26.
49. F. C. Gamst, *The Qemant: a Pagan-Hebraic Peasantry of Ethiopia*, New York, 1969.
50. *Washington Post*, 24 November 1994.
51. www.guihon.org
52. C. Bader, *Les Yibro: Mages somali. Les juifs oubliés de la corne de l'Afrique?* Paris, 2000.

Conclusion

1. In a recent article in the *Jerusalem Post*, 12 September 2001, Michael Freund, who worked in the Prime Minister's office as Deputy Director of Communications & Policy Planning from 1996 to 1999, urged the State of Israel to do something for the aspiring Jews of India and Burma, of Uganda and the United States, of Japan, Africa and South America. He wrote, 'But rather than neglecting these people, it is time for Israel to start reaching out to them, assessing their claims to Jewish ancestry and acting to help those worthy of assistance. The various organs of the State, such as the Jewish Agency, the Chief Rabbinate and the Foreign Ministry, need to look more carefully at this issue and give it serious consideration. For a country struggling to find potential new sources of immigration, groups such as the Bnei Menashe and others like them might very well provide the answer.'
2. S. L. Lyman, 'Postmodernism and the Construction of Ethnocultural Identity: the Jewish-Indian theory and the Lost Tribes of Israel', in *Sociological Spectrum*, 1997, no. 17, p. 263.

3. A. Piatgorsky, *Who's Afraid of Freemasons: the Phenomenon of Freemasonry*, London, 1997, p. 35.
4. D. Cannadine, *Ornamentalism*, pp. 5–6.
5. P. D. Morgan, 'Encounters between British and "Indigenous" peoples, *c.* 1500–*c.* 1800', in *Empire and Others: British Encounters with Indigenous Peoples 1600–1850*, M. J. Daunton and R. Halpern, London, 1999, p. 68.
6. *The Invention of Tradition*, eds E. Hobsbawm and T. Ranger, Cambridge, 1983.
7. Marie-France Rouart, *Le Mythe du Juif errant dans l'Europe du XIXe siècle*, Paris, 1988, pp. 8–9.

INDEX